The DevOps 2.3 Toolkit

Kubernetes: Deploying and managing highly-available and fault-tolerant applications at scale

Viktor Farcic

BIRMINGHAM MUMBAI

The DevOps 2.3 Toolkit

Acquisition Editor: Dominic Shakeshaft
Technical Editor: Nidhisha Shetty
Indexer: Tejal Daruwale Soni
Production Coordinator: Sandip Tadge

First published: September 2018
Production reference: 1100918

Published by Packt Publishing Ltd.
Livery Place
35 Livery Street
Birmingham
B3 2PB, UK.

ISBN 978-1-78913-550-3

www.packtpub.com

To my daughter Sara who just got her first MacBook, and to my wife Eva who still supports me and loves me, even when I don't have enough energy to tell her how much she means to me.

– Viktor Farcic

About the author

Viktor Farcic is a Senior Consultant at CloudBees (`https://www.cloudbees.com/`), a member of the Docker Captains (`https://www.docker.com/docker-captains`) group, and author. He coded using a plethora of languages starting with Pascal (yes, he is old), Basic (before it got Visual prefix), ASP (before it got .Net suffix), C, C++, Perl, Python, ASP.Net, Visual Basic, C#, JavaScript, Java, Scala, and so on. He never worked with Fortran. His current favorite is Go. His big passions are Microservices, Continuous Deployment and **Test-Driven Development (TDD)**. He often speaks at community gatherings and conferences. He wrote *The DevOps 2.0 Toolkit: Automating the Continuous Deployment Pipeline with Containerized Microservices* (`https://www.amazon.com/dp/B01BJ4V66M`), *The DevOps 2.1 Toolkit: Docker Swarm: Building, testing, deploying, and monitoring services inside Docker Swarm clusters* (`https://www.amazon.com/dp/1542468914`), *The DevOps 2.2 Toolkit: Self-Sufficient Docker Clusters: Building Self-Adaptive And Self-Healing Docker Clusters* (`https://www.amazon.com/dp/1979347190`), and *Test-Driven Java Development* (`https://www.packtpub.com/application-development/test-driven-java-development`). His random thoughts and tutorials can be found in his blog `TechnologyConversations.com` (`https://technologyconversations.com/`).

Packt is searching for authors like you

If you're interested in becoming an author for Packt, please visit `authors.packtpub.com` and apply today. We have worked with thousands of developers and tech professionals, just like you, to help them share their insight with the global tech community. You can make a general application, apply for a specific hot topic that we are recruiting an author for, or submit your own idea.

`mapt.io`

Mapt is an online digital library that gives you full access to over 5,000 books and videos, as well as industry leading tools to help you plan your personal development and advance your career. For more information, please visit our website.

Why subscribe?

- Spend less time learning and more time coding with practical eBooks and Videos from over 4,000 industry professionals

- Improve your learning with Skill Plans built especially for you

- Get a free eBook or video every month

- Mapt is fully searchable

- Copy and paste, print, and bookmark content

PacktPub.com

Did you know that Packt offers eBook versions of every book published, with PDF and ePub files available? You can upgrade to the eBook version at `www.PacktPub.com` and as a print book customer, you are entitled to a discount on the eBook copy. Get in touch with us at `service@packtpub.com` for more details.

At `www.PacktPub.com`, you can also read a collection of free technical articles, sign up for a range of free newsletters, and receive exclusive discounts and offers on Packt books and eBooks.

Table of Contents

Preface

If you read one of the other books in *The DevOps Toolkit Series* (`http://www.devopstoolkitseries.com/`), you already know that I am a huge fan of containers, schedulers, and orchestrators. *The DevOps 2.0 Toolkit: Automating the Continuous Deployment Pipeline with Containerized Microservices* (`https://www.amazon.com/dp/B01BJ4V66M`) started as an overview of many different DevOps tools and practices, with containers having an important, but not a decisive role. In the meantime, I fell in utter and complete love with Docker and Swarm, so I chose to write *The DevOps 2.1 Toolkit: Docker Swarm: Building, testing, deploying, and monitoring services inside Docker Swarm clusters* (`https://www.amazon.com/dp/1542468914`). By the time I finished it, I felt that some advanced topics were not explored and deserve a book on its own. *The DevOps 2.2 Toolkit: Self-Sufficient Docker Clusters: Building Self-Adaptive And Self-Healing Docker Clusters* (`https://www.amazon.com/dp/1979347190`) was born.

All those books were (directly or indirectly) focused on Docker Swarm, and I felt that Kubernetes deserves its own space. Truth be told, I was negative about it a few years ago. It was too complicated for most use cases. It was enough to try installing it and, after days of struggle, give up. However, Kubernetes has come a long way since then. Even though its founding principles are the same, with time, it became more mature, more straightforward, and much bigger. Today, it is the biggest and the most adopted container orchestration platform. Some of the most prominent software companies rallied around it. Many startups emerged with new solutions. The open source community behind Kubernetes is one of the biggest in the history of software development. The community is vibrant, fast moving, and with a lot of vested interest in seeing Kubernetes succeed. Even Docker chose to support it and join the community. Kubernetes has a bright future ahead, and no one should ignore it.

If you already chose a different container scheduler (for example, Docker Swarm, Mesos, Nomad, or something else), you might wonder whether it makes sense for you to invest time learning Kubernetes. I think it does. We should always be on a lookout for different solutions. Otherwise, we're being forced to choose one blindly. No matter whether you decide to adopt Kubernetes or to stick with something else, I'll argue that you should know how it works and what it offers. It's all about making an educated decision.

Overview

The goal of this book is not to convince you to adopt Kubernetes but to provide a detailed overview of its features. I want you to become confident in your Kubernetes knowledge and only then choose whether to embrace it. That is, unless you already made up your mind and stumbled upon this book in search of Kubernetes guidance.

The plan is to cover all aspects behind Kubernetes, from basic to advanced features. We'll go not only through the tools behind the official project but also third-party add-ons. I hope that, by the time you finish reading this book, you will be able to call yourself "Kubernetes ninja". I cannot say that you will know everything there is to know about the Kubernetes ecosystem. That would be impossible to accomplish since its growing faster than any single person could follow. What I can say is that you will be very confident in running a Kubernetes cluster of any scale in production.

Like all my other books, this one is very hands-on. There will be just enough theory for you to understand the principles behind each topic. The book is packed with examples, so I need to give you a heads up. Do not buy this book if you're planning to read it on a bus or in bed before going to sleep. You will need to be in front of your computer. A terminal will be your best friend. `kubectl` will be your lover.

The book assumes that you feel comfortable with containers, especially Docker. We won't go into details how to build an image, what is container registry, and how to write Dockerfile. I hope you already know all that. If that's not the case, you might want to postpone reading this and learn at least basic container operations. This book is about things that happen after you built your images and stored them in a registry.

This book is about running containers at scale and not panicking when problems arise. It is about the present and the future of software deployment and monitoring. It's about embracing the challenges and staying ahead of the curve.

Eventually, you might get stuck and will be in need of help. Or you might want to write a review or comment on the book's content. Please join the DevOps20 (`http://slack.devops20toolkit.com/`) Slack channel and post your thoughts, ask questions, or participate in a discussion. If you prefer a more one-on-one communication, you can use Slack to send me a private message or send an email to `viktor@farcic.com`. All the books I wrote are very dear to me, and I want you to have a good experience reading them. Part of that experience is the option to reach out to me. Don't be shy.

Please note that this one, just as the previous books, is self-published. I believe that having no intermediaries between the writer and the reader is the best way to go. It allows me to write faster, update the book more frequently, and have a more direct communication with you. Your feedback is part of the process. No matter whether you purchased the book while only a few or all chapters were written, the idea is that it will never be truly finished. As time passes, it will require updates so that it is aligned with the change in technology or processes. When possible, I will try to keep it up to date and release updates whenever that makes sense. Eventually, things might change so much that updates are not a good option anymore, and that will be a sign that a whole new book is required. I will keep writing as long as I continue getting your support.

Download the example code files

You can download the example code files for this book from your account at `www.packtpub.com`. If you purchased this book elsewhere, you can visit `www.packtpub.com/support` and register to have the files emailed directly to you.

You can download the code files by following these steps:

1. Log in or register at `www.packtpub.com`.
2. Select the **SUPPORT** tab.
3. Click on **Code Downloads & Errata**.
4. Enter the name of the book in the **Search** box and follow the onscreen instructions.

Once the file is downloaded, please make sure that you unzip or extract the folder using the latest version of:

- WinRAR/7-Zip for Windows
- Zipeg/iZip/UnRarX for Mac
- 7-Zip/PeaZip for Linux

The code bundle for the book is also hosted on GitHub at `https://github.com/PacktPublishing/The-DevOps-2.3-Toolkit`. We also have other code bundles from our rich catalog of books and videos available at `https://github.com/PacktPublishing/`. Check them out!

Download the color images

We also provide a PDF file that has color images of the screenshots/diagrams used in this book. You can download it here: `https://www.packtpub.com/sites/default/files/downloads/TheDevOps2.3Toolkit_ColorImages.pdf`.

Conventions used

There are a number of text conventions used throughout this book.

`CodeInText`: Indicates code words in text, database table names, folder names, filenames, file extensions, pathnames, dummy URLs, user input, and Twitter handles. Here is an example: "Even though we executed the `docker` command inside a container, the output clearly shows the images from the host."

A block of code is set as follows:

```
global:
  scrape_interval:      15s

scrape_configs:
  - job_name: Prometheus
    metrics_path: /prometheus/metrics
    static_configs:
      - targets:
        - localhost:9090
```

When we wish to draw your attention to a particular part of a code block, the relevant lines or items are set in bold:

```
global:
  scrape_interval:      15s

scrape_configs:
  - job_name: Prometheus
    metrics_path: /prometheus/metrics
    static_configs:
      - targets:
        - localhost:9090
```

Any command-line input or output is written as follows:

```
docker container exec -it $ID \
    curl node-exporter:9100/metrics
```

Bold: Indicates a new term, an important word, or words that you see onscreen. For example, words in menus or dialog boxes appear in the text like this. Here is an example: "Please type `test` in the **item name** field, select `Pipeline` as the **type**, and click the **OK** button."

Warnings or important notes appear like this.

Tips and tricks appear like this.

Get in touch

Feedback from our readers is always welcome.

General feedback: Email `feedback@packtpub.com` and mention the book title in the subject of your message. If you have questions about any aspect of this book, please email us at `questions@packtpub.com`.

Errata: Although we have taken every care to ensure the accuracy of our content, mistakes do happen. If you have found a mistake in this book, we would be grateful if you would report this to us. Please visit `www.packtpub.com/submit-errata`, selecting your book, clicking on the Errata Submission Form link, and entering the details.

Piracy: If you come across any illegal copies of our works in any form on the Internet, we would be grateful if you would provide us with the location address or website name. Please contact us at `copyright@packtpub.com` with a link to the material.

If you are interested in becoming an author: If there is a topic that you have expertise in and you are interested in either writing or contributing to a book, please visit `authors.packtpub.com`.

How Did We Get Here? 1

A small percentage of companies live in the present. Most of us are stuck in the past, with obsolete technology and outdated processes. If we stay in the past for too long, we might lose our chance to come back to the present. We might move into an alternate timeline and cease to exist.

Every company is a software company. That applies even to those that do not yet realize it. We are all running and continuously increasing our speed. It's a race without a finish line. There are no winners but rather those that fall and do not get up. We live an era of an ever-increasing speed of change. Companies are created and destroyed overnight. No one is safe. No one can allow status quo.

Technology is changing so fast that it is very hard, if not impossible to follow. The moment we learn about a new technology, it is already obsolete and replaced with something else. Take containers as an example. Docker appeared only a few years ago, and everyone is already using it for a myriad of scenarios. Still, even though it is a very young product, it changed many times over. Just when we learned how to use `docker run`, we were told that it is obsolete and should be replaced with `docker-compose up`. We started converting all our `docker run` commands into Compose YAML format. The moment we finished the conversion, we learned that containers should not be run directly. We should use a container scheduler instead. To make things more complicated, we had to make a selection between Mesos and Marathon, Docker Swarm, or Kubernetes.

We can choose to ignore the trends but that would mean that we would fall behind the rest of the competition. There is no alternative to a constant struggle to be competitive. Once we drop our guard and stop learning and improving, the competition will take over our business. Everyone is under pressure to improve, even highly regulated industries. Innovation is impossible until we manage to get to the present tense. Only once we master what others are doing today, can we move forward and come up with something new. Today, container schedulers are a norm. They are not the thing of the future. They are the present. They are here to stay even though it is likely that they will change a lot in the coming months and years. Understanding container schedulers are paramount. Among them, Kubernetes is the most widely used and with a massive community behind it.

Before we dive into Kubernetes, it might be worthwhile going through some history in an attempt to understand some of the problems we were trying to solve, as well as some of the challenges we were facing.

A glimpse from the past

Picture a young boy. He just finished a few months worth of work. He's proud of what he accomplished but, at the same time, fearful whether it will work. He did not yet try it out on a "real" server. This will be the first time he'll deliver the fruits of his work.

He takes a floppy disk out from a drawer, inserts it into his computer, and copies the files he compiled previously. He feels fortunate that perforated cards are a thing of the past.

He gets up from his desk, exits the office, and walks towards his car. It will take him over two hours to get to the building with servers. He's not happy with the prospect of having to drive for two hours, but there is no better alternative. He could have sent the floppy with a messenger, but that would do no good since he wants to install the software himself. He needs to be there. There is no remote option.

A while later, he enters the room with the servers, inserts the floppy disk, and copies and installs the software. Fifteen minutes later, his face shows signs of stress. Something is not working as expected. There is an unforeseen problem. He's collecting outputs and writing notes. He's doing his best to stay calm and gather as much info as he can. He's dreading a long ride back to his computer and days, maybe even weeks, until he figures out what caused the problem and fixes it. He'll be back and install the fix. Perhaps it will work the second time. More likely it won't.

A short history of infrastructure management

A long time ago in a galaxy far, far away...

We would order servers and wait for months until they arrive. To make our misery worse, even after they come, we'd wait for weeks, sometimes even months, until they are placed in racks and provisioned. Most of the time we were waiting for something to happen. Wait for servers, wait until they are provisioned, wait until you get approval to deploy, then wait some more. Only patient people could be software engineers. And yet, that was the time after perforated cards and floppy disks. We had internet or some other way to connect to machines remotely. Still, everything required a lot of waiting.

Given how long it would take to have a fully functioning server, it came as no surprise that only a select few had access to them. If someone does something that should not be done, we could face an extended downtime. On top of that, nobody knew what was running on those servers. Since everything was being done manually, after a while, those servers would become a dumping ground. Things get accumulated over time. No matter how much effort is put into documentation, given enough time, the state of the servers would always diverge from the documentation. That is the nature of manual provisioning and installations. Sysadmin became a god-like person. He was the only one who knew everything or, more likely, faked that he does. He was the dungeon keeper. He had the keys to the kingdom. Everyone was replaceable but him.

Then came configuration management tools. We got CFEngine. It was based on promise theory and was capable of putting a server into the desired state no matter what its actual state was. At least, that was the theory. Even with its shortcomings, CFEngine fulfilled its primary objective. It allowed us to specify the state of static infrastructure and have a reasonable guarantee that it will be achieved. Aside from its main goal, it was an advance towards documented servers setup. Instead of manual hocus-pocus type of actions which resulted in often significant discrepancies between documentation and the actual state, CFEngine allowed us to have a specification that (almost) entirely matches the actual state. Another big advantage it provided is the ability to have, more or less, the same setup for different environments. Servers dedicated to testing could be (almost) the same as those assigned to production. Unfortunately, usage of CFEngine and similar tools were not yet widespread. We had to wait for virtual machines before automated configuration management become a norm. However, CFEngine was not designed for virtual machines. They were meant to work with static, bare metal servers. Still, CFEngine was a massive contribution to the industry even though it failed to get widespread adoption.

After CFEngine came Chef, Puppet, Ansible, Salt, and other similar tools. Life was good until virtual machines came into being or, to be more precise, became widely used. We'll go back to those tools soon. For now, let's turn to the next evolutionary improvement.

Besides forcing us to be patient, physical servers were a massive waste in resource utilization. They came in predefined sizes and, since waiting time was considerable, we often opted for big ones. The bigger, the better. That meant that an application or a service usually required less CPU and memory than the server offered. Unless you do not care about costs, that meant that we'd deploy multiple applications to a single server. The result was a dependencies nightmare. We had to choose between freedom and standardization.

Freedom meant that different applications could use different runtime dependencies. One service could require JDK3 while the other might need JDK4. A third one might be compiled with C. You probably understand where this is going. The more applications we host on a single server, the more dependencies there are. More often than not, those dependencies were conflicting and would produce side effects no one expected. Thanks to our inherent need to convert any expertise into a separate department, those in charge of infrastructure were quick to dismiss freedom in favour of reliability. That translates into "the easier it is for me, the more reliable it is for you." Freedom lost, standardization won.

Standardization starts with systems architects deciding the only right way to develop and deploy something. They are a curious bunch of people. With the risk of putting everyone in the same group and ridiculing the profession, I'll describe an average systems architect as a (probably experienced) coder that decided to climb his company's ladder. While on the subject of ladders, there are often two of those. One is the management ladder that requires an extensive knowledge of Microsoft Word and Excel. Expert knowledge of all MS Office tools is a bonus. Those who mastered MS Project were considered the ultimate experts. Oh, I forgot about email skills. They had to be capable of sending at least fifteen emails a day asking for status reports.

Most expert coders (old timers) would not choose that path. Many preferred to remain technical. That meant taking over systems architect role. The problem is that the "technical path" was often a deceit. Architects would still have to master all the management skills (for example, Word, Excel, and email) with the additional ability to draw diagrams. That wasn't easy. A systems architect had to know how to draw a rectangle, a circle, and a triangle. He had to be proficient in coloring them as well as in connecting them with lines. There were dotted and full lines. Some had to end like an arrow. Choosing the direction of an arrow was a challenge in itself so the lines would often end up with arrows at both ends.

The important part of being an architect is that drawing diagrams and writing countless pages of Word documents was so time demanding, that coding stopped being something they do. They stopped learning and exploring beyond Google search and comparative tables. The net result is that the architecture would reflect knowledge an architect had before they jumped to the new position.

Why am I talking about architects? The reason is simple. They were in charge of standardization demanded by sysadmins. They would draw their diagrams and choose the stack, developers would use. Whatever that stack was, it was to be considered Bible and followed to the letter. Sysadmins were happy since there was a standard and a predefined way to set up a server. Architects were thrilled because their diagrams served a purpose. Since those stacks were supposed to last forever, developers were excited since there was no need for them to learn anything new. Standardization killed innovation, but everyone was happy. Happiness is necessary, isn't it? Why do we need Java 6 if JDK2 works great? It's been proven by countless diagrams.

Then came Virtual machines and broke everyone's happiness.

Virtual machines (VMs) were a massive improvement over bare metal infrastructure. They allowed us to be more precise with hardware requirements. They could be created and destroyed quickly. They could differ. One could host Java application, and the other could be dedicated to Ruby on Rails. We could get them in a matter of minutes, instead of waiting for months. Still, it took quite a while until "could" became "can". Even though the advantages brought by VMs were numerous, years passed until they were widely adopted. Even then, the adoption was usually wrong. Companies often moved the same practices used with bare metal servers into virtual machines. That is not to say that adopting VMs did not bring immediate value. Waiting time for servers dropped from months to weeks. If it wasn't for administrative tasks, manual operations, and operational bottlenecks, they could have reduced waiting time to minutes. Still, waiting for weeks was better than waiting for months. Another benefit is that we could have identical servers in different environments. Companies started copying VMs. While that was much better than before, it did not solve the problem of missing documentation and the ability to create VMs from scratch. Still, multiple identical environments are better than one, even if that meant that we don't know what's inside.

While the adoption of VMs was increasing, so did the number of configuration management tools. We got Chef, Puppet, Ansible, Salt, and so on. Some of them might have existed before VMs. Still, virtual machines made them popular. They helped spread the adoption of "infrastructure as code" principles. However, those tools were based on the same principles as CFEngine. That means that they were designed with static infrastructure in mind. On the other hand, VMs opened the doors to dynamic infrastructure where VMs are continuously created and destroyed. Mutability and constant creation and destruction were clashing. Mutable infrastructure is well suited for static infrastructure. It does not respond well to challenges brought with dynamic nature of modern data centers. Mutability had to give way to immutability.

When ideas behind immutable infrastructure started getting traction, people began combining them with the concepts behind configuration management. However, tools available at that time were not fit for the job. They (Chef, Puppet, Ansible, and the like) were designed with the idea that servers are brought into the desired state at runtime. Immutable processes, on the other hand, assume that (almost) nothing is changeable at runtime. Artifacts were supposed to be created as immutable images. In case of infrastructure, that meant that VMs are created from images, and not changed at runtime. If an upgrade is needed, new image should be created followed with a replacement of old VMs with new ones based on the new image. Such processes brought speed and reliability. With proper tests in place, immutable is always more reliable than mutable.

Hence, we got tools capable of building VM images. Today, they are ruled by Packer. Configuration management tools quickly jumped on board, and their vendors told us that they work equally well for configuring images as servers at runtime. However, that was not the case due to the logic behind those tools. They are designed to put a server that is in an unknown state into the desired state. They assume that we are not sure what the current state is. VM images, on the other hand, are always based on an image with a known state. If for example, we choose Ubuntu as a base image, we know what's inside it. Adding additional packages and configurations is easy. There is no need for things like "if this then that, otherwise something else." A simple shell script is as good as any configuration management tool when the current state is known. Creating a VM image is reasonably straightforward with Packer alone. Still, not all was lost for configuration management tools. We could still use them to orchestrate the creation of VMs based on images and, potentially, do some runtime configuration that couldn't be baked in. Right?

The way we orchestrate infrastructure had to change as well. A higher level of dynamism and elasticity was required. That became especially evident with the emergence of cloud hosting providers like **Amazon Web Services** (**AWS**) and, later on, Azure and GCE. They showed us what can be done. While some companies embraced the cloud, others went into defensive positions. "We can build an internal cloud", "AWS is too expensive", "I would, but I can't because of legislation", and "our market is different", are only a few ill-conceived excuses often given by people who are desperately trying to maintain status quo. That is not to say that there is no truth in those statements but that, more often than not, they are used as an excuse, not for real reasons.

Still, the cloud did manage to become the way to do things, and companies moved their infrastructure to one of the providers. Or, at least, started thinking about it. The number of companies that are abandoning on-premise infrastructure is continuously increasing, and we can safely predict that the trend will continue. Still, the question remains. How do we manage infrastructure in the cloud with all the benefits it gives us? How do we handle its highly dynamic nature? The answer comes in the form of vendor-specific tools like CloudFormation or agnostic solutions like Terraform. When combined with tools that allow us to create images, they represent a new generation of configuration management. We are talking about full automation backed by immutability.

 We're living in an era without the need to SSH into servers.

Today, modern infrastructure is created from immutable images. Any upgrade is performed by building new images and performing rolling updates that will replace VMs one by one. Infrastructure dependencies are never changed at runtime. Tools like Packer, Terraform, CloudFormation, and the like are the answer to today's problems.

One of the inherent benefits behind immutability is a clear division between infrastructure and deployments. Until not long ago, the two meshed together into an inseparable process. With infrastructure becoming a service, deployment processes can be clearly separated, thus allowing different teams, individuals, and expertise to take control.

We'll need to go back in time one more time and discuss the history of deployments. Did they change as much as infrastructure?

A short history of deployment processes

In the beginning, there were no package managers. There were no JAR, WAR, RPM, DEB, and other package formats. At best, we could zip files that form a release. More likely, we'd manually copy files from one place to another. When this practice is combined with bare-metal servers which were intended to last forever, the result was living hell. After some time, no one knew what was installed on the servers. Constant overwrites, reconfigurations, package installations, and mutable types of actions resulted in unstable, unreliable, and undocumented software running on top of countless OS patches.

The emergence of configuration management tools (for example, CFEngine, Chef, Puppet, and so on) helped to decrease the mess. Still, they improved OS setups and maintenance, more than deployments of new releases. They were never designed to do that even though the companies behind them quickly realized that it would be financially beneficial to extend their scope.

Even with configuration management tools, the problems with having multiple services running on the same server persisted. Different services might have different needs, and sometimes those needs clash. One might need JDK6 and the other JDK7. A new release of the first one might require JDK to be upgraded to a new version, but that might affect some other service on the same server. Conflicts and operational complexity were so common that many companies would choose to standardize. As we discussed, standardization is innovation killer. The more we standardize, the less room there is for coming up with better solutions. Even if that's not a problem, standardization with clear isolation means that it is very complicated to upgrade something. Effects could be unforeseen and the sheer work involved to upgrade everything at once is so significant that many choose not to upgrade for a long time (if ever). Many end up stuck with old stacks for a long time.

We needed process isolation that does not require a separate VM for each service. At the same time, we had to come up with an immutable way to deploy software. Mutability was distracting us from our goal to have reliable environments. With the emergence of virtual machines, immutability became feasible. Instead of deploying releases by doing updates at runtime, we could create new VMs with not only OS and patches but also our own software baked in. Each time we wanted to release something, we could create a new image, and instantiate as many VMs as we need. We could do immutable rolling updates. Still, not many of us did that. It was too expensive, both regarding resources as well as time. The process was too long. Even if that would not matter, having a separate VM for each service would result in too much unused CPU and memory.

Fortunately, Linux got namespaces, cgroups, and other things that are together known as containers. They were lightweight, fast, and cheap. They provided process isolation and quite a few other benefits. Unfortunately, they were not easy to use. Even though they've been around for a while, only a handful of companies had the know-how required for their beneficial utilization. We had to wait for Docker to emerge to make containers easy to use and thus accessible to all.

Today, containers are the preferable way to package and deploy services. They are the answer to immutability, we were so desperately trying to implement. They provide necessary isolation of processes, optimized resource utilization, and quite a few other benefits. And yet, we already realized that we need much more. It's not enough to run containers. We need to be able to scale them, to make them fault tolerant, to provide transparent communication across a cluster, and many other things. Containers are only a low-level piece of the puzzle. The real benefits are obtained with tools that sit on top of containers. Those tools are today known as container schedulers. They are our interface. We do not manage containers, they do.

In case you are not already using one of the container schedulers, you might be wondering what they are.

What is a container scheduler?

Picture me as a young teenager. After school, we'd go a courtyard and play soccer. That was an exciting sight. A random number of us running around the yard without any orchestration. There was no offense and no defense. We'd just run after a ball. Everyone moves forward towards the ball, someone kicks it to the left, and we move in that direction, only to start running back because someone kicked the ball again. The strategy was simple. Run towards the ball, kick it if you can, wherever you can, repeat. To this day I do not understand how anyone managed to score. It was complete randomness applied to a bunch of kids. There was no strategy, no plan, and no understanding that winning required coordination. Even a goalkeeper would be in random locations on the field. If he caught the ball around the goal he's guarding, he'd continue running with the ball in front of him. Most of the goals were scored by shooting at an empty goal. It was an "every man for himself" type of ambition. Each one of us hoped to score and bring glory to his or her name. Fortunately, the main objective was to have fun so winning as a team did not matter that much. If we were a "real" team, we'd need a coach. We'd need someone to tell us what the strategy is, who should do what, and when to go on the offense or fall back to defend the goal. We'd need someone to orchestrate us. The field (a cluster) had a random number of people (services) with the common goal (to win). Since anyone could join the game at any time, the number of people (services) was continually changing.

Someone would be injured and would have to be replaced or, when there was no replacement, the rest of us would have to take over his tasks (self-healing). Those football games can be easily translated into clusters. Just as we needed someone to tell us what to do (a coach), clusters need something to orchestrate all the services and resources. Both need not only to make up-front decisions, but also to continuously watch the game/cluster, and adapt the strategy/scheduling depending on the internal and external influences. We needed a coach and clusters need a scheduler. They need a framework that will decide where a service should be deployed and make sure that it maintains the desired run-time specification.

A cluster scheduler has quite a few goals. It's making sure that resources are used efficiently and within constraints. It's making sure that services are (almost) always running. It provides fault tolerance and high availability. It makes sure that the specified number of replicas are deployed. The list can go on for a while and varies from one solution to another. Still, no matter the exact list of cluster scheduler's responsibilities, they can be summarized through the primary goal. A scheduler is making sure that the desired state of a service or a node is (almost) always fulfilled. Instead of using imperative methods to achieve our goals, with schedulers we can be declarative. We can tell a scheduler what the desired state is, and it will do its best to ensure that our desire is (almost) always fulfilled. For example, instead of executing a deployment process five times hoping that we'll have five replicas of a service, we can tell a scheduler that our desired state is to have the service running with five replicas.

The difference between imperative and declarative methods might seem subtle but, in fact, is enormous. With a declarative expression of the desired state, a scheduler can monitor a cluster and perform actions whenever the actual state does not match the desired. Compare that to an execution of a deployment script. Both will deploy a service and produce the same initial result. However, the script will not make sure that the result is maintained over time. If an hour later, one of the replicas fail, our system will be compromised. Traditionally, we were solving that problem with a combination of alerts and manual interventions. An operator would receive a notification that a replica failed, he'd login to the server, and restart the process. If the whole server is down, the operator might choose to create a new one, or he might deploy the failed replica to one of the other servers. But, before doing that, he'd need to check which server has enough available memory and CPU. All that, and much more, is done by schedulers without human intervention. Think of schedulers as operators who are continually monitoring the system and fixing discrepancies between the desired and the actual state. The difference is that schedulers are infinitely faster and more accurate. They do not get tired, they do not need to go to the bathroom, and they do not require paychecks. They are machines or, to be more precise, software running on top of them.

That leads us to container schedulers. How do they differ from schedulers in general?

Container schedulers are based on the same principles as schedulers in general. The significant difference is that they are using containers as the deployment units. They are deploying services packaged as container images. They are trying to collocate them depending on desired memory and CPU specifications. They are making sure that the desired number of replicas are (almost) always running. All in all, they do what other schedulers do but with containers as the lowest and the only packaging unit. And that gives them a distinct advantage. They do not care what's inside. From scheduler's point of view, all containers are the same.

Containers provide benefits that other deployment mechanisms do not. Services deployed as containers are isolated and immutable. Isolation provides reliability. Isolation helps with networking and volume management. It avoids conflicts. It allows us to deploy anything, anywhere, without worrying whether that something will clash with other processes running on the same server. Schedulers, combined with containers and virtual machines, provide the ultimate cluster management nirvana. That will change in the future but, for now, container schedulers are the peak of engineering accomplishments. They allow us to combine the developer's necessity for rapid and frequent deployments with a sysadmin's goals of stability and reproducibility. And that leads us to Kubernetes.

What is Kubernetes?

To understand Kubernetes, it is important to realize that running containers directly is a bad option for most use cases. Containers are low-level entities that require a framework on top. They need something that will provide all the additional features we expect from services deployed to clusters. In other words, containers are handy but are not supposed to be run directly. The reason is simple. Containers, by themselves, do not provide fault tolerance. They cannot be deployed easily to the optimum spot in a cluster, and, to cut a long story short, are not operator friendly. That does not mean that containers by themselves are not useful. They are, but they require much more if we are to harness their real power. If we need to operate containers at scale and if we need them to be fault tolerant and self-healing, and have the other features we expect from modern clusters, we need more. We need at least a scheduler, probably more.

Kubernetes was first developed by a team at Google. It is based on their experience from running containers at scale for years. Later on, it was donated to `Cloud Native Computing Foundation` (`CNCF`) (https://www.cncf.io/). It is a true open source project with probably the highest velocity in history.

Kubernetes is a container scheduler and quite a lot more. We can use it to deploy our services, to roll out new releases without downtime, and to scale (or de-scale) those services. It is portable. It can run on a public or private cloud. It can run on-premise or in a hybrid environment. Kubernetes, in a way, makes your infrastructure vendor agnostic. We can move a Kubernetes cluster from one hosting vendor to another without changing (almost) any of the deployment and management processes. Kubernetes can be easily extended to serve nearly any needs. We can choose which modules we'll use, and we can develop additional features ourselves and plug them in.

If we choose to use Kubernetes, we decide to relinquish control. Kubernetes will decide where to run something and how to accomplish the state we specify. Such control allows Kubernetes to place replicas of a service on the most appropriate server, to restart them when needed, to replicate them, and to scale them. We can say that self-healing is a feature included in its design from the start. On the other hand, self-adaptation is coming as well. At the time of this writing, it is still in its infancy. Soon it will be an integral part of the system.

Zero-downtime deployments, fault tolerance, high availability, scaling, scheduling, and self-healing should be more than enough to see the value in Kubernetes. Yet, that is only a fraction of what it provides. We can use it to mount volumes for stateful applications. It allows us to store confidential information as secrets. We can use it to validate the health of our services. It can load balance requests and monitor resources. It provides service discovery and easy access to logs. And so on and so forth. The list of what Kubernetes does is long and rapidly increasing. Together with Docker, it is becoming a platform that envelops whole software development and deployment lifecycle.

The Kubernetes project has just started. It is in its infancy, and we can expect vast improvements and new features coming soon. Still, do not be fooled with "infancy". Even though the project is young, it has one of the biggest communities behind it and is used in some of the biggest clusters in the world. Do not wait. Adopt it now!

2

Running Kubernetes Cluster Locally

One of my goals in this book is to limit the learning expense to a minimum. True to that spirit, we'll run local Kubernetes clusters for as long as possible. At one point we'll have to switch to a hosted, multi-node Kubernetes cluster. I'll do my best to postpone that for as long as possible without limiting your learning experience. For now, we'll create a local Kubernetes cluster on your laptop.

There are quite a few ways to set up a local Kubernetes cluster. We could, for example, create a few nodes with Vagrant (`https://www.vagrantup.com/`) and execute quite a few shell commands that would convert them into a Kubernetes cluster. We could go even further and create a VirtualBox image that would have all the required software pre-installed and use it to create Vagrant VMs. We could also use Ansible to run provisioning of those images as well as to execute all the commands required to join VMs into a cluster. There are many other things that we could do, but we won't.

At this point, the idea is not to teach you all the intricacies of setting up a Kubernetes cluster. Instead, I want to get you up to speed as fast as possible and let you experience Kubernetes without sidelining that experience with installation details.

If the subject of this book would be Docker Swarm (as it was in *The DevOps 2.1 Toolkit: Docker Swarm*), we'd have Docker for Mac or Windows (or run it natively on Linux) and execute a single `docker swarm init` command. That's all that's needed to create a local Docker Swarm cluster. Can we accomplish the same simplicity with Kubernetes?

In October of 2017, Docker announced initial support for Kubernetes in Docker for Mac and Windows. At the time of this writing, it is available only for Mac in the edge channel.

Minikube creates a single-node cluster inside a VM on your laptop. While that is not ideal since we won't be able to demonstrate some of the features Kubernetes provides in a multi-node setup, it should be more than enough to explain most of the concepts behind Kubernetes. Later on, we'll move into a more production-like environment and explore the features that cannot be demonstrated in Minikube.

A note to Windows users

Please run all the examples from *GitBash* (installed through *Git*). That way the commands you'll see throughout the book will be same as those that should be executed on *MacOS* or any *Linux* distribution. If you're using Hyper-V instead of VirtualBox, you may need to run the *GitBash* window as an Administrator.

Before we dive into Minikube installation, there are a few prerequisites we should set up. The first in line is `kubectl`.

Installing kubectl

Kubernetes' command-line tool, `kubectl`, is used to manage a cluster and applications running inside it. We'll use `kubectl` a lot throughout the book, so we won't go into details just yet. Instead, we'll discuss its commands through examples that will follow shortly. For now, think of it as your interlocutor with a Kubernetes cluster.

Let's install `kubectl`.

All the commands from this chapter are available in the `02-minikube.sh` (`https://gist.github.com/vfarcic/77ca05f4d16125b5a5a5dc30a1ade7f c`) Gist.

Feel free to skip the installation steps if you already have `kubectl`. Just make sure that it is version 1.8 or above.

If you are a **MacOS user**, please execute the commands that follows:

```
curl -LO https://storage.googleapis.com/kubernetes-release/release/`curl -s
https://storage.googleapis.com/kubernetes-release/release/stable.txt`/bin/d
arwin/amd64/kubectl
chmod +x ./kubectl
sudo mv ./kubectl /usr/local/bin/kubectl
```

If you already have Homebrew (`https://brew.sh/`) package manager installed, you can "brew" it with the command that follows:

```
brew install kubectl
```

If, on the other hand, you're a **Linux user**, the commands that will install kubectl are as follows:

```
curl -LO https://storage.googleapis.com/kubernetes-release/release/$(curl -
s
https://storage.googleapis.com/kubernetes-release/release/stable.txt)/bin/l
inux/amd64/kubectl
chmod +x ./kubectl
sudo mv ./kubectl /usr/local/bin/kubectl
```

Finally, **Windows users** should download the binary through the command that follows.

```
curl -LO https://storage.googleapis.com/kubernetes-release/release/$(curl -
s
https://storage.googleapis.com/kubernetes-release/release/stable.txt)/bin/w
indows/amd64/kubectl.exe
```

Feel free to copy the binary to any directory. The important thing is to add it to your PATH.

Let's check kubectl version and, at the same time, validate that it is working correctly. No matter which OS you're using, the command is as follows:

```
kubectl version
```

The output is as follows:

```
Client Version: version.Info{Major:"1", Minor:"9", GitVersion:"v1.9.0",
GitCommit:"925c127ec6b946659ad0fd596fa959be43f0cc05",
GitTreeState:"clean", BuildDate:"2017-12-15T21:07:38Z",
GoVersion:"go1.9.2",
Compiler:"gc", Platform:"darwin/amd64"}
```

The connection to the server localhost:8080 was refused-did you specify the right host or port?

That is a very ugly and unreadable output. Fortunately, kubectl can use a few different formats for its output. For example, we can tell it to output the command in yaml format

```
kubectl version --output=yaml
```

The output is as follows:

```
clientVersion:
  buildDate: 2017-12-15T21:07:38Z
  compiler: gc
  gitCommit: 925c127ec6b946659ad0fd596fa959be43f0cc05
  gitTreeState: clean
  gitVersion: v1.9.0
  goVersion: go1.9.2
  major: "1"
  minor: "9"
  platform: darwin/amd64
The connection to the server localhost:8080 was refused - did you specify
the right host or port?
```

That was a much better (more readable) output.

We can see that the client version is 1.9. At the bottom is the error message stating that `kubectl` could not connect to the server. That is expected since we did not yet create a cluster. That's our next step.

 At the time of writing this book kubectl version was 1.9.0. Your version might be different when you install.

Installing Minikube

Minikube supports several virtualization technologies. We'll use VirtualBox throughout the book since it is the only virtualization supported in all operating systems. If you do not have it already, please head to the **Download VirtualBox** (https://www.virtualbox.org/wiki/Downloads) page and get the version that matches your OS. Please keep in mind that for VirtualBox or HyperV to work, virtualization must be enabled in the BIOS. Most laptops should have it enabled by default.

Finally, we can install Minikube.

If you're using **MacOS**, please execute the command that follows:

```
brew cask install minikube
```

If, on the other hand, you prefer **Linux**, the command is as follows:

```
curl -Lo minikube
```

```
https://storage.googleapis.com/minikube/releases/latest/minikube-"linux-amd
64 && chmod +x minikube && sudo mv minikube "/usr/local/bin/
```

Finally, you will not get a command if you are a Windows user. Instead, download the latest release from of the `minikube-windows-amd64.exe` (`https://storage.googleapis.com/minikube/releases/latest/minikube-windows-amd64.exe`) file, rename it to `minikube.exe`, and add it to your path.

We'll test whether Minikube works by checking its version.

```
minikube version
```

The output is as follows:

```
minikube version: v0.23.0
```

Now we're ready to give the cluster a spin.

Creating a local Kubernetes cluster with Minikube

The folks behind Minikube made creating a cluster as easy as it can get. All we need to do is to execute a single command. Minikube will start a virtual machine locally and deploy the necessary Kubernetes components into it. The VM will get configured with Docker and Kubernetes via a single binary called localkube.

```
minikube start --vm-driver=virtualbox
```

A note to Windows users
You might experience problems with `virtualbox`. If that's the case, you might want to use `hyperv` instead. Open a Powershell Admin Window and execute the `Get-NetAdapter` command, noting the name of your network connection. Create a `hyperv` virtual switch `New-VMSwitch -name NonDockerSwitch -NetAdapterName Ethernet -AllowManagementOS $true` replacing `Ethernet` with your network connection name. Then create the Minikube vm: `minikube start --vm-driver=hyperv --hyperv-virtual-switch "NonDockerSwitch" --memory=4096`. Other minikube commands such as `minikube start`, `minikube stop`, and `minikube delete` all work the same whether you're using VirutalBox or Hyper-V.

A few moments later, a new Minikube VM will be created and set up, and a cluster will be ready for use.

When we executed the `minikube start` command, it created a new VM based on the Minikube image. That image contains a few binaries. It has both `Docker` (https://www.docker.com/) and `rkt` (https://coreos.com/rkt/) container engines as well as `localkube` library. The library includes all the components necessary for running Kubernetes. We'll go into details of all those components later. For now, the important thing is that localkube provides everything we need to run a Kubernetes cluster locally.

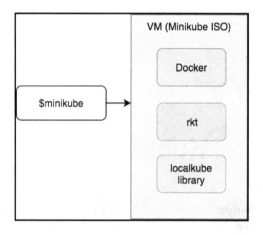

Figure 2-1: Minikube simplified architecture

Remember that this is a single-node cluster. While that is unfortunate, it is still the easiest way (as far as I know) to "play" with Kubernetes locally. It should do, for now. Later on, we'll explore ways to create a multi-node cluster that will be much closer to a production setup.

Let's take a look at the status of the cluster:

```
minikube status
```

The output is as follows:

```
minikube: Running
cluster: Running
kubectl: Correctly Configured: pointing to minikube-vm at 192.168.99.100
```

Minikube is running, and it initialized a Kubernetes cluster. It even configured `kubectl` so that it points to the newly created VM.

You won't see much UI in this book. I believe that a terminal is the best way to operate a cluster. More importantly, I am convinced that one should master a tool through its commands first. Later on, once we feel comfortable and understand how the tool works, we can choose to use a UI on top of it. We'll explore the Kubernetes UI in one of the later chapters. For now, I'll let you have a quick glimpse of it.

```
minikube dashboard
```

Feel free to explore the UI but don't take too long. You'll only get confused with concepts that we did not yet study. Once we learn about pods, replica-sets, services, and a myriad of other Kubernetes components, the UI will start making much more sense.

Figure 2-2: Kubernetes dashboard

Another useful Minikube command is `docker-env`.

```
minikube docker-env
```

The output is as follows:

```
export DOCKER_TLS_VERIFY="1"
export DOCKER_HOST="tcp://192.168.99.100:2376"
export DOCKER_CERT_PATH="/Users/vfarcic/.minikube/certs"
export DOCKER_API_VERSION="1.23"
```

```
# Run this command to configure your shell:
# eval $(minikube docker-env)
```

If you worked with Docker Machine, you'll notice that the output is the same. Both `docker-machine env` and `minikube docker-env` serve the same purpose. They output the environment variables required for a local Docker client to communicate with a remote Docker server. In this case, that Docker server is the one inside a VM created by Minikube. I assume that you already have Docker installed on your laptop. If that's not the case, please go to the install Docker (`https://docs.docker.com/install/`) page and follow the instructions for your operating system. Once Docker is installed, we can connect the client running on your laptop with the server in the Minikube VM.

```
eval $(minikube docker-env)
```

We evaluated (created) the environment variables provided through the `minikube docker-env` command. As a result, every command we send to our local Docker client will be executed on the Minikube VM. We can test that easily by, for example, listing all the running containers on that VM.

```
docker container ls
```

The containers listed in the output are those required by Kubernetes. We can, in a way, consider them system containers. We won't discuss each of them. As a matter of fact, we won't discuss any of them. At least, not right away. All you need to know, at this point, is that they make Kubernetes work.

Since almost everything in that VM is a container, pointing the local Docker client to the service inside it should be all you need (besides `kubectl`). Still, in some cases, you might want to SSH into the VM.

```
minikube ssh
docker container ls
exit
```

We entered into the Minikube VM, listed containers, and got out. There's no reason to do anything else beyond showing that SSH is possible, even though you probably won't use it.

What else is there to verify? We can, for example, confirm that `kubectl` is also pointing to the Minikube VM.

```
kubectl config current-context
```

The output should be a single word, `minikube`, indicating that `kubectl` is configured to talk to Kubernetes inside the newly created cluster.

As an additional verification, we can list all the nodes of the cluster.

```
kubectl get nodes
```

The output is as follows:

```
NAME      STATUS ROLES  AGE VERSION
minikube Ready   <none> 31m v1.8.0
```

It should come as no surprise that there is only one node, conveniently called `minikube`.

If you are experienced with Docker Machine or Vagrant, you probably noticed the similar pattern. Minikube commands are almost exactly the same as those from Docker Machine which, on the other hand, are similar to those from Vagrant.

Let's make a sneak peek into the components currently running in our tiny cluster.

```
kubectl get all --all-namespaces
```

Behold, the cluster in all its glory. It's made out of many building blocks we are yet to explore. Moreover, those are only the beginning. We'll be adding more as our needs and knowledge increase. For now, remember that there are many moving pieces. We won't go into details just yet. That would be too much to start with.

Going back to minikube, we can do all the common things we would expect from a virtual machine. For example, we can stop it.

```
minikube stop
```

We can start it again.

```
minikube start
```

We can delete it.

```
minikube delete
```

One interesting feature is the ability to specify which Kubernetes version we'd like to use.

Since Kubernetes is still a young project, we can expect quite a lot of changes at a rapid pace. That will often mean that our production cluster might not be running the latest version. On the other hand, we should strive to have our local environment as close to production as possible (within reason).

We can list all the available versions with the command that follows:

```
minikube get-k8s-versions
```

The output, limited to the first few lines, is as follows:

```
The following Kubernetes versions are available:
        - v1.9.0
        - v1.8.0
        - v1.7.5
        - v1.7.4
        - v1.7.3
        - v1.7.2
        - v1.7.0
        . . .
```

Now that we know which versions are available, we can create a new cluster based on, let's say, Kubernetes v1.7.0.

```
minikube start \
    --vm-driver=virtualbox \
    --kubernetes-version="v1.7.0"
kubectl version --output=yaml
```

We created a new cluster and output versions of the client and the server.

The output of the latter command is as follows:

```
clientVersion:
  buildDate: 2017-10-24T19:48:57Z
  compiler: gc
  gitCommit: bdaeafa71f6c7c04636251031f93464384d54963
  gitTreeState: clean
  gitVersion: v1.8.2
  goVersion: go1.8.3
  major: "1"
  minor: "8"
  platform: darwin/amd64
serverVersion:
  buildDate: 2017-10-04T09:25:40Z
  compiler: gc
  gitCommit: d3ada0119e776222f11ec7945e6d860061339aad
  gitTreeState: dirty
  gitVersion: v1.7.0
  goVersion: go1.8.3
  major: "1"
  minor: "7"
  platform: linux/amd64
```

If you focus on the `serverVersion` section, you'll notice that the `major` version is 1 and the `minor` is 7.

What now?

We are finished with a short introduction to Minikube. Actually, this might be called a long introduction as well. We use it to create a single-node Kubernetes cluster, launch the UI, do common VM operations like `stop`, `restart`, and `delete`, and so on. There's not much more to it. If you are familiar with Vagrant or Docker Machine, the principle is the same, and the commands are very similar.

Before we leave, we'll destroy the cluster. The next chapter will start fresh. That way, you can execute commands from any chapter at any time.

```
minikube delete
```

That's it. The cluster is no more.

3

Creating Pods

Pods are equivalent to bricks we use to build houses. Both are uneventful and not much by themselves. Yet, they are fundamental building blocks without which we could not construct the solution we are set to build.

If you used Docker or Docker Swarm, you're probably used to thinking that a container is the smallest unit and that more complex patterns are built on top of it. With Kubernetes, the smallest unit is a Pod. A Pod is a way to represent a running process in a cluster. From Kubernetes' perspective, there's nothing smaller than a Pod.

A Pod encapsulates one or more containers. It provides a unique network IP, it attaches storage resources, and it decides how containers should run. Everything in a Pod is tightly coupled.

We should clarify that containers in a Pod are not necessarily made by Docker. Other container runtimes are supported as well. Still, at the time of this writing, Docker is the most commonly used container runtime, and all our examples will use it.

From this chapter onward, we will break the publishing tradition of having a long explanation of concepts before diving into practical examples. Instead, we'll try to learn theory through practice. One step at a time.

We'll move straight into hands-on exercises. Since we cannot create Pods without a Kubernetes cluster, our first order of business is to create one.

Creating a Cluster

We'll create a local Kubernetes cluster using Minikube.

 All the commands from this chapter are available in the 03-pods.sh (https://gist.github.com/vfarcic/d860631d0dd3158c32740e9260c7add 0) Gist.

```
minikube start --vm-driver=virtualbox
kubectl get nodes
```

The output of the latter command is as follows:

```
NAME       STATUS ROLES   AGE VERSION
minikube Ready   <none> 47s v1.8.0
```

To simplify the process and save you from writing all the configuration files, we'll clone the GitHub repository vfarcic/k8s-specs (https://github.com/vfarcic/k8s-specs). It contains everything we'll need for this chapter, as well as for most of the others in this book.

```
git clone https://github.com/vfarcic/k8s-specs.git
cd k8s-specs
```

We cloned the repository and entered into the directory that was created.

Now we can run our first Pod.

Quick and dirty way to run Pods

Just as we can execute docker run to create containers, kubectl allows us to create Pods with a single command. For example, if we'd like to create a Pod with a Mongo database, the command is as follows.

```
kubectl run db --image mongo
```

You'll notice that the output says that deployment "db" was created. Kubernetes runs more than a single Pod. It created a Deployment and a few other things. We won't go into all the details just yet. What matters, for now, is that we created a Pod. We can confirm that by listing all the Pods in the cluster:

```
kubectl get pods
```

The output is as follows:

```
NAME                    READY STATUS             RESTARTS AGE
db-59d5f5b96b-kch6p 0/1    ContainerCreating 0          1m
```

We can see the name of the Pod, its readiness, the status, the number of times it restarted, and for how long it has existed (its age). If you were fast enough, or your network is slow, none of the pods might be ready. We expect to have one Pod, but there's zero running at the moment. Since the `mongo` image is relatively big, it might take a while until it is pulled from Docker Hub. After a while, we can retrieve the Pods one more time to confirm that the Pod with the Mongo database is running.

```
kubectl get pods
```

The output is as follows:

```
NAME                    READY STATUS  RESTARTS AGE
db-59d5f5b96b-kch6p 1/1    Running 0          6m
```

We can see that, this time, the Pod is ready and we can start using the Mongo database.

We can confirm that a container based on the `mongo` image is indeed running inside the cluster.

```
eval $(minikube docker-env)
docker container ls -f ancestor=mongo
```

We evaluated `minikube` variables so that our local Docker client is using Docker server running inside the VM. Further on, we listed all the containers based on the `mongo` image. The output is as follows (IDs are removed for brevity):

```
IMAGE COMMAND                    CREATED        STATUS        PORTS NAMES
mongo "docker-entrypoint.s..." 5 minutes ago Up 5 minutes        k8s
  _db_db-...
```

As you can see, the container defined in the Pod is running.

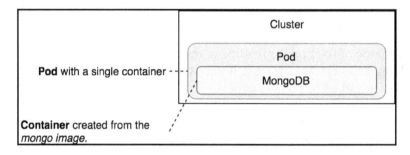

Figure 3-1: A Pod with a single container

That was not the best way to run Pods so we'll delete the deployment which, in turn, will delete everything it envelops, including the Pod.

```
kubectl delete deployment db
```

The output is as follows:

```
deployment "db" deleted
```

Why did I say that was not the best way to run Pods? We used the imperative way to tell Kubernetes what to do. Even though there are cases when that might be useful, most of the time we want to leverage the declarative approach. We want to have a way to define what we need in a file and pass that information to Kubernetes. That way, we can have a documented and repeatable process, that can (and should) be version controlled as well. Moreover, the `kubectl run` was reasonably simple. In real life, we need to declare much more than the name of the deployment and the image. Commands like `kubectl` can quickly become too long and, in many cases, very complicated. Instead, we'll write specifications in YAML format. Soon, we'll see how we can accomplish a similar result using declarative syntax.

Defining Pods through declarative syntax

Even though a Pod can contain any number of containers, the most common use case is to use the single-container-in-a-Pod model. In such a case, a Pod is a wrapper around one container. From Kubernetes' perspective, a Pod is the smallest unit. We cannot tell Kubernetes to run a container. Instead, we ask it to create a Pod that wraps around a container.

Let's take a look at a simple Pod definition:

```
cat pod/db.yml
```

The output is as follows:

```
apiVersion: v1
kind: Pod
metadata:
  name: db
  labels:
    type: db
    vendor: Mongo Labs
spec:
  containers:
  - name: db
    image: mongo:3.3
    command: ["mongod"]
    args: ["--rest", "--httpinterface"]
```

We're using `v1` of Kubernetes Pods API. Both `apiVersion` and `kind` are mandatory. That way, Kubernetes knows what we want to do (create a Pod) and which API version to use.

The next section is `metadata`. It provides information that does not influence how the Pod behaves. We used `metadata` to define the name of the Pod (`db`) and a few labels. Later on, when we move into Controllers, labels will have a practical purpose. For now, they are purely informational.

The last section is the `spec` in which we defined a single container. As you might have guessed, we can have multiple containers defined as a Pod. Otherwise, the section would be written in singular (`container` without s). We'll explore multi-container Pods later.

In our case, the container is defined with the name (`db`), the image (`mongo`), the command that should be executed when the container starts (`mongod`), and, finally, the set of arguments. The arguments are defined as an array with, in this case, two elements (`--rest` and `--httpinterface`).

We won't go into details of everything you can use to define a Pod. Throughout the book, you'll see quite a few other commonly (and not so commonly) used things we should define in Pods. Later on, when you decide to learn all the possible arguments you can apply, explore the official, and ever-changing, `Pod v1 core`

(`https://v1-9.docs.kubernetes.io/docs/reference/generated/kubernetes-api/v1.9/#pod-v1-core`) documentation.

Let's create the Pod defined in the `db.yml` file.

```
kubectl create -f pod/db.yml
```

You'll notice that we did not need to specify `pod` in the command. The command will create the kind of resource defined in the `pod/db.yml` file. Later on, you'll see that a single YAML file can contain definitions of multiple resources.

Let's take a look at the Pods in the cluster:

```
kubectl get pods
```

The output is as follows:

```
NAME READY STATUS   RESTARTS AGE
db   1/1   Running 0        11s
```

Our Pod named `db` is up and running.

In some cases, you might want to retrieve a bit more information by specifying `wide` output.

```
kubectl get pods -o wide
```

The output is as follows:

```
NAME READY STATUS   RESTARTS AGE IP         NODE
db   1/1   Running 0        1m  172.17.0.4 minikube
```

As you can see, we got two additional columns; the IP and the node.

If you'd like to parse the output, using `json` format is probably the best option.

```
kubectl get pods -o json
```

The output is too big to be presented in the book, especially since we won't go through all the information provided through the `json` output format.

When we want more information than provided with the default output, but still in a format that is human-friendly, `yaml` output is probably the best choice.

```
kubectl get pods -o yaml
```

Just as with the `json` output, we won't go into details of everything we got from Kubernetes. With time, you'll become familiar with all the information related to Pods. For now, we want to focus on the most important aspects.

Let's introduce a new `kubectl` sub-command.

```
kubectl describe pod db
```

The `describe` sub-command returned details of the specified resource. In this case, the resource is the Pod named `db`.

The output is too big for us to go into every detail. Besides, most of it should be self-explanatory if you're familiar with containers. Instead, we'll briefly comment on the last section called `events`.

```
. . .
Events:
  Type      Reason              Age   From                 Message
  ----      ------              ----  ----                 -------
  Normal    Scheduled           2m    default-scheduler    Successfully
assigned db to minikube
  Normal    SuccessfulMountVolume 2m    kubelet, minikube    MountVolume.SetUp
succeeded for volume "default-token-x27md"
  Normal    Pulling             2m    kubelet, minikube    pulling image
"mongo:3.3"
  Normal    Pulled              2m    kubelet, minikube    Successfully
pulled image "mongo:3.3"
  Normal    Created             2m    kubelet, minikube    Created container
  Normal    Started             2m    kubelet, minikube    Started container
```

We can see that the Pod was created and went through several stages as shown in the following sequence diagram. Even though the process was simple from a user's perspective, quite a few things happened in the background.

This might be a right moment to pause with our exercises, discuss some of the details of Kubernetes components, and try to get an understanding of how Pod scheduling works.

Three major components were involved in the process.

The *API server* is the central component of a Kubernetes cluster and it runs on the master node. Since we are using Minikube, both master and worker nodes are baked into the same virtual machine. However, a more serious Kubernetes cluster should have the two separated on different hosts.

All other components interact with API server and keep watch for changes. Most of the coordination in Kubernetes consists of a component writing to the API Server resource that another component is watching. The second component will then react to changes almost immediately.

The *scheduler* is also running on the master node. Its job is to watch for unassigned pods and assign them to a node which has available resources (CPU and memory) matching Pod requirements. Since we are running a single-node cluster, specifying resources would not provide much insight into their usage so we'll leave them for later.

Kubelet runs on each node. Its primary function is to make sure that assigned pods are running on the node. It watches for any new Pod assignments for the node. If a Pod is assigned to the node Kubelet is running on, it will pull the Pod definition and use it to create containers through Docker or any other supported container engine.

The sequence of events that transpired with the `kubectl create -f pod/db.yml` command is as follows:

1. Kubernetes client (`kubectl`) sent a request to the API server requesting creation of a Pod defined in the `pod/db.yml` file.
2. Since the scheduler is watching the API server for new events, it detected that there is an unassigned Pod.
3. The scheduler decided which node to assign the Pod to and sent that information to the API server.
4. Kubelet is also watching the API server. It detected that the Pod was assigned to the node it is running on.
5. Kubelet sent a request to Docker requesting the creation of the containers that form the Pod. In our case, the Pod defines a single container based on the `mongo` image.
6. Finally, Kubelet sent a request to the API server notifying it that the Pod was created successfully.

The process might not make much sense right now since we are running a single-node cluster. If we had more VMs, scheduling might have happened somewhere else, and the complexity of the process would be easier to grasp. We'll get there in due time.

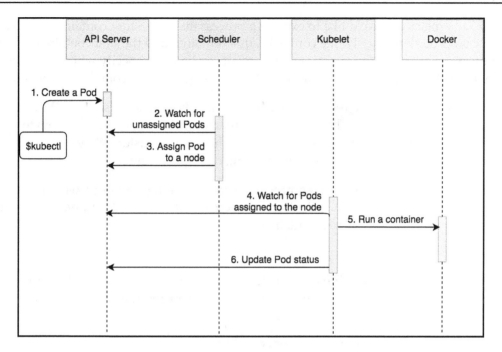

Figure 3-2: Pod scheduling sequence

In many cases, it is more useful to describe resources by referencing the file that defines them. That way there is no confusion nor need to remember the names of resources. We could have executed the command that follows:

```
kubectl describe -f pod/db.yml
```

The output should be the same since, in both cases, kubectl sent a request to Kubernetes API requesting information about the Pod named db.

Just as with Docker, we can execute a new process inside a running container inside a Pod.

```
kubectl exec db ps aux
```

The output is as follows:

```
USER PID %CPU %MEM    VSZ    RSS TTY STAT START TIME COMMAND
root    1  0.5  2.9 967452 59692 ?   Ssl  21:47 0:03 mongod --rest --
httpinterface
root   31  0.0  0.0  17504  1980 ?   Rs   21:58 0:00 ps aux
```

We told Kubernetes that we'd like to execute a process inside the first container of the Pod db. Since our Pod defines only one container, this container and the first container are one and the same. The `--container` (or `-c`) argument can be set to specify which container should be used. That is particularly useful when running multiple containers in a Pod.

Apart from using Pods as the reference, `kubectl exec` is almost the same as the `docker container exec` command. The significant difference is that `kubectl` allows us to execute a process in a container running in any node inside a cluster, while `docker container exec` is limited to containers running on a specific node.

Instead of executing a new short-lived process inside a running container, we can enter into it. For example, we can make the execution interactive with `-i` (`stdin`) and `-t` (terminal) arguments and run `shell` inside a container.

```
kubectl exec -it db sh
```

We're inside the `sh` process inside the container. Since the container hosts a Mongo database, we can, for example, execute `db.stats()` to confirm that the database is indeed running.

```
echo 'db.stats()' | mongo localhost:27017/test
```

We used `mongo` client to execute `db.stats()` for the database `test` running on `localhost:27017`. Since we're not trying to learn Mongo (at least not in this book), the only purpose of this exercise was to prove that the database is up-and-running. Let's get out of the container.

```
exit
```

Logs should be shipped from containers to a central location. However, since we did not yet explore that subject, it would be useful to be able to see logs of a container in a Pod.

The command that outputs logs of the only container in the db Pod is as follows:

```
kubectl logs db
```

The output is too big and not that important in its entirety. One of the last line is as follows:

```
...
2017-11-10T22:06:20.039+0000 I NETWORK  [thread1] waiting for connections
on port 27017
...
```

With the -f (or --follow) we can follow the logs in real-time. Just as with the exec sub-command, if a Pod defines multiple containers, we can specify which one to use with the -c argument.

What happens when a container inside a Pod dies? Let's simulate a failure and observe what happens.

```
kubectl exec -it db pkill mongod
kubectl get pods
```

We killed the main process of the container and listed all the Pods. The output is as follows:

```
NAME READY STATUS   RESTARTS AGE
db   1/1   Running 1        13m
```

The container is running (1/1). Kubernetes guarantees that the containers inside a Pod are (almost) always running. Please note that the RESTARTS field now has the value of 1. Every time a container fails, Kubernetes will restart it:

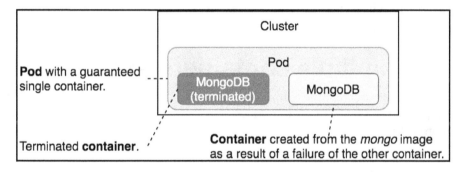

Figure 3-3: Pod with a failed container

Finally, we can delete a Pod if we don't need it anymore.

```
kubectl delete -f pod/db.yml
kubectl get pods
```

We removed the Pods defined in db.yml and retrieved the list of all the Pods in the cluster. The output of the latter command is as follows:

```
NAME READY STATUS      RESTARTS AGE
db   0/1   Terminating 1        3h
```

The number of ready containers dropped to 0, and the status of the db Pod is terminating.

When we sent the instruction to delete a Pod, Kubernetes tried to terminate it gracefully. The first thing it did was to send the `TERM` signal to all the main processes inside the containers that form the Pod. From there on, Kubernetes gives each container a period of thirty seconds so that the processes in those containers can shut down gracefully. Once the grace period expires, the `KILL` signal is sent to terminate all the main processes forcefully and, with them, all the containers. The default grace period can be changed through the `gracePeriodSeconds` value in YAML definition or `--grace-period` argument of the `kubectl delete` command.

If we repeat the `get pods` command thirty seconds after we issued the `delete` instruction, the Pod should be removed from the system:

```
kubectl get pods
```

This time, the output is different.

```
No resources found.
```

The only Pod we had in the system is no more.

Running multiple containers in a single Pod

Pods are designed to run multiple cooperative processes that should act as a cohesive unit. Those processes are wrapped in containers. All the containers that form a Pod are running on the same machine. A Pod cannot be split across multiple nodes.

All the processes (containers) inside a Pod share the same set of resources, and they can communicate with each other through `localhost`. One of those shared resources is storage. A volume defined in a Pod can be accessed by all the containers thus allowing them all to share the same data. We'll explore storage in more depth later on. For now, let's take a look at the `pod/go-demo-2.yml` specification:

```
cat pod/go-demo-2.yml
```

The output is as follows:

```
apiVersion: v1
kind: Pod
metadata:
  name: go-demo-2
  labels:
    type: stack
spec:
  containers:
```

```
      - name: db
        image: mongo:3.3
      - name: api
        image: vfarcic/go-demo-2
        env:
        - name: DB
          value: localhost
```

The YAML file defines a Pod with two containers named `db` and `api`. The service inside the `vfarcic/go-demo-2` image uses environment variable `DB` to know where the database is. The value is `localhost` since all the containers in the same Pod are reachable through it.

Let's create the Pod:

```
kubectl create -f pod/go-demo-2.yml
kubectl get -f pod/go-demo-2.yml
```

We created a new Pod defined in the `go-demo-2.yml` file and retrieved its information from Kubernetes. The output of the latter command is as follows:

```
NAME        READY STATUS  RESTARTS AGE
go-demo-2 2/2   Running 0          2m
```

We can see from the `READY` column that, this time, the Pod has two containers (`2/2`).

This might be an excellent opportunity to introduce formatting to retrieve specific information.

Let's say that we want to retrieve the names of the containers in a Pod. The first thing we'd have to do is get familiar with Kubernetes API. We can do that by going to `Pod v1 core` (https://v1-9.docs.kubernetes.io/docs/reference/generated/kubernetes-api/v1.9/#pod-v1-core) documentation. While reading the documentation will become mandatory sooner or later, we'll use a simpler route and inspect the output from Kubernetes.

```
kubectl get -f pod/go-demo-2.yml -o json
```

The output is too big to be presented in a book, so we'll focus on the task at hand. We need to retrieve the names of the containers in the Pod. Therefore, the part of the output we're looking for is as follows:

```
{
    . . .
    "spec": {
        "containers": [
            {
                . . .
                "name": "db",
```

```
                        . . .
            },
            {
                        . . .
                  "name": "api",
                        . . .
            }
         ],
         . . .
      },
      . . .
   }
```

The `get` command that would filter the output and retrieve only the names of the containers is as follows:

```
kubectl get -f pod/go-demo-2.yml \
    -o jsonpath="{.spec.containers[*].name}"
```

The output is as follows:

```
db api
```

We used `jsonpath` as the output format and specified that we want to retrieve names of all the `containers` from the `spec`. The ability to filter and format information might not look that important right now but, once we move into more complex scenarios, it will prove to be invaluable. That will become especially evident when we try to automate the processes and requests sent to Kubernetes API.

How would we execute a command inside the Pod? Unlike the previous examples that did a similar task, this time we have two containers in the Pod, so we need to be more specific.

```
kubectl exec -it -c db go-demo-2 ps aux
```

The output should display the processes inside the `db` container. Namely, the `mongod` process.

How about logs from a container? As you might have guessed, we cannot execute something like `kubectl logs go-demo-2` since the Pod hosts multiple containers. Instead, we need to be specific and name the container from which we want to see the logs:

```
kubectl logs go-demo-2 -c db
```

How about scaling? How would we, for example, scale the service so that there are two containers of the API and one container for the database?

One option could be to define two containers in the Pod. Let's take a look at a Pod definition that might accomplish what we need.

```
cat pod/go-demo-2-scaled.yml
```

The output is as follows:

```
apiVersion: v1
kind: Pod
metadata:
  name: go-demo-2
  labels:
    type: stack
spec:
  containers:
  - name: db
    image: mongo:3.3
  - name: api-1
    image: vfarcic/go-demo-2
    env:
    - name: DB
      value: localhost
  - name: api-2
    image: vfarcic/go-demo-2
    env:
    - name: DB
      value: localhost
```

We defined two containers for the API and named them `api-1` and `api-2`. The only thing left is to create the Pod. But, we're not going to do that.

We should not think of Pods as resources that should do anything beyond a definition of the smallest unit in our cluster. A Pod is a collection of containers that share the same resources. Not much more. Everything else should be accomplished with higher-level constructs. We'll explore how to scale Pods without changing their definition in one of the next chapters.

Let's go back to our original multi-container Pod that defined `api` and `db` containers. That was a terrible design choice since it tightly couples one with the other. As a result, when we explore how to scale Pods (not containers), both would need to match. If, for example, we scale the Pod to three, we'd have three APIs and three DBs. Instead, we should have defined two Pods, one for each container (`db` and `api`). That would give us enough flexibility to treat each independently from the other.

There are quite a few other reasons not to put multiple containers in the same Pod. For now, just be patient. Most of the scenarios where you might think that multi-container Pod is a good solution will probably be solved through other resources.

 A Pod is a collection of containers. However, that does not mean that multi-container Pods are common. They are rare. Most Pods you'll create will be single container units.

Does that mean that multi-container Pods are useless? They're not. There are scenarios when having multiple containers in a Pod is a good idea. However, they are very specific and, in most cases, are based on one container that acts as the main service and the rest serving as side-cars. A frequent use case are multi-container Pods used for **continuous integration (CI)**, **delivery (CD)**, or **deployment (CDP)** processes. We'll explore them later. For now, we'll focus on single-container Pods.

Let's remove the Pod before we move onto container health.

```
kubectl delete -f pod/go-demo-2.yml
```

Monitoring health

The `vfarcic/go-demo-2` Docker image is designed to fail on the first sign of trouble. In cases like that, there is no need for any health checks. When things go wrong, the main process stops, the container hosting it stops as well, and Kubernetes restarts the failed container. However, not all services are designed to fail fast. Even those that are might still benefit from additional health checks. For example, a back-end API can be up and running but, due to a memory leak, serve requests much slower than expected. Such a situation might benefit from a health check that would verify whether the service responds within, for example, two seconds. We can exploit Kubernetes liveness and readiness probes for that.

`livenessProbe` can be used to confirm whether a container should be running. If the probe fails, Kubernetes will kill the container and apply restart policy which defaults to `Always`. `readinessProbe`, on the other hand, should be used as an indication that the service is ready to serve requests. When combined with `Services` construct, only containers with the `readinessProbe` state set to `Success` will receive requests. We'll leave `readinessProbe` for later since it is directly tied to `Services`. Instead, we'll explore `livenessProbe`. Both are defined in the same way so the experience with one of them can be easily applied to the other.

Let's take a look at an updated definition of the Pod we used thus far:

```
cat pod/go-demo-2-health.yml
```

The output is as follows:

```
apiVersion: v1
kind: Pod
metadata:
  name: go-demo-2
  labels:
    type: stack
spec:
  containers:
  - name: db
    image: mongo:3.3
  - name: api
    image: vfarcic/go-demo-2
    env:
    - name: DB
      value: localhost
    livenessProbe:
      httpGet:
        path: /this/path/does/not/exist
        port: 8080
      initialDelaySeconds: 5
      timeoutSeconds: 2 # Defaults to 1
      periodSeconds: 5 # Defaults to 10
      failureThreshold: 1 # Defaults to 3
```

Don't get confused by seeing two containers in this Pod. I stand by my words. Those two should be defined in separate Pods. However, since that would require knowledge we are yet to obtain, and `vfarcic/go-demo-2` doesn't work without a database, we'll have to stick with the example that specifies two containers. It won't take long until we break it into pieces.

The additional definition is inside the `livenessProbe`.

We defined that the action should be `httpGet` followed with the `path` and the `port` of the service. Since `/this/path/does/not/exist` is true to itself, the probe will fail, thus showing us what happens when a container is unhealthy. The `host` is not specified since it defaults to the Pod IP.

Further down, we declared that the first execution of the probe should be delayed by five seconds (`initialDelaySeconds`), that requests should timeout after two seconds (`timeoutSeconds`), that the process should be repeated every five seconds (`periodSeconds`), and (`failureThreshold`) define how many attempts it must try before giving up.

Let's take a look at the probe in action.

```
kubectl create \
    -f pod/go-demo-2-health.yml
```

We created the Pod with the probe. Now we must wait until the probe fails a few times. A minute is more than enough. Once we're done waiting, we can describe the Pod:

```
kubectl describe \
    -f pod/go-demo-2-health.yml
```

The bottom of the output contains events. They are as follows:

```
...
Events:
  Type     Reason               Age           From               Message
  ----     ------               ----          ----               -------
  Normal   Scheduled            6m            default-scheduler
Successfully assigned go-demo-2 to minikube
  Normal   SuccessfulMountVolume 6m           kubelet, minikube
MountVolume.SetUp succeeded for volume "default-token-7jc7q"
  Normal   Pulling              6m            kubelet, minikube
pulling image "mongo"
  Normal   Pulled               6m            kubelet, minikube
Successfully pulled image "mongo"
  Normal   Created              6m            kubelet, minikube
Created container
  Normal   Started              6m            kubelet, minikube
Started container
  Normal   Created              5m (x3 over 6m) kubelet, minikube
Created container
  Normal   Started              5m (x3 over 6m) kubelet, minikube
Started container
  Warning  Unhealthy            5m (x3 over 6m) kubelet, minikube
```

```
Liveness probe failed: HTTP probe failed with statuscode: 404
    Normal    Pulling                  5m (x4 over 6m)   kubelet, minikube
pulling image "vfarcic/go-demo-2"
    Normal    Killing                  5m (x3 over 6m)   kubelet, minikube
Killing container with id docker://api:Container failed live ness probe..
Container will be killed and recreated.
    Normal    Pulled                   5m (x4 over 6m)   kubelet, minikube
Successfully pulled image "vfarcic/go-demo-2"
```

We can see that, once the container started, the probe was executed, and that it failed. As a result, the container was killed only to be created again. In the preceding output, we can see that the process was repeated three times (`3x over ...`).

Please visit `Probe v1 core`
(`https://v1-9.docs.kubernetes.io/docs/reference/generated/kubernetes-api/v1.9/#probe-v1-core`) if you'd like to learn all the available options.

Pods are (almost) useless (by themselves)

Pods are fundamental building blocks in Kubernetes. In most cases, you will not create Pods directly. Instead, you'll use higher level constructs like Controllers.

Pods are disposable. They are not long lasting services. Even though Kubernetes is doing its best to ensure that the containers in a Pod are (almost) always up-and-running, the same cannot be said for Pods. If a Pod fails, gets destroyed, or gets evicted from a Node, it will not be rescheduled. At least, not without a Controller. Similarly, if a whole node is destroyed, all the Pods on it will cease to exist. Pods do not heal by themselves. Excluding some special cases, Pods are not meant to be created directly.

 Do not create Pods by themselves. Let one of the controllers create Pods for you.

What now?

We'll remove the cluster and start the next chapter fresh.

```
minikube delete
```

Please take some time to get more familiar with Pods. They are the most basic and, arguably, the essential building block in Kubernetes. Since, by now, you have a solid understanding what the Pods are, a good next step might be to go through PodSpec v1 core (`https://v1-9.docs.kubernetes.io/docs/reference/generated/kubernetes-api/v1.9/#pod-v1-core`) documentation.

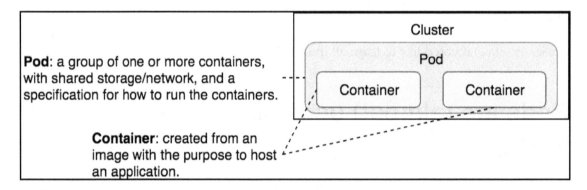

Figure 3-4: The components explored so far

4
Scaling Pods With ReplicaSets

Most applications should be scalable and all must be fault tolerant. Pods do not provide those features, ReplicaSets do.

We learned that Pods are the smallest unit in Kubernetes. We also learned that Pods are not fault tolerant. If a Pod is destroyed, Kubernetes will do nothing to remedy the problem. That is, if Pods are created without Controllers.

The first Controller we'll explore is called *ReplicaSet*. Its primary, and pretty much only function, is to ensure that a specified number of replicas of a Pod matches the actual state (almost) all the time. That means that ReplicaSets make Pods scalable.

We can think of ReplicaSets as a self-healing mechanism. As long as elementary conditions are met (for example, enough memory and CPU), Pods associated with a ReplicaSet are guaranteed to run. They provide fault-tolerance and high availability.

It is worth mentioning ReplicaSet is the next-generation ReplicationController. The only significant difference is that ReplicaSet has extended support for selectors. Everything else is the same. ReplicationController is considered deprecated, so we'll focus only on ReplicaSet.

ReplicaSet's primary function is to ensure that the specified number of replicas of a service are (almost) always running.

Let's explore ReplicaSet through examples and see how it works and what it does.

The first step is to create a Kubernetes cluster.

Creating a Cluster

We'll continue using Minikube to simulate a cluster locally.

 All the commands from this chapter are available in the `04-rs.sh` (https://gist.github.com/vfarcic/f6588da3d1c8a82100a81709295d4a93) Gist.

```
minikube start --vm-driver=virtualbox
kubectl config current-context
```

We created a single-node cluster and configured `kubectl` to use it.

Before we explore the first ReplicaSet example, we'll enter into the local copy of the `vfarcic/k8s-spec` repository and pull the latest version. Who knows, maybe I added some new stuff since the last time you checked it out.

```
cd k8s-specs
git pull
```

Now that the cluster is running and the repository with the specs is up-to-date, we can create our first ReplicaSet.

Creating ReplicaSets

Let's take a look at a ReplicaSet based on the Pod we created in the previous chapter:

```
cat rs/go-demo-2.yml
```

The output is as follows:

```
apiVersion: apps/v1beta2
kind: ReplicaSet
metadata:
  name: go-demo-2
spec:
  replicas: 2
  selector:
    matchLabels:
      type: backend
      service: go-demo-2
  template:
    metadata:
      labels:
```

```
          type: backend
          service: go-demo-2
          db: mongo
          language: go
      spec:
        containers:
        - name: db
          image: mongo:3.3
        - name: api
          image: vfarcic/go-demo-2
          env:
          - name: DB
            value: localhost
          livenessProbe:
            httpGet:
              path: /demo/hello
              port: 8080
```

The apiVersion, kind, and metadata fields are mandatory with all Kubernetes objects. ReplicaSet is no exception.

We specified that the apiVersion is apps/v1beta2. At the time of this writing, ReplicaSet is still in beta. Soon it will be considered stable, and you'll be able to replace the value with apps/v1. The kind is ReplicaSet and metadata has the name key set to go-demo-2. We could have extended ReplicaSet metadata with labels. However, we skipped that part since they would serve only for informational purposes. They do not affect the behavior of the ReplicaSet.

You should be familiar with the three fields since we already explored them when we worked with Pods. In addition to them, the spec section is mandatory as well.

The first field we defined in the spec section is replicas. It sets the desired number of replicas of the Pod. In this case, the ReplicaSet should ensure that two Pods should run concurrently. If we did not specify the value of the replicas, it would default to 1.

The next `spec` section is the `selector`. We use it to select which pods should be included in the ReplicaSet. It does not distinguish between the Pods created by a ReplicaSet or some other process. In other words, ReplicaSets and Pods are decoupled. If Pods that match the `selector` exist, ReplicaSet will do nothing. If they don't, it will create as many Pods to match the value of the `replicas` field. Not only that ReplicaSet creates the Pods that are missing, but it also monitors the cluster and ensures that the desired number of `replicas` is (almost) always running. In case there are already more running Pods with the matching `selector`, some will be terminated to match the number set in `replicas`.

We used `spec.selector.matchLabels` to specify a few labels. They must match the labels defined in the `spec.template`. In our case, ReplicaSet will look for Pods with `type` set to `backend` and `service` set to `go-demo-2`. If Pods with those labels do not already exist, it'll create them using the `spec.template` section.

The last section of the `spec` field is the `template`. It is the only required field in the `spec`, and it has the same schema as a Pod specification. At a minimum, the labels of the `spec.template.metadata.labels` section must match those specified in the `spec.selector.matchLabels`. We can set additional labels that will serve informational purposes only. ReplicaSet will make sure that the number of replicas matches the number of Pods with the same labels. In our case, we set `type` and `service` to the same values and added two additional ones (`db` and `language`).

It might sound confusing that the `spec.template.spec.containers` field is mandatory. ReplicaSet will look for Pods with the matching labels created by other means. If we already created a Pod with labels `type: backend` and `service: go-demo-2`, this ReplicaSet would find them and would not create a Pod defined in `spec.template`. The main purpose of that field is to ensure that the desired number of `replicas` is running. If they are created by other means, ReplicaSet will do nothing. Otherwise, it'll create them using the information in `spec.template`.

Finally, the `spec.template.spec` section contains the same `containers` definition we used in the previous chapter. It defines a Pod with two containers (`db` and `api`).

In the previous chapter, I claimed that those two containers should not belong to the same Pod. The same is true for the containers in Pods managed by the ReplicaSet. However, we did not yet have the opportunity to explore ways to allow containers running in different Pods to communicate with each other. So, for now, we'll continue using the same flawed Pods definition.

Let's create the ReplicaSet and experience its advantages first hand.

```
kubectl create -f rs/go-demo-2.yml
```

We got the response that the `replicaset "go-demo-2"` was `created`. We can confirm that by listing all the ReplicaSets in the cluster.

```
kubectl get rs
```

The output is as follows:

```
NAME        DESIRED CURRENT READY AGE
go-demo-2 2         2       0     14s
```

We can see that the desired number of replicas is 2 and that it matches the current value. The value of the `ready` field is still 0 but, after the images are pulled, and the containers are running, it'll change to 2.

Instead of retrieving all the replicas in the cluster, we can retrieve those specified in the `rs/go-demo-2.yml` file.

```
kubectl get -f rs/go-demo-2.yml
```

The output should be the same since, in both cases, there is only one ReplicaSet running inside the cluster.

All the other `kubectl get` arguments we explored in the previous chapter also apply to ReplicaSets or, to be more precise, to all Kubernetes objects. The same is true for `kubectl describe` command:

```
kubectl describe -f rs/go-demo-2.yml
```

The last lines of the output are as follows:

```
...
Events:
  Type    Reason          Age  From                  Message
  ----    ------          ---- ----                  -------
  Normal SuccessfulCreate 3m   replicaset-controller Created pod:
go-demo-2-v59t5
  Normal SuccessfulCreate 3m   replicaset-controller Created pod:
go-demo-2-5fd54
```

Judging by the events, we can see that ReplicaSet created two Pods while trying to match the desired state with the actual state.

Finally, if you are not yet convinced that the ReplicaSet created the missing Pods, we can list all those running in the cluster and confirm it:

```
kubectl get pods --show-labels
```

To be on the safe side, we used the `--show-labels` argument so that we can verify that the Pods in the cluster match those created by the ReplicaSet.

The output is as follows:

```
NAME                    READY STATUS   RESTARTS AGE LABELS
go-demo-2-5fd54 2/2      Running 0               6m  db=mongo,language=go,service=go-
demo-2,type=backend
go-demo-2-v59t5 2/2      Running 0               6m  db=mongo,language=go,service=go-
demo-2,type=backend
```

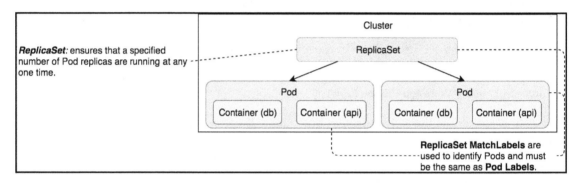

Figure 4-1: A ReplicaSet with two replicas of a Pod

The sequence of events that transpired with the `kubectl create -f rs/go-demo-2.yml` command is as follows:

1. Kubernetes client (`kubectl`) sent a request to the API server requesting the creation of a ReplicaSet defined in the `rs/go-demo-2.yml` file.
2. The controller is watching the API server for new events, and it detected that there is a new ReplicaSet object.
3. The controller creates two new pod definitions because we have configured replica value as 2 in `rs/go-demo-2.yml` file.
4. Since the scheduler is watching the API server for new events, it detected that there are two unassigned Pods.
5. The scheduler decided to which node to assign the Pod and sent that information to the API server.

6. Kubelet is also watching the API server. It detected that the two Pods were assigned to the node it is running on.

7. Kubelet sent requests to Docker requesting the creation of the containers that form the Pod. In our case, the Pod defines two containers based on the mongo and api image. So in total four containers are created.

8. Finally, Kubelet sent a request to the API server notifying it that the Pods were created successfully.

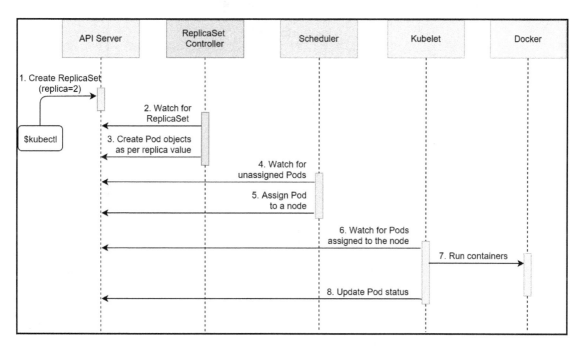

Figure 4-2: The sequence of events followed by request to create a ReplicaSet

The sequence we described is useful when we want to understand everything that happened in the cluster from the moment we requested the creation of a new ReplicaSet. However, it might be too confusing so we'll try to explain the same process through a diagram that more closely represents the cluster.

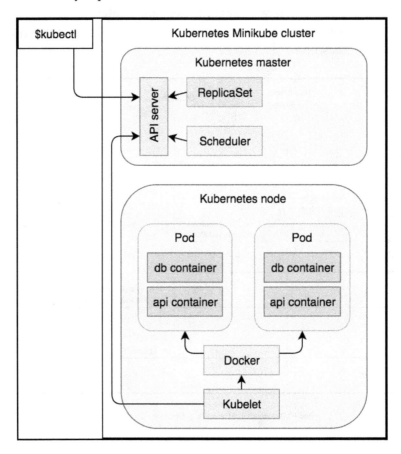

Figure 4-3: The events followed by request to create a ReplicaSet

 Typically, we'd have a multi-node cluster, and the Pods would be distributed across it. For now, while we're using Minikube, there's only one server that acts as both the master and the node. Later on, when we start working on multi-node clusters, the distribution of Pods will become evident. The same can be said for the architecture. We'll explain different Kubernetes components in more detail later on.

Let's see which types of operations we can perform on ReplicaSets.

Operating ReplicaSets

What would happen if we delete the ReplicaSet? As you might have guessed, both the ReplicaSet and everything it created (the Pods) would disappear with a single `kubectl delete -f rs/go-demo-2.yml` command. However, since ReplicaSets and Pods are loosely coupled objects with matching labels, we can remove one without deleting the other. We can, for example, remove the ReplicaSet we created while leaving the two Pods intact.

```
kubectl delete -f rs/go-demo-2.yml \
    --cascade=false
```

We used the `--cascade=false` argument to prevent Kubernetes from removing all the downstream objects. As a result, we got the confirmation that `replicaset "go-demo-2"` was `deleted`. Let's confirm that it is indeed removed from the system.

```
kubectl get rs
```

As expected, the output states that `no resources` were `found`.

If `--cascade=false` indeed prevents Kubernetes from removing the downstream objects, the Pods should continue running in the cluster. Let's confirm the assumption.

```
kubectl get pods
```

The output is as follows:

```
NAME               READY STATUS   RESTARTS AGE
go-demo-2-md5xp 2/2   Running 0           9m
go-demo-2-vnmf7 2/2   Running 0           9m
```

The two Pods created by the ReplicaSet are indeed still running in the cluster even though we removed the ReplicaSet.

The Pods that are currently running in the cluster do not have any relation with the ReplicaSet we created earlier. We deleted the ReplicaSet, and the Pods are still there. Knowing that the ReplicaSet uses labels to decide whether the desired number of Pods is already running in the cluster, should lead us to the conclusion that if we create the same ReplicaSet again, it should reuse the two Pods that are running in the cluster. Let's confirm that.

In addition to the `kubectl create` command we executed previously, we'll also add the `--save-config` argument. It'll save the configuration of the ReplicaSet thus allowing us to perform a few additional operations later on. We'll get to them shortly. For now, the important thing is that we are about to create the same ReplicaSet we had before.

```
kubectl create -f rs/go-demo-2.yml \
    --save-config
```

The output states that the `replicaset "go-demo-2" was created`. Let's see what happened with the Pods.

```
kubectl get pods
```

The output is as follows:

```
NAME             READY STATUS  RESTARTS AGE
go-demo-2-md5xp 2/2    Running 0        10m
go-demo-2-vnmf7 2/2    Running 0        10m
```

If you compare the names of the Pods, you'll see that they are the same as before we created the ReplicaSet. It looked for matching labels, deduced that there are two Pods that match them, and decided that there's no need to create new ones. The matching Pods fulfil the desired number of replicas.

Since we saved the configuration, we can `apply` an updated definition of the ReplicaSet. For example, we can use `rs/go-demo-2-scaled.yml` file that differs only in the number of replicas set to 4. We could have created the ReplicaSet with `apply` in the first place, but we didn't. The `apply` command automatically saves the configuration so that we can edit it later on. The `create` command does not do such thing by default so we had to save it with `--save-config`.

```
kubectl apply -f rs/go-demo-2-scaled.yml
```

This time, the output is slightly different. Instead of saying that the ReplicaSet was created, we can see that it was `configured`:

Let's take a look at the Pods.

```
kubectl get pods
```

The output is as follows:

```
NAME             READY STATUS  RESTARTS AGE
go-demo-2-ckmtv 2/2    Running 0        50s
go-demo-2-1t4qm 2/2    Running 0        50s
go-demo-2-md5xp 2/2    Running 0        11m
```

```
go-demo-2-vnmf7 2/2    Running 0            11m
```

As expected, now there are four Pods in the cluster. If you pay closer attention to the names of the Pods, you'll notice that two of them are the same as before.

When we applied the new configuration with `replicas` set to 4 instead of 2, Kubernetes updated the ReplicaSet which, in turn, evaluated the current state of the Pods with matching labels. It found two with the same labels and decided to create two more so that the new desired state can match the actual state.

Let's see what happens when a Pod is destroyed.

```
POD_NAME=$(kubectl get pods -o name \
    | tail -1)
kubectl delete $POD_NAME
```

We retrieved all the Pods and used `-o name` to retrieve only their names. The result was piped to `tail -1` so that only one of the names is output. The result is stored in the environment variable POD_NAME. The latter command used that variable to remove the Pod as a simulation of a failure.

Let's take another look at the Pods in the cluster:

```
kubectl get pods
```

The output is as follows:

NAME	READY	STATUS	RESTARTS	AGE
go-demo-2-ckmtv	2/2	Running	0	10m
go-demo-2-lt4qm	2/2	Running	0	10m
go-demo-2-md5xp	2/2	Running	0	13m
go-demo-2-t8sfs	2/2	Running	0	30s
go-demo-2-vnmf7	0/2	Terminating	0	13m

We can see that the Pod we deleted is `terminating`. However, since we have a ReplicaSet with `replicas` set to 4, as soon as it discovered that the number of Pods dropped to 3, it created a new one. We just witnessed self-healing in action. As long as there are enough available resources in the cluster, ReplicaSets will make sure that the specified number of Pod replicas are (almost) always up-and-running.

Let's see what happens if we remove one of the Pod labels ReplicaSet uses in its selector.

```
POD_NAME=$(kubectl get pods -o name \
    | tail -1)
kubectl label $POD_NAME service-
kubectl describe $POD_NAME
```

We used the same command to retrieve the name of one of the Pods and executed the command that removed the label `service`. Please note – at the end of the name of the label. It is the syntax that indicates that a label should be removed:

Finally, we described the Pod:

The output of the last command, limited to the labels section, is as follows:

```
...
Labels: db=mongo
        language=go
        type=backend
...
```

As you can see, the label `service` is gone.

Now, let's list the Pods in the cluster and check whether there is any change:

```
kubectl get pods --show-labels
```

The output is as follows:

```
NAME                READY STATUS  RESTARTS AGE LABELS
go-demo-2-ckmtv 2/2   Running 0          24m db=mongo,language=go,service=go-
demo-2,type=backend
go-demo-2-lt4qm 2/2   Running 0          24m db=mongo,language=go,service=go-
demo-2,type=backend
go-demo-2-md5xp 2/2   Running 0          28m
db=mongo,language=go,type=backend
go-demo-2-nrnbh 2/2   Running 0          4m  db=mongo,language=go,service=go-
demo-2,type=backend
go-demo-2-t8sfs 2/2   Running 0          15m db=mongo,language=go,service=go-
demo-2,type=backend
```

The total number of Pods increased to five. The moment we removed the `service` label from one of the Pods, the ReplicaSet discovered that the number of Pods matching the `selector` labels is three and created a new Pod. Right now, we have four Pods controlled by the ReplicaSet and one running freely due to non-matching labels.

What would happen if we add the label we removed?

```
kubectl label $POD_NAME service=go-demo-2
kubectl get pods --show-labels
```

We added the `service=go-demo-2` label and listed all the Pods.

The output of the latter command is as follows:

```
NAME                READY STATUS        RESTARTS AGE LABELS
go-demo-2-ckmtv 2/2   Running      0            28m
db=mongo,language=go,service=go-demo-2,type=backend
go-demo-2-lt4qm 2/2   Running      0            28m
db=mongo,language=go,service=go-demo-2,type=backend
go-demo-2-md5xp 2/2   Running      0            31m
db=mongo,language=go,service=go-demo-2,type=backend
go-demo-2-nrnbh 0/2   Terminating 0            7m
db=mongo,language=go,service=go-demo-2,type=backend
go-demo-2-t8sfs 2/2   Running      0            18m
db=mongo,language=go,service=go-demo-2,type=backend
```

The moment we added the label, the ReplicaSet discovered that there are five Pods with matching selector labels. Since the specification states that there should be four replicas of the Pod, it removed one of the Pods so that the desired state matches the actual state.

The previous few examples showed, one more time, that ReplicaSets and Pods are loosely coupled through matching labels and that ReplicaSets are using those labels to maintain the parity between the actual and the desired state. So far, self-healing worked as expected.

What now?

The good news is that ReplicaSets are relatively straightforward. They provide a guarantee that the specified number of replicas of a Pod will be running in the system as long as there are available resources. That's the primary and, arguably, the only purpose.

The bad news is that ReplicaSets are rarely used independently. You will almost never create a ReplicaSet directly just as you're not going to create Pods. Instead, we tend to create ReplicaSets through Deployments. In other words, we use ReplicaSets to create and control Pods, and Deployments to create ReplicaSets (and a few other things). We'll get to Deployment soon. For now, please delete your local Minikube cluster. The next chapter will start from scratch.

`minikube delete`

 If you'd like to know more about ReplicaSets, please explore ReplicaSet v1 apps (`https://v1-9.docs.kubernetes.io/docs/reference/generated/kubern etes-api/v1.9/#replicaset-v1-apps`) API documentation.

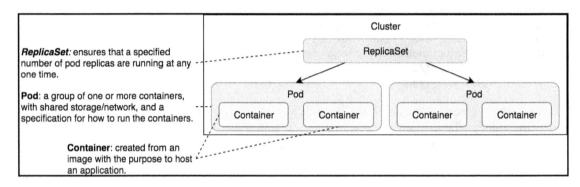

Figure 4-4: The components explored so far

5

Using Services to Enable Communication between Pods

 Applications that cannot communicate with each other or are not accessible to end-users are worthless. Only once the communication paths are established, can applications fulfill their role.

Pods are the smallest unit in Kubernetes and have a relatively short life-span. They are born, and they are destroyed. They are never healed. The system heals itself by creating new Pods (cells) and by terminating those that are unhealthy or those that are surplus. The system is long-living, Pods are not.

Controllers, together with other components like the scheduler, are making sure that the Pods are doing the right thing. They control the scheduler. We used only one of them so far. ReplicaSet is in charge of making sure that the desired number of Pods is always running. If there's too few of them, new ones will be created. If there's too many of them, some will be destroyed. Pods that become unhealthy are terminated as well. All that, and a bit more, is controlled by ReplicaSet.

The problem with our current setup is that there are no communication paths. Our Pods cannot speak with each other. So far, only containers inside a Pod can talk with each other through `localhost`. That led us to the design where both the API and the database needed to be inside the same Pod. That was a lousy solution for quite a few reasons. The main problem is that we cannot scale one without the other. We could not design the setup in a way that there are, for example, three replicas of the API and one replica of the database. The primary obstacle was communication.

Truth be told, each Pod does get its own address. We could have split the API and the database into different Pods and configure the API Pods to communicate with the database through the address of the Pod it lives in. However, since Pods are unreliable, short-lived, and volatile, we cannot assume that the database would always be accessible through the IP of a Pod. When that Pod gets destroyed (or fails), the ReplicaSet would create a new one and assign it a new address. We need a stable, never-to-be-changed address that will forward requests to whichever Pod is currently running.

Kubernetes Services provide addresses through which associated Pods can be accessed.

Let's see Services in action.

Creating a Cluster

You know the drill. Every chapter starts by pulling the latest code from the `vfarcic/k8s-specs` (`https://github.com/vfarcic/k8s-specs`) repository, and with the creation of a new Minikube cluster.

 All the commands from this chapter are available in the `05-svc.sh` (`https://github.com/vfarcic/k8s-specs`) Gist.

```
cd k8s-specs
git pull
minikube start --vm-driver=virtualbox
kubectl config current-context
```

Now we have the latest code pulled and Minikube cluster running (again).

We can proceed with the first example of a Service.

Creating Services by exposing ports

Before we dive into services, we should create a ReplicaSet similar to the one we used in the previous chapter. It'll provide the Pods we can use to demonstrate how Services work.

Let's take a quick look at the ReplicaSet definition:

```
cat svc/go-demo-2-rs.yml
```

The only significant difference is the db container definition. It is as follows.

```
. . .
- name: db
  image: mongo:3.3
  command: ["mongod"]
  args: ["--rest", "--httpinterface"]
  ports:
  - containerPort: 28017
    protocol: TCP
. . .
```

We customized the command and the arguments so that MongoDB exposes the REST interface. We also defined the `containerPort`. Those additions are needed so that we can test that the database is accessible through the Service.

Let's create the ReplicaSet:

```
kubectl create -f svc/go-demo-2-rs.yml
kubectl get -f svc/go-demo-2-rs.yml
```

We created the ReplicaSet and retrieved its state from Kubernetes. The output is as follows:

```
NAME        DESIRED  CURRENT  READY  AGE
go-demo-2   2        2        2      1m
```

You might need to wait until both replicas are up-and-running. If, in your case, the READY column does not yet have the value 2, please wait for a while and get the state again. We can proceed after both replicas are running.

We can use the kubectl expose command to expose a resource as a new Kubernetes service. That resource can be a Deployment, another Service, a ReplicaSet, a ReplicationController, or a Pod. We'll expose the ReplicaSet since it is already running in the cluster.

```
kubectl expose rs go-demo-2 \
    --name=go-demo-2-svc \
    --target-port=28017 \
    --type=NodePort
```

We specified that we want to expose a ReplicaSet (rs) and that the name of the new Service should be go-demo-2-svc. The port that should be exposed is 28017 (the port MongoDB interface is listening to). Finally, we specified that the type of the Service should be NodePort. As a result, the target port will be exposed on every node of the cluster to the outside world, and it will be routed to one of the Pods controlled by the ReplicaSet.

There are other Service types we could have used.

ClusterIP (the default type) exposes the port only inside the cluster. Such a port would not be accessible from anywhere outside. ClusterIP is useful when we want to enable communication between Pods and still prevent any external access. If NodePort is used, ClusterIP will be created automatically. The LoadBalancer type is only useful when combined with cloud provider's load balancer. ExternalName maps a service to an external address (for example, kubernetes.io).

In this chapter, we'll focus on NodePort and ClusterIP types. LoadBalancer will have to wait until we move our cluster to one of the cloud providers and ExternalName has a very limited usage.

The processes that were initiated with the creation of the Service are as follows:

1. Kubernetes client (`kubectl`) sent a request to the API server requesting the creation of the Service based on Pods created through the `go-demo-2` ReplicaSet.
2. Endpoint controller is watching the API server for new service events. It detected that there is a new Service object.
3. Endpoint controller created endpoint objects with the same name as the Service, and it used Service selector to identify endpoints (in this case the IP and the port of `go-demo-2` Pods).
4. kube-proxy is watching for service and endpoint objects. It detected that there is a new Service and a new endpoint object.
5. kube-proxy added iptables rules which capture traffic to the Service port and redirect it to endpoints. For each endpoint object, it adds iptables rule which selects a Pod.
6. The kube-dns add-on is watching for Service. It detected that there is a new service.
7. The kube-dns added `db` container's record to the dns server (skydns).

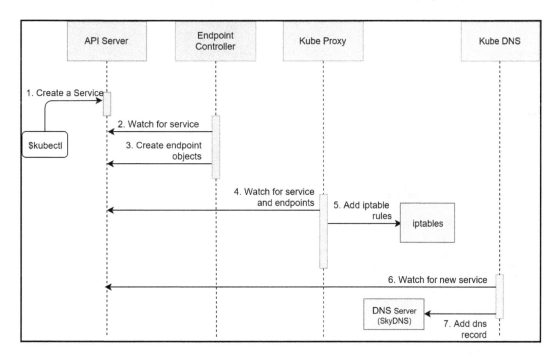

Figure 5-1: The sequence of events followed by request to create a Service

The sequence we described is useful when we want to understand everything that happened in the cluster from the moment we requested the creation of a new Service. However, it might be too confusing so we'll try to explain the same process through a diagram that more closely represents the cluster.

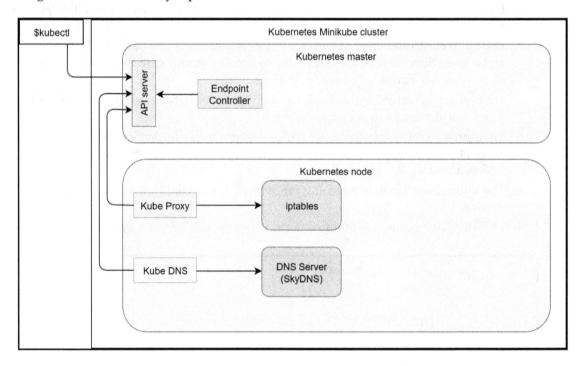

Figure 5-2: The Kubernetes components view when requesting creation of a Service

Let's take a look at our new Service.

```
kubectl describe svc go-demo-2-svc
```

The output is as follows:

```
Name:              go-demo-2-svc
Namespace:         default
Labels:            db=mongo
                   language=go
                   service=go-demo-2
                   type=backend
Annotations:       <none>
Selector:          service=go-demo-2,type=backend
Type:              NodePort
IP:                10.0.0.194
```

```
Port:                     <unset>   28017/TCP
TargetPort:               28017/TCP
NodePort:                 <unset>   31879/TCP
Endpoints:                172.17.0.4:28017,172.17.0.5:28017
Session Affinity:         None
External Traffic Policy:  Cluster
Events:                   <none>
```

We can see the name and the namespace. We did not yet explore namespaces (coming up later) and, since we didn't specify any, it is set to `default`. Since the Service is associated with the Pods created through the ReplicaSet, it inherited all their labels. The selector matches the one from the ReplicaSet. The Service is not directly associated with the ReplicaSet (or any other controller) but with Pods through matching labels.

Next is the `NodePort` type which exposes ports to all the nodes. Since `NodePort` automatically created `ClusterIP` type as well, all the Pods in the cluster can access the `TargetPort`. The `Port` is set to `28017`. That is the port that the Pods can use to access the Service. Since we did not specify it explicitly when we executed the command, its value is the same as the value of the `TargetPort`, which is the port of the associated Pod that will receive all the requests. `NodePort` was generated automatically since we did not set it explicitly. It is the port which we can use to access the Service and, therefore, the Pods from outside the cluster. In most cases, it should be randomly generated, that way we avoid any clashes.

Let's see whether the Service indeed works:

```
PORT=$(kubectl get svc go-demo-2-svc \
    -o jsonpath="{.spec.ports[0].nodePort}")
IP=$(minikube ip)
open "http://$IP:$PORT"
```

A note to Windows users
Git Bash might not be able to use the `open` command. If that's the case, replace the `open` command with `echo`. As a result, you'll get the full address that should be opened directly in your browser of choice.

We used the filtered output of the `kubectl get` command to retrieve the `nodePort` and store it as the environment variable `PORT`. Next, we retrieved the IP of the minikube VM. Finally, we opened MongoDB UI in a browser through the service port.

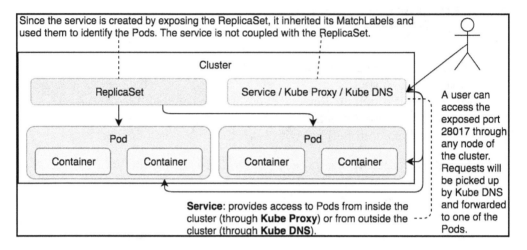

Figure 5-3: The Service created by exposing the ReplicaSet

As I already mentioned in the previous chapters, creating Kubernetes objects using imperative commands is not a good idea unless we're trying some quick hack. The same applies to Services. Even though `kubectl expose` did the work, we should try to use a documented approach through YAML files. In that spirit, we'll destroy the service we created and start over.

```
kubectl delete svc go-demo-2-svc
```

Creating Services through declarative syntax

We can accomplish a similar result as the one using `kubectl expose` through the `svc/go-demo-2-svc.yml` specification.

```
cat svc/go-demo-2-svc.yml
```

The output is as follows:

```
apiVersion: v1
kind: Service
metadata:
  name: go-demo-2
spec:
  type: NodePort
  ports:
  - port: 28017
    nodePort: 30001
    protocol: TCP
  selector:
    type: backend
    service: go-demo-2
```

You should be familiar with the meaning of `apiVersion`, `kind`, and `metadata`, so we'll jump straight into the `spec` section. Since we already explored some of the options through the `kubectl expose` command, the `spec` should be relatively easy to grasp.

The type of the Service is set to `NodePort` meaning that the ports will be available both within the cluster as well as from outside by sending requests to any of the nodes.

The `ports` section specifies that the requests should be forwarded to the Pods on port `28017`. The `nodePort` is new. Instead of letting the service expose a random port, we set it to the explicit value of `30001`. Even though, in most cases, that is not a good practice, I thought it might be a good idea to demonstrate that option as well. The protocol is set to `TCP`. The only other alternative would be to use `UDP`. We could have skipped the protocol altogether since `TCP` is the default value but, sometimes, it is a good idea to leave things as a reminder of an option.

The `selector` is used by the Service to know which Pods should receive requests. It works in the same way as ReplicaSet selectors. In this case, we defined that the service should forward requests to Pods with labels `type` set to `backend` and `service` set to `go-demo`. Those two labels are set in the Pods `spec` of the ReplicaSet.

Now that there's no mystery in the definition, we can proceed and create the Service.

```
kubectl create -f svc/go-demo-2-svc.yml
kubectl get -f svc/go-demo-2-svc.yml
```

We created the Service and retrieved its information from the API server. The output of the latter command is as follows:

```
NAME        TYPE       CLUSTER-IP EXTERNAL-IP PORT(S)        AGE
go-demo-2 NodePort 10.0.0.129 <none>      28017:30001/TCP 10m
```

Now that the Service is running (again), we can double-check that it is working as expected by trying to access MongoDB UI.

```
open "http://$IP:30001"
```

Since we fixed the `nodePort` to `30001`, we did not have to retrieve the Port from the API server. Instead, we used the IP of the Minikube node and the hard-coded port `30001` to open the UI.

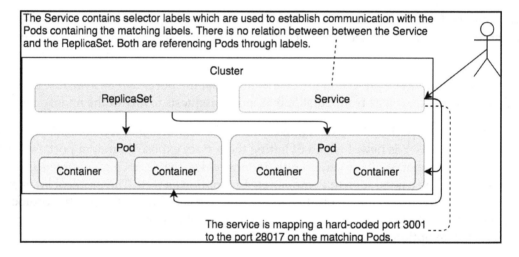

Figure 5-4: The Service with the matching Pods and hard-coded port

Let's take a look at the endpoint. It holds the list of Pods that should receive requests.

```
kubectl get ep go-demo-2 -o yaml
```

The output is as follows:

```
apiVersion: v1
kind: Endpoints
metadata:
  creationTimestamp: 2017-12-12T16:00:51Z
  name: go-demo-2
  namespace: default
  resourceVersion: "5196"
```

```
    selfLink: /api/v1/namespaces/default/endpoints/go-demo-2
    uid: a028b9a7-df55-11e7-a8ef-080027d94e34
  subsets:
  - addresses:
    - ip: 172.17.0.4
      nodeName: minikube
      targetRef:
        kind: Pod
        name: go-demo-2-j8kdw
        namespace: default
        resourceVersion: "5194"
        uid: ac70f868-df4d-11e7-a8ef-080027d94e34
    - ip: 172.17.0.5
      nodeName: minikube
      targetRef:
        kind: Pod
        name: go-demo-2-5vlcc
        namespace: default
        resourceVersion: "5184"
        uid: ac7214d9-df4d-11e7-a8ef-080027d94e34
    ports:
    - port: 28017
      protocol: TCP
```

We can see that there are two subsets, corresponding to the two Pods that contain the same labels as the Service `selector`. Each has a unique IP that is included in the algorithm used when forwarding requests. Actually, it's not much of an algorithm. Requests will be sent to those Pods randomly. That randomness results in something similar to round-robin load balancing. If the number of Pods does not change, each will receive an approximately equal number of requests.

Random requests forwarding should be enough for most use cases. If it's not, we'd need to resort to a third-party solution (for now). However soon, when Kubernetes 1.9 gets released, we'll have an alternative to the *iptables* solution. We'll be able to apply different types of load balancing algorithms like last connection, destination hashing, newer queue, and so on. Still, the current solution is based on *iptables*, and we'll stick with it, for now.

Throughout the book, so far, I repeated a few times that our current Pod design is flawed. We have two containers (an API and a database) packaged together. Among other problems, that prevents us from scaling one without the other. Now that we learned how to use Services, we can redesign our Pod solution.

Before we move on, we'll delete the Service and the ReplicaSet we created:

```
kubectl delete -f svc/go-demo-2-svc.yml
kubectl delete -f svc/go-demo-2-rs.yml
```

Both the ReplicaSet and the Service are gone, and we can start a new.

Splitting the Pod and establishing communication through Services

Let's take a look at a ReplicaSet definition for a Pod with only the database:

```
cat svc/go-demo-2-db-rs.yml
```

The output is as follows:

```
apiVersion: apps/v1beta2
kind: ReplicaSet
metadata:
  name: go-demo-2-db
spec:
  selector:
    matchLabels:
      type: db
      service: go-demo-2
  template:
    metadata:
      labels:
        type: db
        service: go-demo-2
        vendor: MongoLabs
    spec:
      containers:
      - name: db
        image: mongo:3.3
        ports:
        - containerPort: 28017
```

We'll comment only on the things that changed.

Since this ReplicaSet defines only the database, we reduced the number of replicas to 1. Truth be told, MongoDB should be scaled as well, but that's out of the scope of this chapter (and probably the book as well). For now, we'll pretend that one replica of a database is enough.

Since `selector` labels need to be unique, we changed them slightly. The `service` is still `go-demo-2`, but the `type` was changed to `db`.

The rest of the definition is the same except that the `containers` now contain only `mongo`. We'll define the API in a separate ReplicaSet.

Let's create the ReplicaSet before we move to the Service that will reference its Pod.

```
kubectl create \
    -f svc/go-demo-2-db-rs.yml
```

One object was created, three are left to go.

The next one is the Service for the Pod we just created through the ReplicaSet.

```
cat svc/go-demo-2-db-svc.yml
```

The output is as follows:

```
apiVersion: v1
kind: Service
metadata:
  name: go-demo-2-db
spec:
  ports:
  - port: 27017
  selector:
    type: db
    service: go-demo-2
```

This Service definition does not contain anything new. There is no `type`, so it'll default to `ClusterIP`. Since there is no reason for anyone outside the cluster to communicate with the database, there's no need to expose it using the `NodePort` type. We also skipped specifying the `nodePort`, since only internal communication within the cluster is allowed. The same is true for the `protocol`. TCP is all we need, and it happens to be the default one. Finally, the `selector` labels are the same as the labels that define the Pod.

Let's create the Service:

```
kubectl create \
    -f svc/go-demo-2-db-svc.yml
```

We are finished with the database. The ReplicaSet will make sure that the Pod is (almost) always up-and-running and the Service will allow other Pods to communicate with it through a fixed DNS.

Moving to the backend API...

```
cat svc/go-demo-2-api-rs.yml
```

The output is as follows:

```
apiVersion: apps/v1beta2
kind: ReplicaSet
metadata:
  name: go-demo-2-api
spec:
  replicas: 3
  selector:
    matchLabels:
      type: api
      service: go-demo-2
  template:
    metadata:
      labels:
        type: api
        service: go-demo-2
        language: go
    spec:
      containers:
      - name: api
        image: vfarcic/go-demo-2
        env:
        - name: DB
          value: go-demo-2-db
        readinessProbe:
          httpGet:
            path: /demo/hello
            port: 8080
          periodSeconds: 1
        livenessProbe:
          httpGet:
            path: /demo/hello
            port: 8080
```

Just as with the database, this ReplicaSet should be familiar since it's very similar to the one we used before. We'll comment only on the differences.

The number of `replicas` is set to 3. That solves one of the main problems we had with the previous ReplicaSets that defined Pods with both containers. Now the number of replicas can differ, and we have one Pod for the database, and three for the backend API.

The `type` label is set to `api` so that both the ReplicaSet and the (soon to come) Service can distinguish the Pods from those created for the database.

We have the environment variable `DB` set to `go-demo-2-db`. The code behind the `vfarcic/go-demo-2` image is written in a way that the connection to the database is established by reading that variable. In this case, we can say that it will try to connect to the database running on the DNS `go-demo-2-db`. If you go back to the database Service definition, you'll notice that its name is `go-demo-2-db` as well. If everything works correctly, we should expect that the DNS was created with the Service and that it'll forward requests to the database.

In earlier Kubernetes versions it used `userspace` proxy mode. Its advantage is that the proxy would retry failed requests to another Pod. With the shift to the `iptables` mode, that feature is lost. However, `iptables` are much faster and more reliable, so the loss of the retry mechanism is well compensated. That does not mean that the requests are sent to Pods "blindly". The lack of the retry mechanism is mitigated with `readinessProbe`, which we added to the ReplicaSet.

The `readinessProbe` has the same fields as the `livenessProbe`. We used the same values for both, except for the `periodSeconds`, where instead of relying on the default value of 10, we set it to 1. While `livenessProbe` is used to determine whether a Pod is alive or it should be replaced by a new one, the `readinessProbe` is used by the `iptables`. A Pod that does not pass the `readinessProbe` will be excluded and will not receive requests. In theory, Requests might be still sent to a faulty Pod, between two iterations. Still, such requests will be small in number since the `iptables` will change as soon as the next probe responds with HTTP code less than 200, or equal or greater than 400.

Ideally, an application would have different end-points for the `readinessProbe` and the `livenessProbe`. This one doesn't so the same one should do. You can blame it on me being too lazy to add them.

Let's create the ReplicaSet.

```
kubectl create \
    -f svc/go-demo-2-api-rs.yml
```

Only one object is missing, that is service:

```
cat svc/go-demo-2-api-svc.yml
```

The output is as follows:

```
apiVersion: v1
kind: Service
metadata:
  name: go-demo-2-api
spec:
  type: NodePort
  ports:
  - port: 8080
  selector:
    type: api
    service: go-demo-2
```

There's nothing truly new in this definition. The type is set to NodePort since the API should be accessible from outside the cluster. The selector label type is set to api so that it matches the labels defined for the Pods.

That is the last object we'll create (in this section), so let's move on and do it:

```
kubectl create \
    -f svc/go-demo-2-api-svc.yml
```

We'll take a look at what we have in the cluster:

```
kubectl get all
```

The output is as follows:

```
NAME                DESIRED CURRENT READY AGE
rs/go-demo-2-api 3      3       3     18m
rs/go-demo-2-db  1      1       1     48m
rs/go-demo-2-api 3      3       3     18m
rs/go-demo-2-db  1      1       1     48m
NAME                       READY STATUS   RESTARTS AGE
po/go-demo-2-api-6brtz 1/1  Running 0              18m
po/go-demo-2-api-fj9mg 1/1  Running 0              18m
po/go-demo-2-api-vrcxh 1/1  Running 0              18m
po/go-demo-2-db-qcftz  1/1  Running 0              48m
NAME               TYPE        CLUSTER-IP EXTERNAL-IP PORT(S)
AGE
svc/go-demo-2-api NodePort  10.0.0.162 <none>       8080:31256/TCP
2m
svc/go-demo-2-db  ClusterIP 10.0.0.19  <none>       27017/TCP
```

```
48m
svc/kubernetes    ClusterIP 10.0.0.1   <none>      443/TCP
1h
```

Both ReplicaSets for db and api are there, followed by the three replicas of the go-demo-2-api Pods and one replica of the go-demo-2-db Pod. Finally, the two Services are running as well, together with the one created by Kubernetes itself.

 I'm not sure why are the ReplicaSets duplicated in this view. My best guess is that it is a bug that will be corrected soon. To be honest, I haven't spent time investigating that since it does not affect how the cluster and ReplicaSets work. If you execute kubectl get rs, you'll see that there are only two of them, not four.

Before we proceed, it might be worth mentioning that the code behind the vfarcic/go-demo-2 image is designed to fail if it cannot connect to the database. The fact that the three replicas of the go-demo-2-api Pod are running means that the communication is established. The only verification left is to check whether we can access the API from outside the cluster. Let's try that out.

```
PORT=$(kubectl get svc go-demo-2-api \
    -o jsonpath="{.spec.ports[0].nodePort}")
curl -i "http://$IP:$PORT/demo/hello"
```

We retrieved the port of the service (we still have the Minikube node IP from before) and used it to send a request. The output of the last command is as follows:

```
HTTP/1.1 200 OK
Date: Tue, 12 Dec 2017 21:27:51 GMT
Content-Length: 14
Content-Type: text/plain; charset=utf-8
hello, world!
```

We got the response 200 and a friendly hello, world! message indicating that the API is indeed accessible from outside the cluster.

At this point, you might be wondering whether it is overkill to have four YAML files for a single application. Can't we simplify the definitions? Not really. Can we define everything in a single file? Read on.

Before we move further, we'll delete the objects we created. By now, you probably noticed that I like destroying things and starting over. Bear with me. There is a good reason for the imminent destruction:

```
kubectl delete -f svc/go-demo-2-db-rs.yml
```

```
kubectl delete -f svc/go-demo-2-db-svc.yml
kubectl delete -f svc/go-demo-2-api-rs.yml
kubectl delete -f svc/go-demo-2-api-svc.yml
```

Everything we created is gone, and we can start over.

Defining multiple objects in the same YAML file

The `vfarcic/go-demo-2` and `mongo` images form the same stack. They work together and having four YAML definitions is confusing. It would get even more confusing later on since we are going to add more objects to the stack. Things would be much simpler and easier if we would move all the objects we created thus far into a single YAML definition. Fortunately, that is very easy to accomplish.

Let's take a look at yet another YAML file:

```
cat svc/go-demo-2.yml
```

We won't display the output since it is the same as the contents of the previous four YAML files combined. The only difference is that each object definition is separated by three dashes (`---`).

If you're as paranoid as I am, you'd like to double check that everything works as expected, so let's create the objects defined in that file:

```
kubectl create -f svc/go-demo-2.yml
kubectl get -f svc/go-demo-2.yml
```

The output of the latter command is as follows:

```
NAME             DESIRED CURRENT READY AGE
rs/go-demo-2-db 1        1       1     1m
NAME             TYPE        CLUSTER-IP EXTERNAL-IP PORT(S)    AGE
svc/go-demo-2-db ClusterIP 10.0.0.250 <none>      27017/TCP 1m
NAME             DESIRED CURRENT READY AGE
rs/go-demo-2-api 3        3       3     1m
NAME             TYPE        CLUSTER-IP EXTERNAL-IP PORT(S)
AGE
svc/go-demo-2-api NodePort 10.0.0.99  <none>      8080:31726/TCP
1m
```

The two ReplicaSets and the two Services were created, and we can rejoice in replacing four files with one.

Finally, to be on the safe side, we'll also double check that the stack API is up-and-running and accessible.

```
PORT=$(kubectl get svc go-demo-2-api \
    -o jsonpath="{.spec.ports[0].nodePort}")
curl -i "http://$IP:$PORT/demo/hello"
```

The response is `200` indicating that everything works as expected.

Before we finish the discussion about Services, we might want to go through the discovery process.

Discovering Services

Services can be discovered through two principal modes; environment variables and DNS.

Every Pod gets environment variables for each of the active Services. They are provided in the same format as what Docker links expect, as well with the simpler Kubernetes-specific syntax.

Let's take a look at the environment variables available in one of the Pods we're running.

```
POD_NAME=$(kubectl get pod \
    --no-headers \
    -o=custom-columns=NAME:.metadata.name \
    -l type=api,service=go-demo-2 \
    | tail -1)
kubectl exec $POD_NAME env
```

The output, limited to the environment variables related to the `go-demo-2-db` service, is as follows:

```
GO_DEMO_2_DB_PORT=tcp://10.0.0.250:27017
GO_DEMO_2_DB_PORT_27017_TCP_ADDR=10.0.0.250
GO_DEMO_2_DB_PORT_27017_TCP_PROTO=tcp
GO_DEMO_2_DB_PORT_27017_TCP_PORT=27017
GO_DEMO_2_DB_PORT_27017_TCP=tcp://10.0.0.250:27017
GO_DEMO_2_DB_SERVICE_HOST=10.0.0.250
GO_DEMO_2_DB_SERVICE_PORT=27017
```

The first five variables are using the Docker format. If you already worked with Docker networking, you should be familiar with them. At least, if you're familiar with the way Swarm (standalone) and Docker Compose operate. Later version of Swarm (Mode) still generate the environment variables but they are mostly abandoned by the users in favour of DNSes.

The last two environment variables are Kubernetes specific and follow the `[SERVICE_NAME]_SERVICE_HOST` and `[SERVICE_NAME]_SERIVCE_PORT` format (service name is upper-cased).

No matter which set of environment variables you choose to use (if any), they all serve the same purpose. They provide a reference we can use to connect to a Service and, therefore to the related Pods.

Things will become more evident when we describe the `go-demo-2-db` Service.

```
kubectl describe svc go-demo-2-db
```

The output is as follows:

```
Name:              go-demo-2-db
Namespace:         default
Labels:            <none>
Annotations:       <none>
Selector:          service=go-demo-2,type=db
Type:              ClusterIP
IP:                10.0.0.250
Port:              <unset>  27017/TCP
TargetPort:        27017/TCP
Endpoints:         172.17.0.4:27017
Session Affinity:  None
Events:            <none>
```

The key is in the `IP` field. That is the IP through which this service can be accessed and it matches the values of the environment variables `GO_DEMO_2_DB_*` and `GO_DEMO_2_DB_SERVICE_HOST`.

The code inside the containers that form the `go-demo-2-api` Pods could use any of those environment variables to construct a connection string towards the `go-demo-2-db` Pods. For example, we could have used `GO_DEMO_2_DB_SERVICE_HOST` to connect to the database. And, yet, we didn't do that. The reason is simple. It is easier to use DNS instead.

Let's take another look at the snippet from the `go-demo-2-api-rs.yml` ReplicaSet definition:

```
cat svc/go-demo-2-api-rs.yml

. . .
env:
- name: DB
  value: go-demo-2-db
. . .
```

We declared an environment variable with the name of the Service (`go-demo-2-db`). That variable is used by the code as a connection string to the database. Kubernetes converts Service names into DNSes and adds them to the DNS server. It is a cluster add-on that is already set up by Minikube.

Let's go through the sequence of events related to service discovery and components involved:

1. When the `api` container `go-demo-2` tries to connect with the `go-demo-2-db` Service, it looks at the nameserver configured in `/etc/resolv.conf`. kubelet configured the nameserver with the kube-dns Service IP (`10.96.0.10`) during the Pod scheduling process.
2. The container queries the DNS server listening to port `53`. `go-demo-2-db` DNS gets resolved to the service IP `10.0.0.19`. This DNS record was added by kube-dns during the service creation process.
3. The container uses the service IP which forwards requests through the iptables rules. They were added by kube-proxy during Service and Endpoint creation process.

4. Since we only have one replica of the `go-demo-2-db` Pod, iptables forwards requests to just one endpoint. If we had multiple replicas, iptables would act as a load balancer and forward requests randomly among Endpoints of the Service.

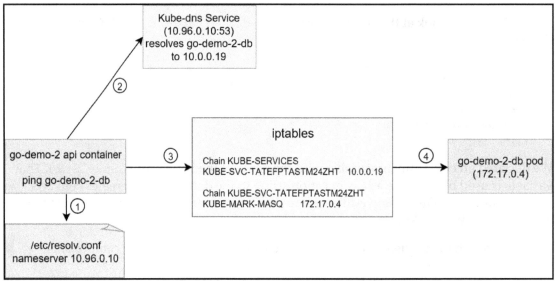

Figure 5-5: Service discovery process and components involved

What now?

That was it. We went through most important aspects of Services. There are a few other cases we did not yet explore, but the current knowledge should be more than enough to get you going.

Services are indispensable objects without which communication between Pods would be hard and volatile. They provide static addresses through which we can access them not only from other Pods but also from outside the cluster. This ability to have fixed entry points is crucial as it provides stability to otherwise dynamic elements of the cluster. Pods come and go, Services stay.

We are one crucial topic away from having a fully functional, yet still simple, strategy for deployment and management of our applications. We are yet to explore how to deploy and update our services without downtime.

We have exhausted this topic and the time has come to destroy everything we did so far.

```
minikube delete
```

 If you'd like to know more about Services, please explore Service v1 core (`https://v1-9.docs.kubernetes.io/docs/reference/generated/kubern etes-api/v1.9/#service-v1-core`) API documentation.

Figure 5-6: The components explored so far

Kubernetes Pods, ReplicaSets, and Services compared to Docker Swarm stacks

Starting from this chapter, we'll compare each Kubernetes feature with Docker Swarm equivalents. That way, Swarm users can have a smoother transition into Kubernetes or, depending on their goals, choose to stick with Swarm.

Please bear in mind that the comparisons will be made only for a specific set of features. You will not (yet) be able to conclude whether Kubernetes is better or worse than Docker Swarm. You'll need to grasp both products in their entirety to make an educated decision. The comparisons like those that follow are useful only as a base for more detailed examinations of the two products.

For now, we'll limit the comparison scope to Pods, ReplicaSets, and Services on the one hand, and Docker Service stacks, on the other.

Let's start with Kubernetes file `go-demo-2.yml` (`https://github.com/vfarcic/k8s-specs/blob/master/svc/go-demo-2.yml`) (the same one we used before).

The definition is as follows:

```
apiVersion: apps/v1beta2
kind: ReplicaSet
metadata:
  name: go-demo-2-db
spec:
  selector:
    matchLabels:
      type: db
      service: go-demo-2
  template:
    metadata:
```

```
          labels:
            type: db
            service: go-demo-2
        spec:
          containers:
          - name: db
            image: mongo:3.3
            ports:
            - containerPort: 28017
---
apiVersion: v1
kind: Service
metadata:
  name: go-demo-2-db
spec:
  ports:
  - port: 27017
  selector:
    type: db
    service: go-demo-2
---
apiVersion: apps/v1beta2
kind: ReplicaSet
metadata:
  name: go-demo-2-api
spec:
  replicas: 3
  selector:
    matchLabels:
      type: api
      service: go-demo-2
  template:
    metadata:
      labels:
        type: api
        service: go-demo-2
    spec:
      containers:
      - name: api
        image: vfarcic/go-demo-2
        env:
        - name: DB
          value: go-demo-2-db
        readinessProbe:
          httpGet:
            path: /demo/hello
            port: 8080
          periodSeconds: 1
```

```
          livenessProbe:
            httpGet:
              path: /demo/hello
              port: 8080
---
apiVersion: v1
kind: Service
metadata:
  name: go-demo-2-api
spec:
  type: NodePort
  ports:
  - port: 8080
  selector:
    type: api
    service: go-demo-2
```

Now, let's take a look at the Docker stack defined in `go-demo-2-swarm.yml` (`https://github.com/vfarcic/k8s-specs/blob/master/svc/go-demo-2-swarm.yml`).

The specification is as follows:

```
version: "3"
services:
  api:
    image: vfarcic/go-demo-2
    environment:
      - DB=db
    ports:
      - 8080
    deploy:
      replicas: 3
  db:
    image: mongo
```

Both definitions accomplish the same result. There is no important difference from the functional point of view, except in Pods. Docker does not have the option to create something similar. When Swarm services are created, they are spread across the cluster, and there is no easy way to specify that multiple containers should run on the same node. Whether multi-container Pods are useful or not is something we'll explore later. For now, we'll ignore that feature.

If we execute something like `docker stack deploy -c svc/go-demo-2-swarm.yml go-demo-2`, the result would be equivalent to what we got when we run `kubectl create -f svc/go-demo-2.yml`. In both cases, we get three replicas of `vfarcic/go-demo-2`, and one replica of `mongo`. Respective schedulers are making sure that the desired state (almost) always matches the actual state. Networking communication through internal DNSes is also established with both solutions. Each node in a cluster would expose a randomly defined port that forwards requests to the `api`. All in all, there are no functional differences between the two solutions.

When it comes to the way services are defined, there is indeed, a considerable difference. Docker's stack definition is much more compact and straight-forward. We defined, in twelve lines, what took around eighty lines in the Kubernetes format.

One might argue that Kubernetes YAML file could have been smaller. Maybe it could. Still, it'll be bigger and more complex no matter how much we simplify it. One might also say that Docker's stack is missing `readinessProbe` and `livenessProbe`. Yes it is, and that is because I decided not to put it there, because the `vfarcic/go-demo-2` image already has `HEALTHCHECK` definition that Docker uses for similar purposes. In most cases, Dockerfile is a better place to define health checks than a stack definition. That does not mean that it cannot be set, or overwritten, in a YAML file. It can, when needed. But, that is not the case in this example.

All in all, if we limit ourselves only to Kubernetes Pods, ReplicaSets, and Services, and their equivalents in Docker Swarm, the latter wins due to a much simpler and more straightforward way to define specs. From the functional perspective, both are very similar.

Should you conclude that Swarm is a better option than Kubernetes? Not at all. At least, not until we compare other features. Swarm won the battle, but the war has just begun. As we progress, you'll see that there's much more to Kubernetes. We only scratched the surface.

6

Deploying Releases with Zero-Downtime

 If we are to survive in the face of competition, we have to release features to production as soon as they are developed and tested. The need for frequent releases fortifies the need for zero-downtime deployments.

We learned how to deploy our applications packaged as Pods, how to scale them through ReplicaSets, and how to enable communication through Services. However, all that is useless if we cannot update those applications with new releases. That is where Kubernetes Deployments come in handy.

The desired state of our applications is changing all the time. The most common reasons for new states are new releases. The process is relatively simple. We make a change and commit it to a code repository. We build it, and we test it. Once we're confident that it works as expected, we deploy it to a cluster. It does not matter whether that deployment is to a development, test, staging, or production environment. We need to deploy a new release to a cluster, even when that is a single-node Kubernetes running on a laptop. No matter how many environments we have, the process should always be the same or, at least, as similar as possible.

The deployment must produce no downtime. It does not matter whether it is performed on a testing or a production cluster. Interrupting consumers is disruptive, and that leads to loss of money and confidence in a product. Gone are the days when users did not care if an application sometimes did not work. There are so many competitors out there that a single bad experience might lead users to another solution. With today's scale, 0.1% of failed requests is considered disastrous. While we might never be able to reach 100% availability, we should certainly not cause downtime ourselves and must minimise other factors that could cause downtime.

Failures caused by circumstances outside of our control are things which, by definition, we can do nothing about. However, failures caused by obsolete practices or negligence are failures which should not happen. Kubernetes Deployments provide us with the tools we need to avoid such failures by allowing us to update our applications without downtime.

Let's explore how Kubernetes Deployments work and the benefits we gain by adopting them.

Creating a Cluster

Creating a cluster at the beginning of each chapter allows us to jump into any part of the book without worrying whether there is a requirement to meet from previous chapters. It also allows us to pause between chapters without stressing our laptops by running a VM that is not in use. The downside is that this is the boring part of every chapter. Therefore, the talk stops here. Let's get it over with.

All the commands from this chapter are available in the `06-deploy.sh` (`https://gist.github.com/vfarcic/677a0d688f65ceb01e31e33db59a440 0`) Gist.

```
cd k8s-specs
git pull
minikube start --vm-driver=virtualbox
kubectl config current-context
```

The code was updated, the cluster is up-and-running, and we can start exploring Deployments.

Deploying new releases

Just as we are not supposed to create Pods directly but using other controllers like ReplicaSet, we are not supposed to create ReplicaSets either. Kubernetes Deployments will create them for us. If you're wondering why, you'll have to wait a little while longer to find out. First, we'll create a few Deployments and, once we are familiar the process and the outcomes, it'll become obvious why they are better at managing ReplicaSets than we are.

Let's take a look at a Deployment specification for the database ReplicaSet we've been using thus far.

```
cat deploy/go-demo-2-db.yml
```

The output is as follows:

```
apiVersion: apps/v1beta2
kind: Deployment
metadata:
  name: go-demo-2-db
spec:
  selector:
    matchLabels:
      type: db
      service: go-demo-2
  template:
    metadata:
      labels:
        type: db
        service: go-demo-2
        vendor: MongoLabs
    spec:
      containers:
      - name: db
        image: mongo:3.3
        ports:
        - containerPort: 28017
```

If you compare this Deployment with the ReplicaSet we created in the previous chapter, you'll probably have a hard time finding a difference. Apart from the kind field, they are the same.

Since, in this case, both the Deployment and the ReplicaSet are the same, you might be wondering what the advantage of using one over the other is.

 We will regularly add --record to the kubectl create commands. This allows us to track each change to our resources such as a Deployments.

Let's create the Deployment and explore what it offers.

```
kubectl create \
    -f deploy/go-demo-2-db.yml \
    --record
kubectl get -f deploy/go-demo-2-db.yml
```

The output of the latter command is as follows:

```
NAME            DESIRED CURRENT UP-TO-DATE AVAILABLE AGE
go-demo-2-db 1      1       1          0         7s
```

The Deployment was created. However, get does not provide us much info, so let's describe it.

```
kubectl describe \
    -f deploy/go-demo-2-db.yml
```

The output, limited to the last few lines, is as follows:

```
. . .
Events:
  Type    Reason          Age  From                   Message
  ----    ------          ---- ----                   -------
  Normal ScalingReplicaSet 2m   deployment-controller Scaled up r
eplica set go-demo-2-db-75fbcbb5cd to 1
```

From the Events section, we can observe that the Deployment created a ReplicaSet. Or, to be more precise, that it scaled it. That is interesting. It shows that Deployments control ReplicaSets. The Deployment created the ReplicaSet which, in turn, created Pods. Let's confirm that by retrieving the list of all the objects:

```
kubectl get all
```

The output is as follows:

```
NAME                       DESIRED  CURRENT  UP-TO-DATE  AVAILABLE  AGE
deploy/go-demo-2-db 1         1        1          1          8m
NAME                       DESIRED  CURRENT  READY  AGE
rs/go-demo-2-db-75fbcbb5cd 1         1        1      8m
NAME                           READY  STATUS   RESTARTS  AGE
po/go-demo-2-db-75fbcbb5cd-k6tz9 1/1  Running  0          8m
NAME            TYPE      CLUSTER-IP  EXTERNAL-IP  PORT(S)  AGE
svc/kubernetes ClusterIP  10.0.0.1    <none>       443/TCP  14m
```

All three objects were created, and you might be wondering why we created the Deployment at all. You might think that we'd have the same result if we created a ReplicaSet directly. You'd be right. So far, from the functional point of view, there is no difference between a ReplicaSet created directly or using a Deployment. The real advantage of Deployments becomes evident if we try to change some of its aspects. For example, we might choose to upgrade MongoDB to version 3.4.

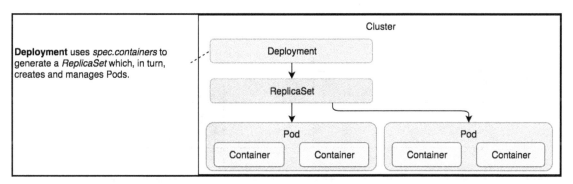

Figure 6-1: Deployment and its cascading effect that creates a ReplicaSet and, though it, Pods

Before we move onto Deployment updates, we'll go through our usual ritual of seeing the process through a sequence diagram. We won't repeat the explanation of the events that happened after the ReplicaSet object was created as those steps were already explained in the previous chapters.

1. Kubernetes client (`kubectl`) sent a request to the API server requesting the creation of a Deployment defined in the `deploy/go-demo-2-db.yml` file
2. The deployment controller is watching the API server for new events, and it detected that there is a new Deployment object
3. The deployment controller creates a new ReplicaSet object

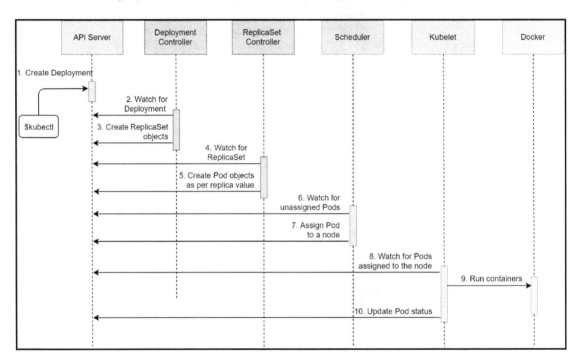

Figure 6-2: The sequence of events followed by request to create a deployment

Updating Deployments

Let's see what happens when we `set` a new image to the `db` Pod.

```
kubectl set image \
    -f deploy/go-demo-2-db.yml \
    db=mongo:3.4 \
    --record
```

It'll take a while until the new image is pulled, so you might as well fetch yourself a coffee. Once you're back, we can `describe` the Deployment by checking the events it created.

```
kubectl describe \
    -f deploy/go-demo-2-db.yml
```

The last few lines of the output are as follows:

```
...
Events:
  Type    Reason            Age   From                   Message
  ----    ------            ----  ----                   -------
  Normal  ScalingReplicaSet 19m   deployment-controller  Scaled
up replica set go-demo-2-db-75fbcbb5cd to 1
  Normal  ScalingReplicaSet 5m    deployment-controller  Scaled
up replica set go-demo-2-db-f8d4b86ff to 1
  Normal  ScalingReplicaSet 0s    deployment-controller  Scaled
down replica set go-demo-2-db-75fbcbb5cd to 0
```

We can see that it created a new ReplicaSet and that it scaled the old ReplicaSet to 0. If, in your case, the last line did not appear, you'll need to wait until the new version of the `mongo` image is pulled.

Instead of operating directly on the level of Pods, the Deployment created a new ReplicaSet which, in turn, produced Pods based on the new image. Once they became fully operational, it scaled the old ReplicaSet to 0. Since we are running a ReplicaSet with only one replica, it might not be clear why it used that strategy. When we create a Deployment for the API, things will become more evident.

To be on the safe side, we might want to retrieve all the objects from the cluster:

```
kubectl get all
```

The output is as follows:

```
NAME                    DESIRED  CURRENT  UP-TO-DATE  AVAILABLE
AGE
deploy/go-demo-2-db     1        1        1           1
3m
NAME                         DESIRED  CURRENT  READY    AGE
rs/go-demo-2-db-75fbcbb5cd   0        0        0        3m
rs/go-demo-2-db-f8d4b86ff    1        1        1        2m
NAME                             READY    STATUS    RESTARTS
AGE
po/go-demo-2-db-f8d4b86ff-qvhgg  1/1      Running   0
2m
NAME            TYPE     CLUSTER-IP  EXTERNAL-IP  PORT(S)
```

```
AGE
svc/kubernetes    ClusterIP    10.0.0.1      <none>         443/TCP
35m
```

As you can see, both ReplicaSets are there. However, one is inactive (scaled to 0).

You'll notice that contained within the name of the Pod is a hash which matches the hash in the name of the new ReplicaSet, namely f8d4b86ff. Even though it might look like it is a random value, it is not. If you destroy the Deployment and create it again, you'll notice that the hash in the Pod name and ReplicaSet name remain consistent. This value is generated by hashing the PodTemplate of the ReplicaSet. As long as the PodTemplate is the same, the hash value will be the same as well. That way a Deployment can know whether anything related to the Pods has changed and, if it does, will create a new ReplicaSet.

The kubectl set image command is not the only way to update a Deployment. We could also have used kubectl edit as well. The command would be as follows. **Please do NOT execute it.** If you do (against my advice), you'll need to type :q followed by the *Enter* key to exit.

```
kubectl edit -f deploy/go-demo-2-db.yml
```

I don't think the above edit command is a good way to update the definition. It is unpractical and undocumented. The kubectl set image is more useful if we'd like to integrate Deployment updates with one of the CI/CD tools. Since we'll have a chapter dedicated to continuous deployment, we'll continue using kubectl set image from now on.

Another alternative would be to update the YAML file and execute the kubectl apply command. While that is a good idea for applications that do not update frequently, it does not fit well with those that change weekly, daily, or even hourly.

MongoDB is one of those that might get updated with a new release only a couple of times a year so having an always up-to-date YAML file in your source code repository is an excellent practice. We used kubectl set image just as a way to introduce you to what's coming next when we explore frequent deployments without downtime.

A simple update of Pod images is far from what Deployment offers. To see its real power, we should deploy the API. Since it can be scaled to multiple Pods, it'll provide us with a much better playground.

Before we move on, let's finish with the database by adding a Service and, therefore, enabling internal cluster communication to it:

```
kubectl create \
    -f deploy/go-demo-2-db-svc.yml \
    --record
```

Zero-Downtime Deployments

Updating a single-replica MongoDB cannot demonstrate true power behind Deployments. We need a scalable service. It's not that MongoDB cannot be scaled (it can), but it is not as straight-forward as an application that was designed to be scalable. We'll jump to the second application in the stack and create a Deployment of the ReplicaSet that will create Pods based on the `vfarcic/go-demo-2` image. But, before we do that, we'll spend a few moments discussing the need for zero-downtime deployments.

On the one hand, our applications are supposed to have very high availability. Depending on the context and the goals, we usually discuss how many nines are coming after 99%. At the very least, an application must have availability of at least 99.9%. More likely, it should be something closer to 99.99 or even 99.999 percent availability. Hundred percent availability is often not possible or too expensive to accomplish. We cannot avoid all failures, but we can reduce them to acceptable limits.

No matter what the availability of SLA is, applications (at least when developed by us) must be scalable. Only when there are multiple replicas, can we hope for any decent availability. Scaled applications can not only spread the load across various instances but ensure that a failure of one replica will not produce downtime. Healthy instances are handling the load until the scheduler recreates failed ones.

> High availability is accomplished through fault tolerance and scalability. If either is missing, any failure might have disastrous effects.

The reason we're discussing failures and scalability lies in the nature of immutable deployments. If a Pod is unchangeable, the only way to update it with a new release is to destroy the old ones and put the Pods based on the new image in their place. Destruction of Pods is not much different from failures. In both cases, they cease to work. On the other hand, fault tolerance (re-scheduling) is a replacement of failed Pods.

The only essential difference is that new releases result in Pods being replaced with new ones based on the new image. As long as the process is controlled, new releases should not result in any downtime when multiple replicas of an application are running and when they are adequately designed.

We should not worry about the frequency of new releases. The process should be the same no matter whether we make releases once a month, once a week, once a day, or every few minutes. If the release process produces any downtime, we might be compelled to deploy new versions infrequently. As a matter of fact, throughout the history of software development, we were taught that releases should be limited in number. A couple a year was the norm. Part of the reasons behind such infrequent releases was due to the downtime they produce. If we can reach zero-downtime deployments, the frequency can change, and we can aim for continuous deployment. We won't go into benefits behind continuous deployment just yet. It's not relevant at this point. Instead, we'll focus on zero-downtime deployments. Given a choice, no one would choose the little-bit-of-downtime strategy, so I'll assume that everyone wants to be able to release without interruptions.

Zero-downtime deployment is a prerequisite for higher frequency releases.

Let's take a look at the Deployment definition of the API:

```
cat deploy/go-demo-2-api.yml
```

The output is as follows:

```
apiVersion: apps/v1beta2
kind: Deployment
metadata:
  name: go-demo-2-api
spec:
  replicas: 3
  selector:
    matchLabels:
      type: api
      service: go-demo-2
  minReadySeconds: 1
  progressDeadlineSeconds: 60
  revisionHistoryLimit: 5
  strategy:
   type: RollingUpdate
    rollingUpdate:
      maxSurge: 1
      maxUnavailable: 1
```

```
template:
  metadata:
    labels:
      type: api
      service: go-demo-2
      language: go
  spec:
    containers:
    - name: api
      image: vfarcic/go-demo-2
      env:
      - name: DB
        value: go-demo-2-db
      readinessProbe:
        httpGet:
          path: /demo/hello
          port: 8080
        periodSeconds: 1
      livenessProbe:
        httpGet:
          path: /demo/hello
          port: 8080
```

We'll skip explaining `apiVersion`, `kind`, and `metadata`, since they always follow the same pattern.

The `spec` section has a few of the fields we haven't seen before, and a few of those we are familiar with. The `replicas` and the `selector` are the same as what we used in the ReplicaSet from the previous chapter.

`minReadySeconds` defines the minimum number of seconds before Kubernetes starts considering the Pods healthy. We put the value of this field to 1 second. The default value is 0, meaning that the Pods will be considered available as soon as they are ready and, when specified, `livenessProbe` returns OK. If in doubt, omit this field and leave it to the default value of 0. We defined it mostly for demonstration purposes.

The next field is `revisionHistoryLimit`. It defines the number of old ReplicaSets we can rollback. Like most of the fields, it is set to the sensible default value of 10. We changed it to 5 and, as a result, we will be able to rollback to any of the previous five ReplicaSets.

The `strategy` can be either the `RollingUpdate` or the `Recreate` type. The latter will kill all the existing Pods before an update. `Recreate` resembles the processes we used in the past when the typical strategy for deploying a new release was first to stop the existing one and then put a new one in its place. This approach inevitably leads to downtime. The only case when this strategy is useful is when applications are not designed for two releases to coexist. Unfortunately, that is still more common than it should be. If you're in doubt whether your application is like that, ask yourself the following question. Would there be an adverse effect if two different versions of my application are running in parallel? If that's the case, a `Recreate` strategy might be a good choice and *you must be aware that you cannot accomplish zero-downtime deployments.*

The `recreate` strategy is much better suited for our single-replica database. We should have set up the native database replication (not the same as Kubernetes ReplicaSet object), but, as explained earlier, that is out of the scope of this chapter (and probably this book).

If we're running the database as a single replica, we must have mounted a network drive volume. That would allow us to avoid data loss when updating it or in case of a failure. Since most databases (MongoDB included) cannot have multiple instances writing to the same data files, killing the old release before creating a new one is a good strategy when replication is absent. We'll apply it later.

The `RollingUpdate` strategy is the default type, for a good reason. It allows us to deploy new releases without downtime. It creates a new ReplicaSet with zero replicas and, depending on other parameters, increases the replicas of the new one, and decreases those from the old one. The process is finished when the replicas of the new ReplicaSet entirely replace those from the old one.

When `RollingUpdate` is the strategy of choice, it can be fine-tuned with the `maxSurge` and `maxUnavailable` fields. The former defines the maximum number of Pods that can exceed the desired number (set using `replicas`). It can be set to an absolute number (for example, 2) or a percentage (for example, `35%`). The total number of Pods will never exceed the desired number (set using `replicas`) and the `maxSurge` combined. The default value is `25%`.

`maxUnavailable` defines the maximum number of Pods that are not operational. If, for example, the number of replicas is set to 15 and this field is set to 4, the minimum number of Pods that would run at any given moment would be 11. Just as the `maxSurge` field, this one also defaults to `25%`. If this field is not specified, there will always be at least 75% of the desired Pods.

In most cases, the default values of the Deployment specific fields are a good option. We changed the default settings only as a way to demonstrate better all the options we can use. We'll remove them from most of the Deployment definitions that follow.

The `template` is the same `PodTemplate` we used before. Best practice is to be explicit with image tags like we did when we set `mongo:3.3`. However, that might not always be the best strategy with the images we're building. Given we employ right practices, we can rely on `latest` tags being stable. Even if we discover they're not, we can remedy that quickly by creating a new `latest` tag. However, we cannot expect the same from third-party images. They must always be tagged to a specific version.

> Never deploy third-party images based on `latest` tags. By being explicit with the release, we have more control over what is running in production, as well as what should be the next upgrade.

We won't always use `latest` for our services, but only for the initial Deployments. Assuming that we are doing our best to maintain the `latest` tag stable and production-ready, it is handy when setting up the cluster for the first time. After that, each new release will be with a specific tag. Our automated continuous deployment pipeline will do that for us in one of the next chapters.

> If you are confident in your ability to maintain `latest` stable, it is handy using it for the first Deployment of an application.

Before we explore rolling updates, we should create the Deployment and, with it, the first release of our application.

```
kubectl create \
    -f deploy/go-demo-2-api.yml \
    --record
kubectl get -f deploy/go-demo-2-api.yml
```

We created the Deployment and retrieved the object from the Kubernetes API server.

The output of the latter command is as follows:

```
NAME           DESIRED CURRENT UP-TO-DATE AVAILABLE AGE
go-demo-2-api  3       3       3          3         1m
```

Please make sure that the number of available Pods is 3. Wait for a few moments, if that's not the case. Once all the Pods are up-and-running, we'll have a Deployment that created a new ReplicaSet which, in turn, created three Pods based on the latest release of the `vfarcic/go-demo-2` image.

Let's see what happens when we set a new image.

```
kubectl set image \
    -f deploy/go-demo-2-api.yml \
    api=vfarcic/go-demo-2:2.0 \
    --record
```

There are a few ways we can observe what is happening during the update. One of those is through the `kubectl rollout status` command.

```
kubectl rollout status -w \
    -f deploy/go-demo-2-api.yml
```

The output is as follows:

```
. . .
deployment "go-demo-2-api" successfully rolled out
```

From the last entry, we can see that the rollout of the new deployment was successful. Depending on the time that passed between setting the new image and displaying the rollout status, you might have seen other entries marking the progress. However, I think that the events from the `kubectl describe` command are painting a better picture of the process that was executed.

```
kubectl describe \
    -f deploy/go-demo-2-api.yml
```

The last lines of the output are as follows:

```
. . .
Replicas: 3 desired | 3 updated | 3 total | 3 available | 0 unava
liable
. . .
OldReplicaSets:  <none>
NewReplicaSet:   go-demo-2-api-68c75f4f5 (3/3 replicas created)
Events:
  Type    Reason            Age    From                    Message
  ----    ------            ----   ----                    -------
  Normal ScalingReplicaSet 2m     deployment-controller Scaled up r
eplica set go-demo-2-api-68df567fb5 to 3
  Normal ScalingReplicaSet 2m     deployment-controller Scaled up r
eplica set go-demo-2-api-68c75f4f5 to 1
```

```
   Normal ScalingReplicaSet 2m    deployment-controller Scaled down
replica set go-demo-2-api-68df567fb5 to 2
   Normal ScalingReplicaSet 2m    deployment-controller Scaled up r
eplica set go-demo-2-api-68c75f4f5 to 2
   Normal ScalingReplicaSet 2m    deployment-controller Scaled down
replica set go-demo-2-api-68df567fb5 to 1
   Normal ScalingReplicaSet 2m    deployment-controller Scaled up r
eplica set go-demo-2-api-68c75f4f5 to 3
   Normal ScalingReplicaSet 2m    deployment-controller Scaled down
replica set go-demo-2-api-68df567fb5 to 0
```

We can see that the number of desired replicas is 3. The same number was updated and all are available.

At the bottom of the output are events associated with the Deployment. The process started by increasing the number of replicas of the new ReplicaSet (go-demo-2-api-68c75f4f5) to 1. Next, it decreased the number of replicas of the old ReplicaSet (go-demo-2-api-68df567fb5) to 2. The same process of increasing replicas of the new, and decreasing replicas of the old ReplicaSet continued until the new one got the desired number (3), and the old one dropped to zero.

There was no downtime throughout the process. Users would receive a response from the application no matter whether they sent it before, during, or after the update. The only important thing is that, during the update, a response might have come from the old or the new release. During the update process, both releases were running in parallel.

Let's take a look at the rollout history:

```
kubectl rollout history \
    -f deploy/go-demo-2-api.yml
```

The output is as follows:

```
deployments "go-demo-2-api"
REVISION CHANGE-CAUSE
1            kubectl create --filename=deploy/go-demo-2-api.yml --rec
ord=true
2            kubectl set image api=vfarcic/go-demo-2:2.0 --filename=d
eploy/go-demo-2-api.yml
```

We can see that, so far, there were two revisions of the software. The change cause shows which command created each of those revisions.

How about ReplicaSets?

```
kubectl get rs
```

The output, limited to `go-demo-2-api`, is as follows.

```
NAME                        DESIRED CURRENT READY AGE
go-demo-2-api-68c75f4f5  3         3         3      4m
go-demo-2-api-68df567fb5 0         0         0      4m
...
```

We can see that the Deployment did not modify the ReplicaSet, but that it created a new one and, at the end of the process, the old one was scaled to zero replicas.

The diagram in the *Figure 6-2* shows the flow of the events that occurred since we executed the `kubectl set image` command. It closely depicts the events we already saw from the `kubectl describe` command.

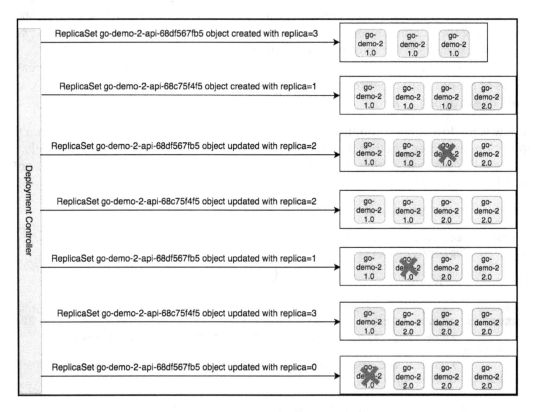

Figure 6-3: Deployment controller rolling update workflow

We made great progress. However, the unexpected can happen at any time, and we must be prepared to deal with it.

Rolling back or rolling forward?

At this point, we are, more or less, capable of deploying new releases to production as soon as they are ready. However, there will be problems. Something unexpected will happen. A bug will sneak in and put our production cluster at risk. What should we do in such a case? The answer to that question largely depends on the size of the changes and the frequency of deployments.

If we are using continuous deployment process, we are deploying new releases to production fairly often. Instead of waiting until features accumulate, we are deploying small chunks. In such cases, fixing a problem might be just as fast as rolling back. After all, how much time would it take you to fix a problem caused by only a few hours of work (maybe a day) and that was discovered minutes after you committed? Probably not much. The problem was introduced by a very recent change that is still in engineer's head. Fixing it should not take long, and we should be able to deploy a new release soon.

You might not have frequent releases, or the amount of changes included is more than a couple of hundreds of lines of code. In such a case, rolling forward might not be as fast as it should be. Still, rolling back might not even be possible. We might not be able to revert the deployment if database schema changed, and it is not compatible with the previous versions of the back-end that uses it. The moment the first transaction enters, we might lose the option to roll-back. At least, not without losing the data generated since the new release.

Rolling back a release that introduced database changes is often not possible. Even when it is, rolling forward is usually a better option when practicing continuous deployment with high-frequency releases limited to a small scope of changes.

I did my best to discourage you from rolling back. Still, in some cases that is a better option. In others, that might be the only option. Luckily, rolling back is reasonably straightforward with Kubernetes.

We'll imagine that we just discovered that the latest release of the `vfarcic/go-demo-2` image is faulty and that we should roll back to the previous release. The command that will do just that is as follows:

```
kubectl rollout undo \
    -f deploy/go-demo-2-api.yml
kubectl describe \
    -f deploy/go-demo-2-api.yml
```

The output of the latter command, limited to the last lines, is as follows:

```
OldReplicaSets:    <none>
NewReplicaSet:     go-demo-2-api-68df567fb5 (3/3 replicas created)
Events:
  Type    Reason              Age            From
Message
  ----    ------              ----           ----
--------
  Normal ScalingReplicaSet   6m             deployment-controller
Scaled up replica set go-demo-2-api-68c75f4f5 to 1
  Normal ScalingReplicaSet   6m             deployment-controller
Scaled down replica set go-demo-2-api-68df567fb5 to 2
  Normal ScalingReplicaSet   6m             deployment-controller
Scaled up replica set go-demo-2-api-68c75f4f5 to 2
  Normal ScalingReplicaSet   6m             deployment-controller
Scaled down replica set go-demo-2-api-68df567fb5 to 1
  Normal ScalingReplicaSet   6m             deployment-controller
Scaled up replica set go-demo-2-api-68c75f4f5 to 3
  Normal ScalingReplicaSet   6m             deployment-controller
Scaled down replica set go-demo-2-api-68df567fb5 to 0
  Normal DeploymentRollback 1m             deployment-controller
Rolled back deployment "go-demo-2-api" to revision 1
  Normal ScalingReplicaSet   1m             deployment-controller
Scaled up replica set go-demo-2-api-68df567fb5 to 1
  Normal ScalingReplicaSet   1m             deployment-controller
Scaled down replica set go-demo-2-api-68c75f4f5 to 2
  Normal ScalingReplicaSet   1m (x2 over 6m) deployment-controller
Scaled up replica set go-demo-2-api-68df567fb5 to 3
  Normal ScalingReplicaSet   1m (x3 over 1m) deployment-controller
(combined from similar events): Scaled down replica set go-demo-2
-api-68c75f4f5 to0
```

We can see from the events section that the Deployment initiated rollback and, from there on, the process we experienced before was reversed. It started increasing the replicas of the older ReplicaSet, and decreasing those from the latest one. Once the process is finished, the older ReplicaSet became active with all the replicas, and the newer one was scaled down to zero.

The end result might be easier to see from the NewReplicaSet entry located just above Events. Before we undid the rollout, the value was go-demo-2-api-68c75f4f5, and now it's go-demo-2-api-68df567fb5.

Knowing only the current state of the latest Deployment is often insufficient, and we might need a list of the past rollouts. We can get it with the kubectl rollout history command.

```
kubectl rollout history \
    -f deploy/go-demo-2-api.yml
```

The output is as follows:

```
REVISION   CHANGE-CAUSE
2          kubectl set image api=vfarcic/go-demo-2:2.0 --filename=
deploy/go-demo-2-api.yml
3          kubectl create --filename=deploy/go-demo-2-api.yml --re
cord=true
```

If you look at the third revision, you'll notice that the change cause is the same command we used to create the Deployment the first time. Before we executed `kubectl rollout undo`, we had two revisions; 1 and 2. The `undo` command checked the second-to-last revision (1). Since new deployments do no destroy ReplicaSets but scale them to 0, all it had to do to undo the last change was to scale it back to the desired number of replicas and, at the same time, scale the current one to zero.

Let's fast track a bit and deploy a few new releases. That will provide us with a broader playground to explore a few additional things we can do with Deployments.

```
kubectl set image \
    -f deploy/go-demo-2-api.yml \
    api=vfarcic/go-demo-2:3.0 \
    --record
kubectl rollout status \
    -f deploy/go-demo-2-api.yml
```

We updated the image to `vfarcic/go-demo-2:3.0` and retrieved the rollout status. The last line of the latter command is as follows:

```
deployment "go-demo-2-api" successfully rolled out
```

The deployment was successfully updated and, as a result, it created a new ReplicaSet and scaled it up to the desired number of replicas. The previously active ReplicaSet was scaled to 0. As a result, we're running tag 3.0 of the `vfarcic/go-demo-2` image.

We'll repeat the process with the tag 4.0:

```
kubectl set image \
    -f deploy/go-demo-2-api.yml \
    api=vfarcic/go-demo-2:4.0 \
    --record
kubectl rollout status \
    -f deploy/go-demo-2-api.yml
```

The output of the last line of the `rollout status` confirmed that the rollout was successful.

Now that we deployed a few releases, we can check the current `rollout history`:

```
kubectl rollout history \
    -f deploy/go-demo-2-api.yml
```

The output is as follows:

```
deployments "go-demo-2-api"
REVISION CHANGE-CAUSE
2         kubectl set image api=vfarcic/go-demo-2:2.0 --filename=d
eploy/go-demo-2-api.yml --record=true
3         kubectl create --filename=deploy/go-demo-2-api.yml --rec
ord=true
4         kubectl set image api=vfarcic/go-demo-2:3.0 --filename=d
eploy/go-demo-2-api.yml --record=true
5         kubectl set image api=vfarcic/go-demo-2:4.0 --filename=deploy/go-
demo-2-api.yml --record=true
```

We can clearly see the commands that produced the changes and, through them, how our application progressed all the way until the current release based on the image `vfarcic/go-demo-2:4.0`.

You saw that we can rollback to the previous release through the `kubectl rollout undo` command. In most cases, that should be the correct action when faced with problems and without the ability to roll forward by creating a new release with the fix. However, sometimes even that is not enough, and we have to go back in time further than the previous release.

Let's say that we discovered not only that the current release is faulty but also that a few before it have bugs as well. Following the same narrative, we'll imagine that the last correct release was based on the image `vfarcic/go-demo-2:2.0`. We can remedy that by executing the command that follows (**please do NOT run it**):

```
kubectl set image \
    -f deploy/go-demo-2-api.yml \
    api=vfarcic/go-demo-2:2.0 \
    --record
```

While that command would certainly fix the problem, there is an easier way to accomplish the same result. We can undo the rollout by moving to the last revision that worked correctly. Assuming that we want to revert to the image vfarcic/go-demo-2:2.0, reviewing the change causes listed in the history tells us we should roll back to revision 2. That can be accomplished through the --to-revision argument. The command is as follows:

```
kubectl rollout undo \
    -f deploy/go-demo-2-api.yml \
    --to-revision=2
kubectl rollout history \
    -f deploy/go-demo-2-api.yml
```

We undid the rollout by moving to revision 2. We also retrieved the history.

The output of the latter command is as follows:

```
deployments "go-demo-2-api"
REVISION   CHANGE-CAUSE
3          kubectl create --filename=deploy/go-demo-2-api.yml --re
cord=true
4          kubectl set image api=vfarcic/go-demo-2:3.0 --filename=
deploy/go-demo-2-api.yml --record=true
5          kubectl set image api=vfarcic/go-demo-2:4.0 --filename=
deploy/go-demo-2-api.yml --record=true
6          kubectl set image api=vfarcic/go-demo-2:2.0 --filename=
deploy/go-demo-2-api.yml --record=true
```

Through the new revision 6, we can see that the currently active Deployment is based on the image vfarcic/go-demo-2:2.0. We successfully moved back to the specific point in time. The problem is solved and, if this was the "real" application running in a production cluster, our users would continue interacting with the version of our software that actually works.

Rolling back failed Deployments

Discovering a critical bug is probably the most common reason for a rollback. Still, there are others. For example, we might be in a situation when Pods cannot be created. An easy to reproduce case would be an attempt to deploy an image with a tag that does not exist.

```
kubectl set image \
    -f deploy/go-demo-2-api.yml \
    api=vfarcic/go-demo-2:does-not-exist \
    --record
```

The output is as follows:

```
deployment "go-demo-2-api" image updated
```

After seeing such a message, you might be under the impression that everything is OK. However, that output only indicates that the definition of the image used in the Deployment was successfully updated. That does not mean that the Pods behind the ReplicaSet are indeed running. For one, I can assure you that the vfarcic/go-demo-2:does-not-exist image does not exist.

Please make sure that at least 60 seconds have passed since you executed the kubectl set image command. If you're wondering why we are waiting, the answer lies in the progressDeadlineSeconds field set in the go-demo-2-api Deployment definition. That's how much the Deployment has to wait before it deduces that it cannot progress due to a failure to run a Pod.

Let's take a look at the ReplicaSets.

```
kubectl get rs -l type=api
```

The output is as follows:

NAME	DESIRED	CURRENT	READY	AGE
go-demo-2-api-5b49d94f9b	0	0	0	8m
go-demo-2-api-68c75f4f5	2	2	2	9m
go-demo-2-api-7cb9bb5675	0	0	0	8m
go-demo-2-api-68df567fb5	0	0	0	9m
go-demo-2-api-dc7877dcd	2	2	0	4m

By now, under different circumstances, all the Pods from the new ReplicaSet (go-demo-2-api-dc7877dcd) should be set to 3, and the Pods of the previous one (go-demo-2-api-68c75f4f5) should have been scaled down to 0. However, the Deployment noticed that there is a problem and stopped the update process.

We should be able to get more detailed information with the `kubectl rollout status` command:

```
kubectl rollout status \
    -f deploy/go-demo-2-api.yml
```

The output is as follows:

```
error: deployment "go-demo-2-api" exceeded its progress deadline
```

The Deployment realized that it shouldn't proceed. The new Pods are not running, and the limit was reached. There's no point to continue trying.

If you expected that the Deployment would roll back after it failed, you're wrong. It will not do such a thing. At least, not without additional add-ons. That does not mean that I would expect you to sit in front of your terminal, wait for timeouts, and check the `rollout status` before deciding whether to keep the new update or to roll back. I expect you to deploy new releases as part of your automated CDP pipeline. Fortunately, the `status` command returns 1 if the deployment failed and we can use that information to decide what to do next. For those of you not living and breathing Linux, any exit code different than 0 is considered an error. Let's confirm that by checking the exit code of the last command:

```
echo $?
```

The output is indeed 1, thus confirming that the rollout failed.

We'll explore automated CDP pipeline soon. For now, just remember that we can find out whether Deployment updates were successful or not.

Now that we discovered that our last rollout failed, we should undo it. You already know how to do that, but I'll remind you just in case you're of a forgetful nature.

```
kubectl rollout undo \
    -f deploy/go-demo-2-api.yml
kubectl rollout status \
    -f deploy/go-demo-2-api.yml
```

The output of the last command confirmed that deployment "go-demo-2-api" was successfully rolled out.

Now that we have learned how to rollback no matter whether the problem is a critical bug or inability to run the new release, we can take a short pause from learning new stuff and merge all the definitions we explored thus far into a single YAML file. But, before we do that, we'll remove the objects we created.

```
kubectl delete \
    -f deploy/go-demo-2-db.yml
kubectl delete \
    -f deploy/go-demo-2-db-svc.yml
kubectl delete \
    -f deploy/go-demo-2-api.yml
```

Merging everything into the same YAML definition

Consider this section a short intermezzo. We'll merge the definitions we used in this chapter into a single YAML file. You already had a similar example before, so there's no need for lengthy explanations.

```
cat deploy/go-demo-2.yml
```

If you start searching for differences with the previous definitions, you will find a few. The `minReadySeconds`, `progressDeadlineSeconds`, `revisionHistoryLimit`, and `strategy` fields are removed from the `go-demo-2-api` Deployment. We used them mostly as a way to demonstrate their usage. But, since Kubernetes has sensible defaults, we omitted them from this definition. You'll also notice that there are two Services even though we created only one in this chapter. We did not need the `go-demo-2-api` Service in our examples since we didn't need to access the API. But, for the sake of completeness, it is included in this definition. Finally, the strategy for deploying the database is set to `recreate`. As explained earlier, it is more suited for a single-replica database, even though we did not mount a volume that would preserve the data.

Let's create the objects defined in `deploy/go-demo-2.yml`. Remember, with `--save-config` we're making sure we can edit the configuration later. The alternative would be to use `kubectl apply` instead.

```
kubectl create \
    -f deploy/go-demo-2.yml \
    --record --save-config
kubectl get -f deploy/go-demo-2.yml
```

The output of the latter command is as follows:

```
NAME                    DESIRED CURRENT UP-TO-DATE AVAILABLE AGE
deploy/go-demo-2-db 1        1       1            1         15s
NAME                TYPE      CLUSTER-IP EXTERNAL-IP PORT(S)    AGE
svc/go-demo-2-db ClusterIP 10.0.0.125 <none>       27017/TCP 15s
NAME                    DESIRED CURRENT UP-TO-DATE AVAILABLE AGE
deploy/go-demo-2-api 3       3       3            3         15s
NAME                TYPE      CLUSTER-IP EXTERNAL-IP PORT(S)
AGE
svc/go-demo-2-api NodePort 10.0.0.57  <none>       8080:31586/TCP
15s
```

All four objects (two Deployments and two Services) were created, and we can move on and explore ways to update multiple objects with a single command.

Updating multiple objects

Even though most of the time we send requests to specific objects, almost everything is happening using selector labels. When we updated the Deployments, they looked for matching selectors to choose which ReplicaSets to create and scale. They, in turn, created or terminated Pods also using the matching selectors. Almost everything in Kubernetes is operated using label selectors. It's just that sometimes that is obscured from us.

We do not have to update an object only by specifying its name or the YAML file where its definition resides. We can also use labels to decide which object should be updated. That opens some interesting possibilities since the selectors might match multiple objects.

Imagine that we are running several Deployments with Mongo databases and that the time has come to update them all to a newer release. Before we explore how we could do that, we'll create another Deployment so that we have at least two with the database Pods.

Let us first take a look at the definition:

```
cat deploy/different-app-db.yml
```

The output is as follows:

```
piVersion: apps/v1beta2
kind: Deployment
metadata:
  name: different-app-db
  labels:
    type: db
    service: different-app
```

```
      vendor: MongoLabs
spec:
  selector:
    matchLabels:
      type: db
      service: different-app
  template:
    metadata:
      labels:
        type: db
        service: different-app
        vendor: MongoLabs
    spec:
      containers:
      - name: db
        image: mongo:3.3
        ports:
        - containerPort: 28017
```

When compared with the `go-demo-2-db` Deployment, the only difference is in the `service` label. Both have the `type` set to `db`.

Let's create the deployment:

```
kubectl create \
    -f deploy/different-app-db.yml
```

Now that we have two deployments with the `mongo:3.3` Pods, we can try to update them both at the same time.

The trick is to find a label (or a set of labels) that uniquely identifies all the Deployments we want to update.

Let's take a look at the list of Deployments with their labels:

```
kubectl get deployments --show-labels
```

The output is as follows:

```
NAME                DESIRED  CURRENT  UP-TO-DATE  AVAILABLE  AGE  LABELS
different-app-db 1      1        1           1          1h   service
=different-app,type=db,vendor=MongoLabs
go-demo-2-api    3      3        3           3          1h   languag
e=go,service=go-demo-2,type=api
go-demo-2-db     1      1        1           1          1h   service
=go-demo-2,type=db,vendor=MongoLabs
```

We want to update `mongo` Pods created using `different-app-db` and `go-demo-2-db` Deployments. Both are uniquely identified with the labels `type=db` and `vendor=MongoLabs`. Let's test that:

```
kubectl get deployments \
    -l type=db,vendor=MongoLabs
```

The output is as follows:

```
NAME             DESIRED  CURRENT  UP-TO-DATE  AVAILABLE  AGE
different-app-db 1        1        1           1          1h
go-demo-2-db     1        1        1           1          1h
```

We can see that filtering with those two labels worked. We retrieved only the Deployments we want to update, so let's proceed and roll out the new release:

```
kubectl set image deployments \
    -l type=db,vendor=MongoLabs \
    db=mongo:3.4 --record
```

The output is as follows:

```
deployment "different-app-db" image updated
deployment "go-demo-2-db" image updated
```

Finally, before we move into the next subject, we should validate that the image indeed changed to `mongo:3.4`:

```
kubectl describe \
    -f deploy/go-demo-2.yml
```

The output, limited to the relevant parts, is as follows:

```
...
  Containers:
   db:
    Image:         mongo:3.4
...
```

As we can see, the update was indeed successful, at least with that Deployment. Feel free to describe the Deployment defined in `deploy/different-app-db.yml`. You should see that its image was also updated to the newer version.

Scaling Deployments

There are quite a few different ways we can scale Deployments. Everything we do in this section is not unique to Deployments and can be applied to any Controller, like ReplicaSet, and those we did not yet explore.

If we decide that the number of replicas changes with relatively low frequency or that Deployments are performed manually, the best way to scale is to write a new YAML file or, even better, modify the existing one. Assuming that we store YAML files in a code repository, by updating existing files we have a documented and reproducible definition of the objects running inside a cluster.

We already performed scaling when we applied the definition from the `go-demo-2-scaled.yml`. We'll do something similar, but with Deployments.

Let's take a look at `deploy/go-demo-2-scaled.yml`.

```
cat deploy/go-demo-2-scaled.yml
```

We won't display the contents of the whole file since it is almost identical to `deploy/go-demo-2.yml`. The only difference is the number of replicas of the `go-demo-2-api` Deployment.

```
. . .
apiVersion: apps/v1beta2
kind: Deployment
metadata:
  name: go-demo-2-api
spec:
  replicas: 5
. . .
```

At the moment, we're running three replicas. Once we apply the new definition, it should increase to five.

```
kubectl apply \
    -f deploy/go-demo-2-scaled.yml
```

Please note that, even though the file is different, the names of the resources are the same so `kubectl apply` did not create new objects. Instead, it updated those that changed. In particular, it changed the number of replicas of the `go-demo-2-api` Deployment.

Let's confirm that there are indeed five replicas of the Pods controlled through the Deployment.

```
kubectl get \
    -f deploy/go-demo-2-scaled.yml
```

The output, limited to the `deploy/go-demo-2-api`, is as follows:

```
. . .
NAME                    DESIRED CURRENT UP-TO-DATE AVAILABLE AGE
deploy/go-demo-2-api 5     5        5            5         11m
. . .
```

The result should come as no surprise. After all, we executed the same process before, when we explored ReplicaSets.

While scaling Deployments using YAML files (or other Controllers) is an excellent way to keep documentation accurate, it rarely fits the dynamic nature of the clusters. We should aim for a system that will scale (and de-scale) services automatically. When scaling is frequent and, hopefully, automated, we cannot expect to update YAML definitions and push them to Git. That would be too inefficient and would probably cause quite a few unwanted executions of delivery pipelines if they are triggered through repository Webhooks. After all, do we really want to push updated YAML files multiple times a day?

The number of `replicas` should not be part of the design. Instead, they are a fluctuating number that changes continuously (or at least often), depending on the traffic, memory and CPU utilization, and so on.

Depending on release frequency, the same can be said for `image`. If we are practicing continuous delivery or deployment, we might be releasing once a week, once a day, or even more often. In such cases, new images would be deployed often, and there is no strong argument for the need to change YAML files every time we make a new release. That is especially true if we are deploying through an automated process (as we should).

We'll explore automation later on. For now, we'll limit ourselves to a command similar to `kubectl set image`. We used it to change the `image` used by Pods with each release. Similarly, we'll use `kubectl scale` to change the number of replicas. Consider this an introduction to automation that is coming later on.

```
kubectl scale deployment \
    go-demo-2-api --replicas 8 --record
```

We scaled the number of replicas associated with the Deployment `go-demo-2-api`. Please note that, this time, we did not use `-f` to reference a file. Since we have two Deployments specified in the same YAML, that would result in scaling of both. Since we wanted to limit it to a particular Deployment, we used its name instead.

Let's confirm that scaling indeed worked as expected.

```
kubectl get -f deploy/go-demo-2.yml
```

The output, limited to Deployments, is as follows:

```
NAME                   DESIRED CURRENT UP-TO-DATE AVAILABLE AGE
deploy/go-demo-2-db 1      1       1              1         33m
NAME                   DESIRED CURRENT UP-TO-DATE AVAILABLE AGE
deploy/go-demo-2-api 8     8       8              8         33m
```

As I mentioned earlier, we'll dedicate quite a lot of time to automation, and you won't have to scale your applications manually. However, I thought that it is useful to know that the `kubectl scale` command exists. For now, you know how to scale Deployments (and other Controllers).

What now?

Everything we learned led us to Deployments. Pods must not be created directly, but through ReplicaSets which, similarly, must not be created directly, but through Deployments. They are the objects that allow us not only to create the ReplicaSets and Pods, but that can also be updated without producing any downtime (when applications are designed accordingly). We combined Deployments with Services so that Pods can communicate with each other, or can be accessed from outside a cluster. All in all, we have everything we need to release our services to production. That is not to say that we understand all the crucial aspects of Kubernetes. We're not even close to that point. But, we do have almost everything we need for running some types of applications in production. What we're missing is networking.

Before we enter the next stage of our knowledge seeking mission, we'll destroy the cluster we're running and give our laptops a break.

```
minikube delete
```

If you'd like to know more about Deployments, please explore Deployment v1 apps (`https://v1-9.docs.kubernetes.io/docs/reference/generated/kubern etes-api/v1.9/#deployment-v1-apps`) API documentation.

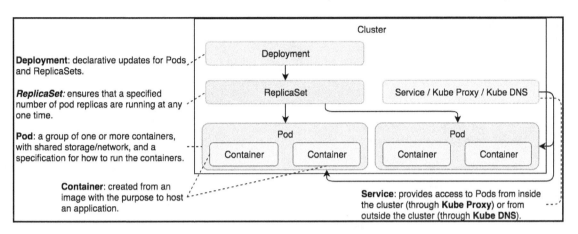

Figure 6-4: The components explored so far

Before we move onto the next chapter, we'll explore the differences between Kubernetes Deployments and Docker Swarm stacks.

Kubernetes Deployments compared to Docker Swarm stacks

If you have already used Docker Swarm, the logic behind Kubernetes Deployments should be familiar. Both serve the same purpose and can be used to deploy new applications or update those that are already running inside a cluster. In both cases, we can easily deploy new releases without any downtime (when application architecture permits that).

Unlike the previous comparison between Kubernetes Pods, ReplicaSets, and Services with Docker Swarm Stacks, Kubernetes Deployments do provide a few potentially important functional differences. But, before we dive into the functional comparison, we'll take a moment to explore differences in how we define objects.

An example Kubernetes Deployment and Service definition is as follows:

```
apiVersion: apps/v1beta2
kind: Deployment
```

```
metadata:
  name: go-demo-2-db
spec:
  selector:
    matchLabels:
     type: db
       service: go-demo-2
  strategy:
    type: Recreate
  template:
    metadata:
      labels:
        type: db
        service: go-demo-2
        vendor: MongoLabs
    spec:
      containers:
      - name: db
        image: mongo:3.3
        ports:
        - containerPort: 28017
---
apiVersion: v1
kind: Service
metadata:
  name: go-demo-2-db
spec:
  ports:
  - port: 27017
  selector:
    type: db
    service: go-demo-2
---
apiVersion: apps/v1beta2
kind: Deployment
metadata:
  name: go-demo-2-api
spec:
  replicas: 3
  selector:
    matchLabels:
      type: api
      service: go-demo-2
  template:
    metadata:
      labels:
        type: api
        service: go-demo-2
```

```
      language: go
  spec:
    containers:
    - name: api
      image: vfarcic/go-demo-2
      env:
      - name: DB
        value: go-demo-2-db
      readinessProbe:
        httpGet:
          path: /demo/hello
          port: 8080
        periodSeconds: 1
      livenessProbe:
        httpGet:
          path: /demo/hello
          port: 8080

---

apiVersion: v1
kind: Service
metadata:
  name: go-demo-2-api
spec:
  type: NodePort
  ports:
  - port: 8080
  selector:
    type: api
    service: go-demo-2
```

An equivalent Docker Swarm stack definition is as follows:

```
version: "3"
services:
  api:
    image: vfarcic/go-demo-2
    environment:
      - DB=db
    ports:
      - 8080
    deploy:
      replicas: 3
  db:
    image: mongo:3.3
```

Both definitions provide, more or less, the same functionality.

It is evident that a Kubernetes Deployment requires a much longer definition with more a complex syntax. It is worth noting that Swarm's equivalent to `readinessProbe` and `livenessProbe` is not present in the stack because it is defined as a `HEALTHCHECK` inside the Dockerfile. Still, even if we remove them, a Kubernetes Deployment remains longer and more complicated.

When comparing only the differences in the ways to define objects, Docker Swarm is a clear **winner**. Let's see what we can conclude from the functional point of view.

Creating the objects is reasonably straight-forward. Both `kubectl create` and `docker stack deploy` will deploy new releases without any downtime. New containers or, in case of Kubernetes, Pods will be created and, in parallel, the old ones will be terminated. So far, both solutions are, more or less, the same.

One of the main differences is what happens in case of a failure. A Kubernetes Deployment will not perform any corrective action in case of a failure. It will stop the update, leaving a combination of new and old Pods running in parallel. Docker Swarm, on the other hand, can be configured to rollback automatically. That might seem like another win for Docker Swarm. However, Kubernetes has something Swarm doesn't. We can use `kubectl rollout status` command to find out whether the update was a success or failure and, in case of the latter, we can `undo` the `rollout`. Even though we need a few commands to accomplish the same result, that might fare better when updates are automated. Knowing whether an update succeeded or failed allows us to not only execute a subsequent rollback action but also notify someone that there is a problem.

Both approaches have their pros and cons. Docker Swarm's automated rollback is better suited in some cases, and Kubernetes update status works better in others. The methods are different, and there is no clear winner, so I'll proclaim it a tie.

Kubernetes Deployments can record history. We can use the `kubectl rollout history` command to inspect past rollout. When updates are working as expected, `history` is not very useful. But, when things go wrong, it might provide additional insight. That can be combined with the ability to rollback to a specific revision, not necessarily the previous one. However, most of the time, we rollback to the previous version. The ability to go back further in time is not very useful. Even when such a need arises, both products can do that. The difference is that Kubernetes Deployments allow us to go to a specific revision (for example, we're on the revision five, rollback to the revision two). With Docker Swarm, we'd have to issue a new update (for example, update the image to the tag 2.0). Since containers are immutable, the result is the same, so the difference is only in the syntax behind a rollback.

The ability to rollback to a specific version or a tag exists in both products. We can argue which syntax is more straightforward or more useful. The differences are minor, and I'll proclaim that there is no winner for that functionality. It's another tie.

Since almost everything in Kubernetes is based on label selectors, it has a feature that Docker Swarm doesn't. We can update multiple Deployments at the same time. We can, for example, issue an update (`kubetl set image`) that uses filters to find all Mongo databases and upgrade them to a newer release. It is a feature that would require a few lines of bash scripting with Docker Swarm. However, while the ability to update all Deployments that match specific labels might sound like a useful feature, it often isn't. More often than not, such actions can produce undesirable effects. If, for example, we have five back-end applications that use Mongo database (one for each), we'd probably want to upgrade them in a more controlled fashion. Teams behind those services would probably want to test each of those upgrades and give their blessings. We probably wouldn't wait until all are finished, but upgrade a single database when the team in charge of it feels confident.

There are the cases when updating multiple objects is useful so I must give this one to Kubernetes. It a minor win, but it still counts.

There are a few other things that are easier to accomplish with Kubernetes. For example, due to the way Kubernetes Services work, creating a blue-green deployment process, instead of using rolling updates, is much easier. However, such a process falls into advanced usage so I'll leave it out of this comparison. It'll (probably) come later.

It's difficult to say which solution provides better results. Docker Swarm continues to shine from the user-friendliness perspective. On the other hand, Kubernetes Deployments offer a few additional features.

It is much simpler and easier to write a Docker Swarm stack file than a Kubernetes Deployment definition. Kubernetes Deployments offer a few additional functional features that Swarm does not have. However, those features are, for most use cases, of minor importance. Those that indeed matter are, more or less, the same.

Don't make a decision based on the differences between Kubernetes Deployments and Docker Swarm stacks. Definition syntax is where Swarm has a clear win, while on the functional front Kubernetes has a tiny edge over Swarm. If you'd make a decision only based on deployments, Swarm might be a slightly better candidate. Or not. It all depends on what matters more in your case. Do you care about YAML syntax? Are those additional Kubernetes Deployment features something you will ever use?

In any case, Kubernetes has much more to offer, and any conclusion based on such a limited comparison scope is bound to be incomplete. We only scratched the surface. Stay tuned for more.

7
Using Ingress to Forward Traffic

 Applications that are not accessible to users are useless. Kubernetes Services provide accessibility with a usability cost. Each application can be reached through a different port. We cannot expect users to know the port of each service in our cluster.

Ingress objects manage external access to the applications running inside a Kubernetes cluster. While, at first glance, it might seem that we already accomplished that through Kubernetes Services, they do not make the applications truly accessible. We still need forwarding rules based on paths and domains, SSL termination and a number of other features. In a more traditional setup, we'd probably use an external proxy and a load balancer. Ingress provides an API that allows us to accomplish these things, in addition to a few other features we expect from a dynamic cluster.

We'll explore the problems and the solutions through examples. For now, we first need to create a cluster.

Creating a cluster

As every other chapter so far, we'll start by creating a Minikube single-node cluster.

 All the commands from this chapter are available in the 07-ingress.sh (https://gist.github.com/vfarcic/54ef6592bce747ff2d1b089834fc755 b) Gist.

```
cd k8s-specs
git pull
minikube start --vm-driver=virtualbox
kubectl config current-context
```

The cluster should be up-and-running, and we can move on.

Exploring deficiencies when enabling external access through Kubernetes services

We cannot explore solutions before we know what the problems are. Therefore, we'll re-create a few objects using the knowledge we already gained. That will let us see whether Kubernetes services satisfy all the needs users of our applications might have. Or, to be more explicit, we'll explore which features we're missing when making our applications accessible to users.

We already discussed that it is a bad practice to publish fixed ports through services. That method is likely to result in conflicts or, at the very least, create the additional burden of carefully keeping track of which port belongs to which service. We already discarded that option before, and we won't change our minds now. Since we've clarified that, let's go back and create the Deployments and the Services from the previous chapter.

```
kubectl create \
    -f ingress/go-demo-2-deploy.yml
kubectl get \
    -f ingress/go-demo-2-deploy.yml
```

The output of the get command is as follows:

```
NAME                 DESIRED CURRENT UP-TO-DATE AVAILABLE AGE
deploy/go-demo-2-db 1        1       1          1         48s
NAME             TYPE      CLUSTER-IP EXTERNAL-IP PORT(S)    AGE
svc/go-demo-2-db ClusterIP 10.0.0.14  <none>      27017/TCP 48s
NAME                 DESIRED CURRENT UP-TO-DATE AVAILABLE AGE
deploy/go-demo-2-api 3       3       3          3         48s
NAME              TYPE      CLUSTER-IP EXTERNAL-IP PORT(S)
AGE
svc/go-demo-2-api NodePort  10.0.0.179 <none>      8080:30417/TCP
48s
```

As you can see, these are the same Services and Deployments we previously created.

Before we move on, we should wait until all the Pods are up and running.

```
kubectl get pods
```

The output is as follows:

```
NAME                            READY STATUS   RESTARTS AGE
go-demo-2-api-68df567fb5-8qcmv  1/1   Running  0        3m
go-demo-2-api-68df567fb5-k55d4  1/1   Running  0        3m
go-demo-2-api-68df567fb5-ws9cj  1/1   Running  0        3m
go-demo-2-db-dd48b7dfc-hdxbz    1/1   Running  0        3m
```

If, in your case, some of the Pods are not yet running, please wait a few moments and re-execute the kubectl get pods command. We'll continue once they're ready.

One obvious way to access the applications is through Services:

```
IP=$(minikube ip)
PORT=$(kubectl get svc go-demo-2-api \
    -o jsonpath="{.spec.ports[0].nodePort}")
curl -i "http://$IP:$PORT/demo/hello"
```

We retrieved the Minikube IP and the port of the go-demo-2-api Service. We used that information to send a request.

The output of the curl command is as follows:

```
HTTP/1.1 200 OK
Date: Sun, 24 Dec 2017 13:35:26 GMT
Content-Length: 14
Content-Type: text/plain; charset=utf-8
hello, world!
```

The application responded with the status code 200 thus confirming that the Service indeed forwards the requests.

While publishing a random, or even a hard-coded port of a single application might not be so bad, if we'd apply the same principle to more applications, the user experience would be horrible. To make the point a bit clearer, we'll deploy another application:

```
kubectl create \
    -f ingress/devops-toolkit-dep.yml \
    --record --save-config
kubectl get \
    -f ingress/devops-toolkit-dep.yml
```

This application follows similar logic to the first. From the latter command, we can see that it contains a Deployment and a Service. The details are of no importance since the YAML definition is very similar to those we used before. What matters is that now we have two applications running inside the cluster.

Let's check whether the new application is indeed reachable:

```
PORT=$(kubectl get svc devops-toolkit \
    -o jsonpath="{.spec.ports[0].nodePort}")
open "http://$IP:$PORT"
```

We retrieved the port of the new Service and opened the application in a browser. You should see a simple front-end with *The DevOps Toolkit* books. If you don't, you might want to wait a bit longer until the containers are pulled, and try again.

A simplified flow of requests is depicted in the *Figure 7-1*. A user sends a request to one of the nodes of the cluster. That request is received by a Service and load balanced to one of the associated Pods. It's a bit more complicated than that, with iptables, kube DNS, kube proxy, and a few other things involved in the process. We explored them in more detail in Chapter 5, *Using Services to Enable Communication Between Pods*, and there's probably no need to go through them all again. For the sake of brevity, the simplified diagram should do:

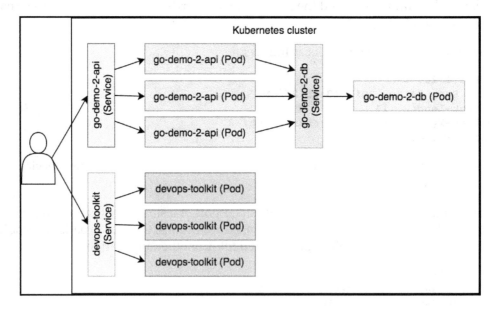

Figure 7-1: Applications access through Services

We cannot expect our users to know specific ports behind each of those applications. Even with only two, that would not be very user-friendly. If that number would rise to tens or even hundreds of applications, our business would be very short-lived.

What we need is a way to make all services accessible through standard HTTP (80) or HTTPS (443) ports. Kubernetes Services alone cannot get us there. We need more.

What we need is to grant access to our services on predefined paths and domains. Our go-demo-2 service could be distinguished from others through the base path /demo. Similarly, the books application could be reachable through the devopstoolkitseries.com domain. If we could accomplish that, we could access them with the commands the follow:

```
curl "http://$IP/demo/hello"
```

The request received the Connection refused response. There is no process listening on port 80, so this outcome is not a surprise. We could have changed one of the Services to publish the fixed port 80 instead assigning a random one. Still, that would provide access only to one of the two applications.

We often want to associate each application with a different domain or sub-domain. Outside the examples we're running, the books application is accessible through the devopstoolkitseries.com (http://www.devopstoolkitseries.com/) domain. Since I'm not going to give you permissions to modify my domain's DNS records, we'll simulate it by adding the domain to the Host header.

The command that should verify whether the application running inside our cluster is accessible through the devopstoolkitseries.com domain is as follows:

```
curl -i \
    -H "Host: devopstoolkitseries.com" \
    "http://$IP"
```

As expected, the request is still refused.

Last, but not least, we should be able to make some, if not all, applications (partly) secure by enabling HTTPS access. That means that we should have a place to store our SSL certificates. We could put them inside our applications, but that would only increase the operational complexity. Instead, we should aim towards SSL offloading somewhere between clients and the applications.

The problems that we are facing are common, and it should come as no surprise that Kubernetes has a solution.

Enabling Ingress controllers

We need a mechanism that will accept requests on pre-defined ports (for example, `80` and `443`) and forward them to Kubernetes services. It should be able to distinguish requests based on paths and domains as well as to be able to perform SSL offloading.

Kubernetes itself does not have a ready-to-go solution for this. Unlike other types of Controllers that are typically part of the `kube-controller-manager` binary, Ingress Controller needs to be installed separately. Instead of a Controller, `kube-controller-manager` offers *Ingress resource* that other third-party solutions can utilize to provide requests forwarding and SSL features. In other words, Kubernetes only provides an *API*, and we need to set up a Controller that will use it.

Fortunately, the community already built a myriad of Ingress controllers. We won't evaluate all of the available options since that would require a lot of space, and it would mostly depend on your needs and your hosting vendor. Instead, we'll explore how Ingress controllers work through the one that is already available in Minikube.

Let's take a look at the list of the Minikube addons:

```
minikube addons list
```

The output is as follows:

```
- kube-dns: enabled
- registry: disabled
- registry-creds: disabled
- dashboard: enabled
- coredns: disabled
- heapster: disabled
- ingress: disabled
- addon-manager: enabled
- default-storageclass: enabled
```

We can see that `ingress` is available as one of the Minikube addons. However, it is disabled by default, so our next action will be to enable it.

 If you used Minikube before, the `ingress` addon might already be enabled. If that's the case, please skip the command that follows.

```
minikube addons enable ingress
```

Now that `ingress` addon is enabled, we'll check whether it is running inside our cluster:

```
kubectl get pods -n kube-system \
    | grep ingress
```

Ignore the `-n` argument. We did not yet explore Namespaces. For now, please note that the output of the command should show that `nginx-ingress-controller-...` Pod is running.

If the output is empty, you might need to wait for a few moments until the containers are pulled, and re-execute the `kubectl get all --namespace ingress-nginx` command again.

 The Ingress controller that ships with Minikube is based on the `gcr.io/google_containers/nginx-ingress-controller` (`https://console.cloud.google.com/gcr/images/google-containers/G LOBAL/nginx-ingress-controller?gcrImageListsize=50`) image hosted in **Google Cloud Platform** (**GCP**) Container Registry. The image is based on NGINX Ingress Controller (`https://github.com/kubernetes/ingress-nginx/blob/master/README. md`). It is one of the only two currently supported and maintained by the Kubernetes community. The other one is GLBC (`https://github.com/kubernetes/ingress- gce/blob/master/README.md`) that comes with **Google Compute Engine** (**GCE**) (`https://cloud.google.com/compute/`) Kubernetes hosted solution.

By default, the Ingress controller is configured with only two endpoints.

If we'd like to check Controller's health, we can send a request to `/healthz`.

```
curl -i "http://$IP/healthz"
```

The output is as follows:

```
HTTP/1.1 200 OK
Server: nginx/1.13.5
Date: Sun, 24 Dec 2017 15:22:20 GMT
Content-Type: text/html
Content-Length: 0
Connection: keep-alive
Strict-Transport-Security: max-age=15724800; includeSubDomains;
```

It responded with the status code `200 OK`, thus indicating that it is healthy and ready to serve requests. There's not much more to it so we'll move to the second endpoint.

The Ingress controller has a default catch-all endpoint that is used when a request does not match any of the other criteria. Since we did not yet create any Ingress Resource, this endpoint should provide the same response to all requests except `/healthz`:

```
curl -i "http://$IP/something"
```

The output is as follows:

```
HTTP/1.1 404 Not Found
Server: nginx/1.13.5
Date: Sun, 24 Dec 2017 15:36:23 GMT
Content-Type: text/plain; charset=utf-8
Content-Length: 21
Connection: keep-alive
Strict-Transport-Security: max-age=15724800; includeSubDomains;
default backend - 404
```

We got the response indicating that the requested resource could not be found.

Now we're ready to create our first Ingress Resource.

Creating Ingress Resources based on paths

We'll try to make our `go-demo-2-api` service available through the port `80`. We'll do that by defining an Ingress resource with the rule to forward all requests with the path starting with `/demo` to the service `go-demo-2-api`.

Let's take a look at the Ingress' YAML definition:

```
cat ingress/go-demo-2-ingress.yml
```

The output is as follows:

```
apiVersion: extensions/v1beta1
kind: Ingress
metadata:
  name: go-demo-2
  annotations:
    ingress.kubernetes.io/ssl-redirect: "false"
    nginx.ingress.kubernetes.io/ssl-redirect: "false"
spec:
  rules:
  - http:
      paths:
      - path: /demo
        backend:
```

```
serviceName: go-demo-2-api
servicePort: 8080
```

This time, `metadata` contains a field we haven't used before. The `annotations` section allows us to provide additional information to the Ingress controller. As you'll see soon, Ingress API specification is concise and limited. That is done on purpose. The specification API defines only the fields that are mandatory for all Ingress controllers. All the additional info an Ingress controller needs is specified through `annotations`. That way, the community behind the Controllers can progress at great speed, while still providing basic general compatibility and standards.

The list of general annotations and the Controllers that support them can be found in the Ingress Annotations page(`https://github.com/kubernetes/ingress-nginx/blob/master/doc s/user-guide/nginx-configuration/annotations.md`). For those specific to the NGINX Ingress controller (`https://github.com/kubernetes/ingress-nginx/blob/master/README. md`), please visit the NGINX Annotations (`https://github.com/kubernetes/ingress-nginx/blob/master/docs/us er-guide/nginx-configuration/annotations.md`)page, and for those specific to GCE Ingress, visit the `ingress-gce` (`https://github.com/kubernetes/ingress-gce`) page. You'll notice that documentation uses `nginx.ingress.kubernetes.io/` annotation prefixes. That is a relatively recent change that, at the time of this writing, applies to the beta versions of the Controller. We're combining it with `ingress.kubernetes.io/` prefixes so that the definitions work in all Kubernetes versions.

We specified only one annotation. `nginx.ingress.kubernetes.io/ssl-redirect:` `"false"` tells the Controller that we do NOT want to redirect all HTTP requests to HTTPS. We're forced to do so since we do not have SSL certificates for the exercises that follow.

Now that we shed some light on the `metadata annotations`, we can move to the `ingress` specification.

We specified a set of `rules` in the `spec` section. They are used to configure Ingress resource. For now, our rule is based on `http` with a single `path` and a `backend`. All the requests with the `path` starting with `/demo` will be forwarded to the service `go-demo-2-api` on the port `8080`.

Now that we had a short tour around some of the Ingress configuration options, we can proceed and create the resource.

```
kubectl create \
    -f ingress/go-demo-2-ingress.yml
kubectl get \
    -f ingress/go-demo-2-ingress.yml
```

The output of the latter command is as follows:

```
NAME        HOSTS ADDRESS        PORTS AGE
go-demo-2 *       192.168.99.100 80    29s
```

We can see that the Ingress resource was created. Don't panic if, in your case, the address is blank. It might take a while for it to obtain it.

Let's see whether requests sent to the base path `/demo` work.

```
IP=$(kubectl get ingress go-demo-2 \
    -o jsonpath="{.status.loadBalancer.ingress[0].ip}")

curl -i "http://$IP/demo/hello"
```

The output is as follows:

```
HTTP/1.1 200 OK
Server: nginx/1.13.5
Date: Sun, 24 Dec 2017 14:19:04 GMT
Content-Type: text/plain; charset=utf-8
Content-Length: 14
Connection: keep-alive
Strict-Transport-Security: max-age=15724800; includeSubDomains;
hello, world!
```

The status code `200 OK` is a clear indication that this time, the application is accessible through the port 80. If that's not enough of assurance, you can observe the `hello, world!` response as well.

The `go-demo-2` service we're currently using is no longer properly configured for our Ingress setup. Using `type: NodePort`, it is configured to export the port `8080` on all of the nodes. Since we're expecting users to access the application through the Ingress Controller on port `80`, there's probably no need to allow external access through the port `8080` as well. We should switch to the `ClusterIP` type. That will allow direct access to the Service only within the cluster, thus limiting all external communication through Ingress.

We cannot just update the Service with a new definition. Once a Service port is exposed, it cannot be un-exposed. We'll delete the `go-demo-2` objects we created and start over. Besides the need to change the Service type, that will give us an opportunity to unify everything in a single YAML file:

```
kubectl delete \
    -f ingress/go-demo-2-ingress.yml
kubectl delete \
    -f ingress/go-demo-2-deploy.yml
```

We removed the objects related to `go-demo-2`, and now we can take a look at the unified definition.

```
cat ingress/go-demo-2.yml
```

We won't go into details of the new definition since it does not have any significant changes. It combines `ingress/go-demo-2-ingress.yml` and `ingress/go-demo-2-deploy.yml` into a single file, and it removes `type: NodePort` from the `go-demo-2` Service.

```
kubectl create \
    -f ingress/go-demo-2.yml \
    --record --save-config
curl -i "http://$IP/demo/hello"
```

We created the objects from the unified definition and sent a request to validate that everything works as expected. The response should be `200 OK` indicating that everything (still) works as expected.

Please note that Kubernetes needs a few seconds until all the objects are running as expected. If you were too fast, you might have received the response `404 Not Found` instead `200 OK`. If that was the case, all you have to do is send the `curl` request again.

Let's see, through a sequence diagram, what happened when we created the Ingress resource.

1. The Kubernetes client (`kubectl`) sent a request to the API server requesting the creation of the Ingress resource defined in the `ingress/go-demo-2.yml` file.
2. The ingress controller is watching the API server for new events. It detected that there is a new Ingress resource.
3. The ingress controller configured the load balancer. In this case, it is nginx which was enabled by `minikube addons enable ingress` command. It modified `nginx.conf` with the values of all `go-demo-2-api` endpoints.

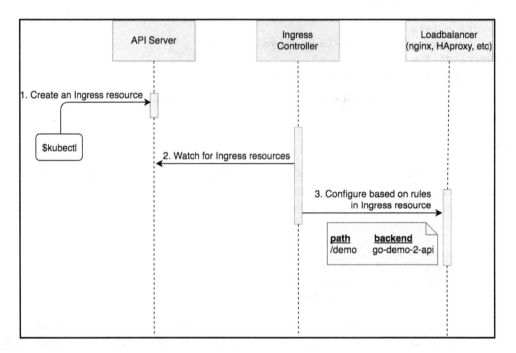

Figure 7-2: The sequence of events followed by the request to create an Ingress resource

Now that one of the applications is accessible through Ingress, we should apply the same principles to the other.

Let's take a look at the full definition of all the objects behind the `devops-toolkit` application.

```
cat ingress/devops-toolkit.yml
```

The output, limited to the Ingress object, is as follows:

```
apiVersion: extensions/v1beta1
kind: Ingress
metadata:
  name: devops-toolkit
  annotations:
    ingress.kubernetes.io/ssl-redirect: "false"
    nginx.ingress.kubernetes.io/ssl-redirect: "false"
spec:
  rules:
  - http:
      paths:
      - path: /
        backend:
          serviceName: devops-toolkit
          servicePort: 80
...
```

The `devops-toolkit` Ingress resource is very similar to `go-demo-2`. The only significant difference is that the `path` is set to `/`. It will serve all requests. It would be a much better solution if we'd change it to a unique base path (for example, `/devops-toolkit`) since that would provide a unique identifier. However, this application does not have an option to define a base path, so an attempt to do so in Ingress would result in a failure to retrieve resources. We'd need to write `rewrite` rules instead. We could, for example, create a rule that rewrites path base `/devops-toolkit` to `/`. That way if, for example, someone sends a request to `/devops-toolkit/something`, Ingress would rewrite it to `/something` before sending it to the destination Service. While such an action is often useful, we'll ignore it for now. I have better plans for this application. Until I decide to reveal them, `/` as the base `path` should do.

Apart from adding Ingress to the mix, the definition removed `type: NodePort` from the Service. This is the same type of action we did previously with the `go-demo-2` service. We do not need external access to the Service.

Let's remove the old objects and create those defined in the `ingress/devops-toolkit.yml` file:

```
kubectl delete \
    -f ingress/devops-toolkit-dep.yml
kubectl create \
    -f ingress/devops-toolkit.yml \
    --record --save-config
```

We removed the old `devops-toolkit` and created new ones.

Let's take a look at the Ingresses running inside the cluster:

```
kubectl get ing
```

The output is as follows:

NAME	HOSTS	ADDRESS	PORTS	AGE
devops-toolkit	*	192.168.99.100	80	20s
go-demo-2	*	192.168.99.100	80	58s

We can see that now we have multiple Ingress resources. The Ingress controller (in this case NGINX) configured itself taking both of those resources into account.

> We can define multiple Ingress resources that will configure a single Ingress controller.

Let's confirm that both applications are accessible through HTTP (port 80).

```
open http://$IP
curl "http://$IP/demo/hello"
```

The first command opened one of the applications in a browser, while the other returned the already familiar `hello, world!` message.

> Ingress is a (kind of) Service that runs on all nodes of a cluster. A user can send requests to any and, as long as they match one of the rules, they will be forwarded to the appropriate Service.

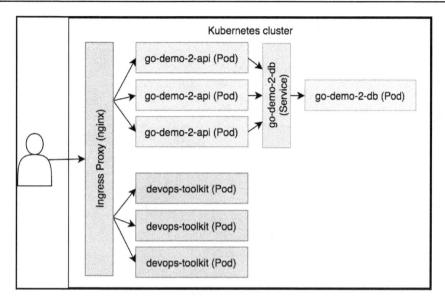

Figure 7-3: Applications accessed through Ingress controller

Even though we can send requests to both applications using the same port (80), that is often a sub-optimal solution. Our users would probably be happier if they could access those applications through different domains.

Creating Ingress resources based on domains

We'll try to refactor our `devops-toolkit` Ingress definition so that the Controller forwards requests coming from the `devopstoolkitseries.com` domain. The change should be minimal, so we'll get down to it right away.

```
cat ingress/devops-toolkit-dom.yml
```

When compared with the previous definition, the only difference is in the additional entry `host: devopstoolkitseries.com`. Since that will be the only application accessible through that domain, we also removed the `path: /` entry.

Let's `apply` the new definition:

```
kubectl apply \
    -f ingress/devops-toolkit-dom.yml \
    --record
```

What would happen if we send a similar domain-less request to the Application? I'm sure you already know the answer, but we'll check it out anyways:

```
curl -I "http://$IP"
```

The output is as follows:

```
HTTP/1.1 404 Not Found
Server: nginx/1.13.5
Date: Sun, 24 Dec 2017 14:50:29 GMT
Content-Type: text/plain; charset=utf-8
Content-Length: 21
Connection: keep-alive
Strict-Transport-Security: max-age=15724800; includeSubDomains;
```

There is no Ingress resource defined to listen to `/`. The updated Ingress will forward requests only if they come from `devopstoolkitseries.com`.

I own the `devopstoolkitseries.com` domain, and I'm not willing to give you the access to my DNS registry to configure it with the IP of your Minikube cluster. Therefore, we won't be able to test it by sending a request to `devopstoolkitseries.com`. What we can do is to "fake" it by adding that domain to the request header:

```
curl -I \
    -H "Host: devopstoolkitseries.com" \
    "http://$IP"
```

The output is as follows:

```
HTTP/1.1 200 OK
Server: nginx/1.13.5
Date: Sun, 24 Dec 2017 14:51:09 GMT
Content-Type: text/html
Content-Length: 12872
Connection: keep-alive
Last-Modified: Thu, 14 Dec 2017 13:59:34 GMT
ETag: "5a3283c6-3248"
Accept-Ranges: bytes
```

Now that Ingress received a request that looks like it's coming from the domain `devopstoolkitseries.com`, it forwarded it to the `devops-toolkit` Service which, in turn, load balanced it to one of the `devops-toolkit` Pods. As a result, we got the response `200 OK`.

Just to be on the safe side, we'll verify whether `go-demo-2` Ingress still works.

```
curl -H "Host: acme.com" \
    "http://$IP/demo/hello"
```

We got the famous `hello, world!` response, thus confirming that both Ingress resources are operational. Even though we "faked" the last request as if it's coming from `acme.com`, it still worked. Since the `go-demo-2` Ingress does not have any `host` defined, it accepts any request with the `path` starting with `/demo`.

We're still missing a few things. One of those is a setup of a default backend.

Creating an Ingress resource with default backends

In some cases, we might want to define a default backend. We might want to forward requests that do not match any of the Ingress rules.

Let's take a look at an example:

```
curl -I -H "Host: acme.com" \
    "http://$IP"
```

So far, we have two sets of Ingress rules in our cluster. One accepts all requests with the base path `/demo`. The other forwards all requests coming from the `devopstoolkitseries.com` domain. The request we just sent does not match either of those rules, so the response was once again **404 Not Found**.

Let's imagine that it would be a good idea to forward all requests with the wrong domain to the `devops-toolkit` application. Of course, by "wrong domain", I mean one of the domains we own, and not one of those that are already included in Ingress rules:

```
cat ingress/default-backend.yml
```

The output is as follows:

```
apiVersion: extensions/v1beta1
kind: Ingress
metadata:
  name: default
  annotations:
    ingress.kubernetes.io/ssl-redirect: "false"
    nginx.ingress.kubernetes.io/ssl-redirect: "false"
spec:
  backend:
    serviceName: devops-toolkit
    servicePort: 80
```

There's no Deployment, nor is there a Service. This time, we're creating only an Ingress resource.

The `spec` has no rules, but only a single `backend`.

> When an Ingress `spec` is without rules, it is considered a default backend. As such, it will forward all requests that do not match paths and/or domains set as rules in the other Ingress resources.

We can use the default backend as a substitute for the default `404` pages or for any other occasion that is not covered by other rules.

You'll notice that the `serviceName` is `devops-toolkit`. The example would be much better if I created a separate application for this purpose. At the risk of you calling me lazy, I'll say that it does not matter for this example. All we want, at the moment, is to see something other than `404 Not Found` response.

```
kubectl create \
    -f ingress/default-backend.yml
```

We created the Ingress resource with the default backend, and now we can test whether it truly works:

```
curl -I -H "Host: acme.com" \
    "http://$IP"
```

This time, the output is different. We got `200 OK` instead of the `404 Not Found` response.

```
HTTP/1.1 200 OK
...
```

What now?

We explored some of the essential functions of Ingress resources and Controllers. To be more concrete, we examined almost all those that are defined in the Ingress API.

One notable feature we did not explore is TLS configuration. Without it, our services cannot serve HTTPS requests. To enable it, we'd need to configure Ingress to offload SSL certificates.

There are two reasons we did not explore TLS. For one, we do not have a valid SSL certificate. On top of that, we did not yet study Kubernetes Secrets. I'd suggest you explore SSL setup yourself once you make a decision which Ingress controller to use. Secrets, on the other hand, will be explained soon.

We'll explore other Ingress controllers once we move our cluster to "real" servers that we'll create with one of the hosting vendors. Until then, you might benefit from reading NGINX Ingress controller (`https://github.com/kubernetes/ingress-nginx/blob/master/README.md`) documentation in more detail. Specifically, I suggest you pay close attention to its annotations (`https://github.com/kubernetes/ingress-nginx/blob/master/docs/user-guide/nginx-configuration/annotations.md`).

Now that another chapter is finished, we'll destroy the cluster and let your laptop rest for a while. It deserves a break.

```
minikube delete
```

 If you'd like to know more about Ingress, please explore Ingress v1beta1 extensions (`https://v1-9.docs.kubernetes.io/docs/reference/generated/kubernetes-api/v1.9/#ingress-v1beta1-extensions`) API documentation.

Before we move into the next chapter, we'll explore the differences between Kubernetes Ingress and its Docker Swarm equivalent.

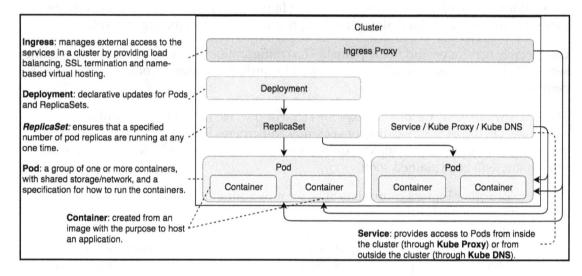

Figure 7-4: The components explored so far

Kubernetes Ingress compared to Docker Swarm equivalent

Both Kubernetes and Docker Swarm have Ingress, and it might sound compelling to compare them and explore the differences. While that, at first glance, might seem like the right thing to do, there is a problem. Ingress works quite differently across the two.

Swarm Ingress networking is much more similar to Kubernetes services. Both can, and should, be used to expose ports to clients both inside and outside a cluster. If we compare the two products, we'll discover that Kubernetes services are similar to a combination of Docker Swarm's Overlay and Ingress networking. The Overlay is used to provide communication between applications inside a cluster, and Swarm's Ingress is a flavor of Overlay network that publishes ports to the outside world. The truth is that Swarm does not have an equivalent to Kubernetes Ingress controllers. That is, *if we do not include Docker Enterprise Edition to the mix.*

The fact that a Kubernetes Ingress equivalent does not ship with Docker Swarm does not mean that similar functionality cannot be accomplished through other means. It can. `Traefik`, for example, can act both as a Kubernetes Ingress Controller, as well as a dynamic Docker Swarm proxy. It provides, more or less, the same functionality no matter which scheduler you choose. If you're looking for a Swarm specific alternative, you might choose Docker Flow Proxy (`http://proxy.dockerflow.com/`) (written by yours truly).

All in all, as soon as we stop comparing Ingress on both platforms and start looking for a similar set of functionality, we can quickly conclude that both Kubernetes and Docker Swarm allow a similar set of features. We can use paths and domains to route traffic from a single set of ports (for example, `80` and `443`) to a specific application that matches the rules. Both allow us to offload SSL certificates, and both provide solutions that make all the necessary configurations dynamically.

If on the functional level both platforms provide a very similar set of features, can we conclude that there is no essential difference between the two schedulers when taking into account only dynamic routing and load balancing? *I would say no*. Some important differences might not be of functional nature.

Kubernetes provides a well-defined Ingress API that third-party solutions can utilize to deliver a seamless experience. Let's take a look at one example:

```
apiVersion: extensions/v1beta1
kind: Ingress
metadata:
  name: devops-toolkit
spec:
  rules:
  - host: devopstoolkitseries.com
    http:
      paths:
      - backend:
          serviceName: devops-toolkit
          servicePort: 80
```

This definition can be used with many different solutions. Behind this Ingress resource could be nginx, voyager, haproxy, or trafficserver Ingress controller. All of them use the same Ingress API to deduce which Services should be used by forwarding algorithms. Even Traefik, known for its incompatibility with commonly used Ingress annotations, would accept that YAML definition.

Having a well-defined API still leaves a lot of room for innovation. We can use `annotations` to provide the additional information our Ingress controller of choice might need. Some of the same annotations are used across different solutions, while the others are specific to a controller.

All in all, Kubernetes Ingress controller combines a well-defined (and simple) specification that all Ingress controllers must accept and, at the same time, it leaves ample room for innovation through custom `annotations` specified in `metadata`.

Docker Swarm does not have anything resembling an Ingress API. Functionality similar to Kubernetes Ingress controllers can be accomplished either by using Swarm Kit or using the Docker API. The problem is that there is no defined API that third-party solutions should follow, so each is a world in itself. For example, understanding how Traefik works will not help you much when trying to switch to Docker Flow Proxy. Each is operated differently in isolation. There is no standard because Docker did not focus on making one.

Docker's approach to scheduling is based entirely on the features baked into Docker Server. There is only one way to do things. Often, that provides a very user-friendly and reliable experience. If Swarm does what you need it to do, it is an excellent choice. However, the problem occurs when you need more. In that case, you might experience difficulties finding a solution with Docker Swarm.

When we compared Kubernetes ReplicaSets, Services, and Deployments with their Docker Swarm equivalents, the result was the same set of features. There was no substantial difference on the functional level. From the user experience perspective, Swarm provided much better results. Its YAML file was much more straightforward and more concise. With only those features in mind, Swarm had the edge over Kubernetes. This time it's different.

Kubernetes strategy is primarily based on API. Once a specific type of a resource is defined, any solution can utilize it to provide the given functionality. That is especially true with Ingress. We can choose among a myriad of solutions. Some of them are developed and maintained by the Kubernetes community (for example, GLBC and NGINX Ingress controllers), while others are provided by third-parties. No matter where the solution comes from, it adheres to the same API and, therefore, to the same YAML definition. As a result, we have a more substantial number of solutions to choose from, without sacrificing consistency in how we define resources.

If we limit the comparison to Kubernetes Ingress controllers and their equivalents in Docker Swarm, the former is a clear winner. Assuming that the current strategy continues, Docker would need to add layer 7 forwarding into Docker Server if it is to get back in the game on this front. If we limit ourselves only to this set of features, Kubernetes wins through its Ingress API that opened the door, not only to internal solutions, but also to third-party Controllers.

We are still at the beginning. There are many more features worth comparing. We only scratched the surface. Stay tuned for more.

8

Using Volumes to Access Host's File System

Having a system without a state is impossible. Even though there is a tendency to develop stateless applications, we still need to deal with the state. There are databases and other stateful third-party applications. No matter what we do, we need to make sure that the state is preserved no matter what happens to containers, Pods, or even whole nodes.

Most of the time, stateful applications store their state on disk. That leaves us with a problem. If a container crashes, `kubelet` will restart it. The problem is that it will create a new container based on the same image. All data accumulated inside a container that crashed will be lost.

Kubernetes volumes solve the need to preserve the state across container crashes. In essence, volumes are references to files and directories made accessible to containers that form a Pod. The significant difference between different types of Kubernetes volumes is in the way these files and directories are created.

While the primary use-case for volumes is the preservation of state, there are quite a few others. For example, we might use volumes to access Docker's socket running on a host. Or we might use them to access configuration residing in a file on the host file system.

We can describe Volumes as a way to access a file system that might be running on the same host or somewhere else. No matter where that file system is, it is external to the containers that mount volumes. There can be many reasons why someone might mount a Volume, with state preservation being only one of them.

There are over twenty-five volume types supported by Kubernetes. It would take us too much time to go through all of them. Besides, even if we'd like to do that, many volume types are specific to a hosting vendor. For example, `awsElasticBlockStore` works only with AWS, `azureDisk` and `azureFile` work only with Azure, and so on and so forth. We'll limit our exploration to volume types that can be used within Minikube. You should be able to extrapolate that knowledge to volume types applicable to your hosting vendor of choice.

Let's get down to it.

Creating a cluster

This time, we'll have an additional action we'll execute in preparation to create a Minikube cluster.

 All the commands from this chapter are available in the `08-volume.sh` (`https://gist.github.com/vfarcic/5acafb64c0124a1965f6d371dd0dedd 1`) Gist.

```
cd k8s-specs

git pull

cp volume/prometheus-conf.yml \
    ~/.minikube/files
```

We'll need the file inside the soon-to-be-created Minikube VM. When it starts, it will copy all the files from `~/.minikube/files` on your host, into the `/files` directory in the VM.

 Depending on your operating system, the `~/.minikube/files` directory might be somewhere else. If that's the case, please adapt the preceding command.

Now that the files are copied to the shared directory, we can repeat the same process we did quite a few times before. Please note that we've added the step from the last chapter that enables the ingress addon.

```
minikube start --vm-driver=virtualbox
minikube addons enable ingress
kubectl config current-context
```

Now that the Minikube cluster is up-and-running, we can explore the first volume type.

Accessing host's resources through hostPath volumes

Sooner or later, we'll have to build our images. A simple solution would be to execute the `docker image build` command directly from a server. However, that might cause problems. Building images on a single host means that there is an uneven resource utilization and that there is a single point of failure. Wouldn't it be better if we could build images anywhere inside a Kubernetes cluster?

Instead of executing the `docker image build` command, we could create a Pod based on the `docker` image. Kubernetes will make sure that the Pod is scheduled somewhere inside the cluster, thus distributing resource usage much better.

Let's start with an elementary example. If we can list the images, we'll prove that running docker commands inside containers works. Since, from Kubernetes' point of view, Pods are the smallest entity, that's what we'll run.

```
kubectl run docker \
    --image=docker:17.11 \
    --restart=Never \
    docker image ls
kubectl get pods --show-all
```

We created a Pod named `docker` and based it on the official `docker` image. Since we want to execute a one-shot command, we specified that it should `Never` restart. Finally, the container command is `docker image ls`. The second command lists all the Pods in the cluster (including failed ones).

The output of the latter command is as follows:

```
NAME    READY STATUS RESTARTS AGE
docker 0/1    Error  0         1m
```

The output should show that the status is `Error`, thus indicating that there is a problem with the container we're running. If, in your case, the status is not yet `Error`, Kubernetes is probably still pulling the image. In that case, please wait a few moments, and re-execute the `kubectl get pods` command.

Let's take a look at the logs of the container:

```
kubectl logs docker
```

The output is as follows:

```
Cannot connect to the Docker daemon at unix:///var/run/docker.sock. Is the
docker daemon running?
```

Docker consists of two main pieces. There is a client, and there is a server. When we executed `docker image ls`, we invoked the client who tried to communicate with the server through its API. The problem is that Docker server is not running in that container. What we should do is tell the client (inside a container) to use Docker server that is already running on the host (Minikube VM).

By default, the client sends instructions to the server through the socket located in `/var/run/docker.sock`. We can accomplish our goal if we mount that file from the host into a container.

Before we try to enable communication between a Docker client in a container and Docker server on a host, we'll delete the Pod we created a few moments ago:

```
kubectl delete pod docker
```

Let's take a look at the Pod definition stored in `volume/docker.yml`:

```
cat volume/docker.yml
```

The output is as follows:

```
apiVersion: v1
kind: Pod
metadata:
  name: docker
spec:
  containers:
  - name: docker
    image: docker:17.11
    command: ["sleep"]
    args: ["100000"]
    volumeMounts:
    - mountPath: /var/run/docker.sock
      name: docker-socket
```

```
volumes:
- name: docker-socket
  hostPath:
    path: /var/run/docker.sock
    type: Socket
```

Part of the definition closely mimics the `kubectl run` command we executed earlier. The only significant difference is in the `volumeMounts` and `volumes` sections.

The `volumeMounts` field is relatively straightforward and is the same no matter which type of volume we're using. In this section, we're specifying the `mountPath` and the name of the volume. The former is the path we expect to mount inside this container. You'll notice that we are not specifying the type of the volume nor any other specifics inside the `VolumeMounts` section. Instead, we simply have a reference to a volume called `docker-socket`.

The volume configuration specific to each type is defined in the `volumes` section. In this case, we're using the `hostPath` volume type.

`hostPath` allows us to mount a file or a directory from a host to Pods and, through them, to containers. Before we discuss the usefulness of this type, we'll have a short discussion about use-cases when this is not a good choice.

 Do not use `hostPath` to store a state of an application. Since it mounts a file or a directory from a host into a Pod, it is not fault-tolerant. If the server fails, Kubernetes will schedule the Pod to a healthy node, and the state will be lost.

For our use case, `hostPath` works just fine. We're not using it to preserve state, but to gain access to Docker server running on the same host as the Pod.

The `hostPath` type has only two fields. The `path` represents the file or a directory we want to mount from the host. Since we want to mount a socket, we set the `type` accordingly. There are other types we could use.

The `Directory` type will mount a directory from the host. It must exist on the given path. If it doesn't, we might switch to `DirectoryOrCreate` type which serves the same purpose. The difference is that `DirectoryOrCreate` will create the directory if it does not exist on the host.

The `File` and `FileOrCreate` are similar to their `Directory` equivalents. The only difference is that this time we'd mount a file, instead of a directory.

The other supported types are `Socket`, `CharDevice`, and `BlockDevice`. They should be self-explanatory. If you don't know what character or block devices are, you probably don't need those types.

Last, but not least, we changed the command and the arguments to `sleep 100000`. That will give us more freedom since we'll be able to create the Pod, enter inside its only container, and experiment with different commands.

Let's create the Pod and check whether, this time, we can execute Docker commands from inside the container it'll create:

```
kubectl create \
    -f volume/docker.yml
```

Since the image is already pulled, starting the Pod should be almost instant.

Let's see whether we can retrieve the list of Docker images:

```
kubectl exec -it docker \
    -- docker image ls \
    --format "{{.Repository}}"
```

We executed `docker image ls` command and shortened the output by limiting its formatting only to `Repository`. The output is as follows:

```
Docker
gcr.io/google_containers/nginx-ingress-controller
gcr.io/google_containers/k8s-dns-sidecar-amd64
gcr.io/google_containers/k8s-dns-kube-dns-amd64
gcr.io/google_containers/k8s-dns-dnsmasq-nanny-amd64
gcr.io/google_containers/kubernetes-dashboard-amd64
gcr.io/google_containers/kubernetes-dashboard-amd64
gcr.io/google-containers/kube-addon-manager
gcr.io/google_containers/defaultbackend
gcr.io/google_containers/pause-amd64
```

Even though we executed the `docker` command inside a container, the output clearly shows the images from the host. We proved that mounting the Docker socket (`/var/run/docker.sock`) as a volume allows communication between Docker client inside the container, and Docker server running on the host.

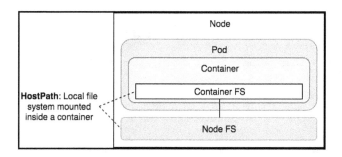

Figure 8-1: HostPath mounted inside a container

Let's enter the container and see whether we can build a Docker image.

```
kubectl exec -it docker sh
```

To build an image, we need a `Dockerfile` as well as an application's source code. We'll continue using `go-demo-2` as the example, so our first action will be to clone the repository:

```
apk add -U git
git clone \
    https://github.com/vfarcic/go-demo-2.git
cd go-demo-2
```

We used `apk add` to install `git`. `docker` and many other images use `alpine` as the base. If you're not familiar with `alpine`, it is a very slim and efficient base image, and I strongly recommend that you use it when building your own. Images like `debian`, `centos`, `ubuntu`, `redhat`, and similar base images are often a terrible choice made because of a misunderstanding of how containers work.

`alpine` uses `apk` package management, so we invoked it to install `git`. Next, we cloned the `vfarcic/go-demo-2` repository, and, finally, we entered into the `go-demo-2` directory:

Let's take a quick look at the `Dockerfile`:

```
cat Dockerfile
```

The output is as follows:

```
FROM golang:1.9 AS build
ADD . /src
WORKDIR /src
RUN go get -d -v -t
RUN go test --cover -v ./... --run UnitTest
RUN go build -v -o go-demo
```

```
FROM alpine:3.4
MAINTAINER      Viktor Farcic viktor@farcic.com

RUN mkdir /lib64 &amp;&amp; ln -s /lib/libc.musl-x86_64.so.1 /lib64/ld-
linux-x86-64.so.2

EXPOSE 8080
ENV DB db
CMD ["go-demo"]
HEALTHCHECK --interval=10s CMD wget -qO- localhost:8080/demo/hello

COPY --from=build /src/go-demo /usr/local/bin/go-demo
RUN chmod +x /usr/local/bin/go-demo
```

Since this book is dedicated to Kubernetes, we won't go into details behind this Dockerfile, but only comment that it uses Docker's multi-stage builds. The first stage downloads the dependencies, it runs unit tests, and it builds the binary. The second stage starts over. It builds a fresh image with the go-demo binary copied from the previous stage.

I sincerely hope you're proficient with Docker and there's no need to explain image building further. If that's not the case, you might want to explore the official documentation or one of my previous books. This one is focused only on Kubernetes.

Let's test whether building an image indeed works.

```
docker image build \
    -t vfarcic/go-demo-2:beta .

docker image ls \
    --format "{{.Repository}}"
```

We executed the docker image build command, followed by docker image ls. The output of the latter command is as follows:

```
vfarcic/go-demo-2
<none>
golang
docker
alpine
gcr.io/google_containers/nginx-ingress-controller
gcr.io/google_containers/k8s-dns-sidecar-amd64
gcr.io/google_containers/k8s-dns-kube-dns-amd64
gcr.io/google_containers/k8s-dns-dnsmasq-nanny-amd64
gcr.io/google_containers/kubernetes-dashboard-amd64
gcr.io/google_containers/kubernetes-dashboard-amd64
gcr.io/google-containers/kube-addon-manager
```

```
gcr.io/google_containers/defaultbackend
gcr.io/google_containers/pause-amd64
```

If we compare this with the previous `docker image ls` output, we'll notice that, this time, a few new images are listed. The `golang` and `alpine` images are used as a basis for each of the build stages. The `vfarcic/go-demo-2` is the result of our build. Finally, `<none>` is only a left-over of the process and it can be safely removed.

```
docker system prune -f

docker image ls \
    --format "{{.Repository}}"
```

The `docker system prune` command removes all unused resources. At least, all those created and unused by Docker. We confirmed that by executing `docker image ls` again. This time, we can see the `<none>` image is gone.

We'll destroy the `docker` Pod and explore other usages of the `hostPath` volume type:

```
Exit
kubectl delete \
    -f volume/docker.yml
```

 `hostPath` is a great solution for accessing host resources like `/var/run/docker.sock`, `/dev/cgroups`, and others. That is, as long as the resource we're trying to reach is on the same node as the Pod.

Let's see whether we can find other use-cases for `hostPath`.

Using hostPath volume type to inject configuration files

We are about to deploy Prometheus (`https://prometheus.io/`) for the first time (in this book). We won't go into details behind the application except to say that it's fantastic and that you should consider it for your monitoring and alerting needs. At the risk of disappointing you, I will have to say that Prometheus is not in the scope of this chapter, and probably not even the book. We're using it only to demonstrate a few Kubernetes concepts. We're not trying to learn how to operate it.

Let's take a look the application's definition:

```
cat volume/prometheus.yml
```

The output is as follows:

```
apiVersion: extensions/v1beta1
kind: Ingress
metadata:
  name: Prometheus
  annotations:
    ingress.kubernetes.io/ssl-redirect: "false"
    nginx.ingress.kubernetes.io/ssl-redirect: "false"
spec:
  rules:
  - http:
      paths:
      - path: /Prometheus
        backend:
          serviceName: Prometheus
          servicePort: 9090


---


apiVersion: apps/v1beta2
kind: Deployment
metadata:
  name: Prometheus
spec:
  selector:
    matchLabels:
      type: monitor
      service: Prometheus
  strategy:
    type: Recreate
  template:
    metadata:
      labels:
        type: monitor
        service: Prometheus
    spec:
      containers:
      - name: Prometheus
        image: prom/prometheus:v2.0.0
        command:
        - /bin/Prometheus
        args:
        - "--config.file=/etc/prometheus/prometheus.yml"
```

```
        - "--storage.tsdb.path=/prometheus"
        - "--web.console.libraries=/usr/share"
        - "--web.external-url=http://192.168.99.100/prometheus"


    ---

apiVersion: v1
kind: Service
metadata:
  name: Prometheus
spec:
  ports:
  - port: 9090
  selector:
    type: monitor
    service: Prometheus
```

There's nothing genuinely new in that YAML file. It defines an Ingress, a deployment, and a service. There is, however, one thing we might need to change. Prometheus needs a full external-url if we want to change the base path. At the moment, it's set to the IP of my Minikube VM. In your case, that IP might be different. We'll fix that by adding a bit of sed "magic" that will make sure the IP matches that of your Minikube VM.

```
cat volume/prometheus.yml | sed -e \
    "s/192.168.99.100/$(minikube ip)/g" \
    | kubectl create -f - \
    --record --save-config

kubectl rollout status deploy prometheus
```

We output the contents of the volume/prometheus.yml file, we used sed to replace the hard-coded IP with the actual value of your Minikube instance, and we passed the result to kubectl create. Please note that, this time, the create command has dash (–) instead of the path to the file. That's an indication that stdin should be used instead.

Once we created the application, we used the kubectl rollout status command to confirm that the deployment finished.

Now we can open Prometheus in a browser.

```
open "http://$(minikube ip)/prometheus"
```

At first glance, the application seems to be running correctly. However, since the targets are the crucial part of the application, we should check them as well. For those not familiar with Prometheus, it pulls data from targets (external data sources) and, by default, comes with only one target pre-configured: Prometheus itself. Prometheus will always pull data from this target unless we configure it otherwise.

Let's take a look at its targets.

```
open "http://$(minikube ip)/prometheus/targets"
```

There's something wrong. The default target is not reachable. Before we start panicking, we should take a closer look at its configuration.

```
open "http://$(minikube ip)/prometheus/config"
```

The problem is with the `metrics_path` field. By default, it is set to `/metrics`. However, since we changed the base path to `/prometheus`, the field should have `/prometheus/metrics` as the value.

Long story short, we must change Prometheus configuration.

We could, for example, enter the container, update the configuration file, and send the reload request to Prometheus. That would be a terrible solution since it would last only until the next time we update the application, or until the container fails, and Kubernetes decides to reschedule it.

Let's explore alternative solutions. We could, for example, use `hostPath` volume for this as well. If we can guarantee that the correct configuration file is inside the VM, the Pod could attach it to the `prometheus` container. Let's try it out.

```
cat volume/prometheus-host-path.yml
```

The output, limited to relevant parts, is as follows:

```
apiVersion: apps/v1beta2
kind: Deployment
metadata:
  name: Prometheus
spec:
  selector:
    ...
    spec:
      containers:
        ...
        volumeMounts:
        - mountPath: /etc/prometheus/prometheus.yml
```

```
        name: prom-conf
    volumes:
    - name: prom-conf
      hostPath:
        path: /files/prometheus-conf.yml
        type: File
...
```

The only significant difference, when compared with the previous definition, is in the added `volumeMounts` and `volumes` fields. We're using the same schema as before, except that, this time, the `type` is set to `File`. Once we apply this Deployment, the file `/files/prometheus-conf.yml` on the host will be available as `/etc/prometheus/prometheus.yml` inside the container.

If you recall, we copied one file to the `~/.minikube/files` directory, and Minikube copied it to the `/files` directory inside the VM.

 In some cases, files might end up being copied to the VM's root (`/`), instead of to `/files`. If this has happened to you, please enter the VM (`minikube ssh`), and move the files to `/files`, by executing the commands that follow (only if the `/files` directory does not exist or is empty).

```
minikube ssh
sudo mkdir /files
sudo mv /prometheus-conf.yml  /files/
exit
```

The time has come to take a look at the content of the file.

```
minikube ssh sudo chmod +rw \
    /files/prometheus-conf.yml
```

```
minikube ssh cat \
    /files/prometheus-conf.yml
```

We changed the permissions of the file and displayed its content.

The output is as follows:

```
global:
  scrape_interval:      15s

scrape_configs:
  - job_name: Prometheus
    metrics_path: /prometheus/metrics
```

```
static_configs:
  - targets:
    - localhost:9090
```

This configuration is almost identical to what Prometheus uses by default. The only difference is in the `metrics_path`, which is now pointing to `/prometheus/metrics`.

Let's see whether Prometheus with the new configuration works as expected:

```
cat volume/prometheus-host-path.yml \
    | sed -e \
    "s/192.168.99.100/$(minikube ip)/g" \
    | kubectl apply -f -
kubectl rollout status deploy Prometheus
open http://$(minikube ip)/prometheus/targets
```

We applied the new definition (after the `sed` "magic"), we waited until the `rollout` finished, and we then opened the Prometheus targets in a browser. This time, with the updated configuration, Prometheus is successfully pulling data from the only target currently configured:

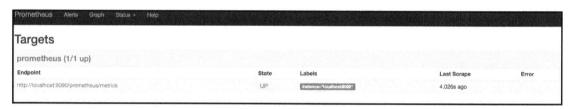

Figure 8-2: Prometheus targets screen

The next logical step would be to configure Prometheus with additional targets. Specifically, you may want to configure it to fetch metrics that are already made available through the Kubernetes API. We, however, will *NOT* be doing this. First of all, this chapter is not about monitoring and alerting. The second, and the more important reason, is that using the `hostPath` volume type to provide configuration is *NOT* a good idea.

 A `hostPath` volume maps a directory from a host to where the Pod is running. Using it to "inject" configuration files into containers would mean that we'd have to make sure that the file is present on every node of the cluster.

Working with Minikube can be potentially misleading. The fact that we're running a single-node cluster means that every Pod we run will be scheduled on one node. Copying a configuration file to that single node, as we did in our example, ensures that it can be mounted in any Pod. However, the moment we add more nodes to the cluster, we'd experience side effects. We'd need to make sure that each node in our cluster has the same file we wish to mount, as we would not be able to predict where individual Pods would be scheduled. This would introduce far too much unnecessary work and added complexity.

An alternative solution would be to mount an NFS drive to all the nodes and store the file there. That would provide the guarantee that the file will be available on all the nodes, as long as we do *NOT* forget to mount NFS on each.

Another solution could be to create a custom Prometheus image. It could be based on the official image, with a single `COPY` instruction that would add the configuration. The advantage of that solution is that the image would be entirely immutable. Its state would not be polluted with unnecessary volume mounts. Anyone could run that image and expect the same result. That is my preferred solution. However, in some cases, you might want to deploy the same application with a slightly different configuration. Should we, in those cases, fall back to mounting an NFS drive on each node and continue using `hostPath`?

Even though mounting an NFS drive would solve some of the problems, it is still not a great solution. In order to mount a file from NFS, we need to use the `nfs` (`https://kubernetes.io/docs/concepts/storage/volumes/#nfs`) volume type instead of `hostPath`. Even then it would be a sub-optimal solution. A much better approach would be to use `configMap`. We'll explore it in the next chapter.

> Do use `hostPath` to mount host resources like `/var/run/docker.sock` and `/dev/cgroups`. Do not use it to inject configuration files or store the state of an application.

We'll move onto a more exotic volume type. But, before that, we'll remove the Pod we're currently running:

```
kubectl delete \
    -f volume/prometheus-host-path.yml
```

Using gitRepo to mount a Git repository

The `gitRepo` volume type is probably not going to be on your list of top three volume types. Or, maybe it will. It all depends on your use cases. I like it since it demonstrates how a concept of a volume can be extended to a new and innovative solution.

Let's see it in action through the `volume/github.yml` definition:

```
cat volume/github.yml
```

The output is as follows:

```
apiVersion: v1
kind: Pod
metadata:
  name: github
spec:
  containers:
  - name: github
    image: docker:17.11
    command: ["sleep"]
    args: ["100000"]
    volumeMounts:
    - mountPath: /var/run/docker.sock
      name: docker-socket
    - mountPath: /src
      name: github
  volumes:
  - name: docker-socket
    hostPath:
      path: /var/run/docker.sock
      type: Socket
  - name: github
    gitRepo:
      repository: https://github.com/vfarcic/go-demo-2.git
      directory: .
```

This Pod definition is very similar to `volume/docker.yml`. The only significant difference is that we added the second `volumeMount`. It will mount the directory `/src` inside the container, and will use the volume named `github`. The volume definition is straightforward. The `gitRepo` type defines the Git `repository` and the `directory`. If we skipped the latter, we'd get the repository mounted as `/src/go-demo-2`.

The `gitRepo` volume type allows a third field which we haven't used. We could have set a specific `revision` of the repository. But, for demo purposes, the `HEAD` should do.

Let's create the Pod.

```
kubectl create \
    -f volume/github.yml
```

Now that we created the Pod, we'll enter its only container, and check whether `gitRepo` indeed works as expected:

```
kubectl exec -it github sh

cd /src

ls -l
```

We entered into the container of the Pod, switched to the `/src` directory, and listed all the files and directories inside it. That proved that `gitRepo` mounted a volume with the contents of the `vfarcic/go-demo-2` GitHub repository.

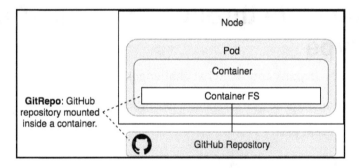

Figure 8-3: GitHub repository mounted inside a container

Since the Pod container is based on the `docker` image, and the socket is mounted as well, we should be able to build the image using the source code provided by the `gitRepo` volume:

```
docker image build \
    -t vfarcic/go-demo-2:beta .
```

This time, the build should be very fast since we already have the same image on the host, and the source code did not change in the meantime. You should see a `Using cache` notification for each layer of the image we're building.

Since we now proved the point, let's get out of the container and remove the Pod:

```
Exit
```

```
kubectl delete \
    -f volume/github.yml
```

gitRepo is a nifty little addition to the volume types. It does not save us a lot of work, nor does it provide something truly exceptional. We could accomplish the same result by using an image with git and execute a simple git clone command. Still, the volume type might come in handy on a few occasions. The more we have defined in YAML files, the less we depend on ad-hoc commands. That way, we can aim towards fully documented processes.

 The gitRepo volume type helps us move git commands (for example, git clone) into the YAML definition. It also removes the need for the git binary inside containers. While gitRepo might not always be the best option, it is indeed something worth considering.

Persisting state through the emptyDir volume type

This time we'll deploy Jenkins and see what challenges we will face.

Let's take a look at the volume/jenkins.yml definition:

```
cat volume/jenkins.yml
```

The output is as follows:

```
apiVersion: extensions/v1beta1
kind: Ingress
metadata:
  name: Jenkins
  annotations:
    ingress.kubernetes.io/ssl-redirect: "false"
    nginx.ingress.kubernetes.io/ssl-redirect: "false"
spec:
  rules:
  - http:
      paths:
      - path: /Jenkins
        backend:
          serviceName: Jenkins
          servicePort: 8080

---
```

```
apiVersion: apps/v1beta2
kind: Deployment
metadata:
  name: Jenkins
spec:
  selector:
    matchLabels:
      type: master
      service: Jenkins
  strategy:
    type: Recreate
  template:
    metadata:
      labels:
        type: master
        service: Jenkins
    spec:
      containers:
      - name: Jenkins
        image: vfarcic/Jenkins
        env:
        - name: JENKINS_OPTS
          value: --prefix=/jenkins

---

apiVersion: v1
kind: Service
metadata:
  name: Jenkins
spec:
  ports:
  - port: 8080
  selector:
    type: master
    service: jenkins
```

There's nothing special in that YAML file. It defines an Ingress with /jenkins path, a Deployment, and a Service. We won't waste time with it. Instead, we'll move on and create the objects.

```
kubectl create \
    -f volume/jenkins.yml \
    --record --save-config

kubectl rollout status deploy jenkins
```

We created the objects and waited until the processes finished. Now we can open Jenkins in our browser of choice:

```
open "http://$(minikube ip)/jenkins"
```

Jenkins UI opened, thus confirming that the application is deployed correctly. Jenkins' primary function is to execute jobs, so it's only fair to create one:

```
open "http://$(minikube ip)/jenkins/newJob"
```

Please type `test` in the **item name** field, select `Pipeline` as the type, and click the **OK** button.

There's no need to make the Pipeline do any specific set of tasks. For now, you should be fine if you just **Save** the job.

Let's explore what happens if the main process inside the Jenkins container dies:

```
POD_NAME=$(kubectl get pods \
    -l service=jenkins,type=master \
    -o jsonpath="{.items[*].metadata.name}")

kubectl exec -it $POD_NAME kill 1
```

We retrieved the name of the Pod, and we used it to execute `kill 1` inside its only container. The result is a simulation of a failure. Soon afterward, Kubernetes detected the failure and recreated the container. Let's double-check all that.

```
kubectl get pods
```

The output is as follows:

```
NAME                        READY STATUS   RESTARTS AGE
jenkins-76d59945d8-zcz8m 1/1    Running 1           12m
```

We can see that a container is running. Since we killed the main process and, with it, the first container, the number of restarts was increased to one.

Let's go back to Jenkins UI and check what happened to the job. I'm sure you already know the answer, but we'll double check it anyways.

```
open "http://$(minikube ip)/jenkins"
```

As expected, the job we created is gone. When Kubernetes recreated the failed container, it created a new one from the same image. Everything we generated inside the running container is no more. We reset to the initial state:

Let's take a look at a slightly updated YAML definition:

```
cat volume/jenkins-empty-dir.yml
```

The output, limited to the relevant parts, is as follows:

```
...
kind: Deployment
...
spec:
  ...
  template:
    ...
    spec:
      containers:
        ...
        volumeMounts:
        - mountPath: /var/jenkins_home
          name: jenkins-home
      volumes:
      - emptyDir: {}
        name: jenkins-home
...
```

We added a mount that references the `jenkins-home` volume. The volume type is, this time, `emptyDir`. We'll discuss the new volume type soon. But, before we dive into explanations, we'll try to experience its effects:

```
kubectl apply \
    -f volume/jenkins-empty-dir.yml

kubectl rollout status deploy jenkins
```

We applied the new definition and waited until the rollout finished.

Now we can open the **New Job** Jenkins screen and repeat the same process we followed before:

```
open "http://$(minikube ip)/jenkins/newJob"
```

Please type `test` in the **item name** field, select `Pipeline` as the type, click the **OK** button, and finish by clicking the **Save** button.

Now we'll kill the container and see what happens:

```
POD_NAME=$(kubectl get pods \
    -l service=jenkins,type=master \
    -o jsonpath="{.items[*].metadata.name}")

kubectl exec -it $POD_NAME kill 1

kubectl get pods
```

The output should show that there is a container running or, in other words, that Kubernetes detected the failure and created a new container.

Finally, let's open Jenkins' Home screen one more time:

```
open "http://$(minikube ip)/jenkins"
```

This time, the `test` job is there. The state of the application was preserved even when the container failed, and Kubernetes created a new one:

Figure 8-4: Jenkins with preserved state

Now let's talk about the `emptyDir` volume. It is considerably different from those we explored thus far.

An emptyDir Volume is created when a Pod is assigned to a node. It will exist for as long as the Pod continues running on that server.

What that means is that `emptyDir` can survive container failures. When a container crashes, a Pod is not removed from the node. Instead, Kubernetes will recreate the failed container inside the same Pod and, thus, preserve the `emptyDir` Volume. All in all, this volume type is only partially fault-tolerant.

If `emptyDir` is not entirely fault-tolerant, you might be wondering why we are discussing it in the first place.

The `emptyDir` volume type is closest we can get to fault-tolerant volumes without using a network drive. Since we do not have any, we had to resort to `emptyDir` as the-closest-we-can-get-to-fault-tolerant-persistence type of Volume.

As you start deploying third-party applications, you'll discover that many of them come with the recommended YAML definition. If you pay closer attention, you'll notice that many are using `emptyDir` volume type. It's not that `emptyDir` is the best choice, but that it all depends on your needs, your hosting provider, your infrastructure, and quite a few other things. There is no one-size-fits-all type of persistent and fault-tolerant volume type. On the other hand, `emptyDir` always works. Since it has no external dependencies, it is safe to put it as an example, with the assumption that people will change to whichever type fits them better.

There is an unwritten assumption that `emptyDir` is used for testing purposes, and will be changed to something else before it reaches production.

As long as we're using Minikube to create a Kubernetes cluster, we'll use `emptyDir` as a solution for persistent volumes. Do not despair. Later on, once we move into a "more serious" cluster setup, we'll explore better options for persisting state. For now, you have a taste. The full (and persistent) meal is coming later.

What now?

With the exception of `emptyDir`, our choice of volume type demonstrated in this chapter was not simply based on the ability to use them in a Minikube cluster. Each of these three volume types will be an essential piece in the chapters that follow. We'll use `hostPath` to access Docker server from inside containers. The `gitRepo` volume type will be very significant once we start designing a continuous deployment pipeline. The `emptyDir` type will be required as long as we're using Minikube. Until we have a better solution for creating a Kubernetes cluster, `emptyDir` will continue to be used in our Minikube examples.

We have only scratched the surface with volumes. There are at least two more that we should explore inside Minikube, and one (or more) when we change to a different solution for creating a cluster. The volumes that we'll explore throughout the rest of the book are long enough subjects to deserve a separate chapter or, as we already mentioned, require that we get rid of Minikube. For now, we'll just destroy the cluster and take a break.

```
minikube delete
```

If you'd like to know more about Volumes, please explore Volume v1 core (`https://v1-9.docs.kubernetes.io/docs/reference/generated/kubernetes-api/v1.9/#volume-v1-core`) API documentation.

The next chapter is dedicated to the `configMap` volume type. It will, hopefully, solve a few problems and provide better solutions to some use-cases than those we employed in this chapter. ConfigMaps deserve a full chapter, so they're getting one.

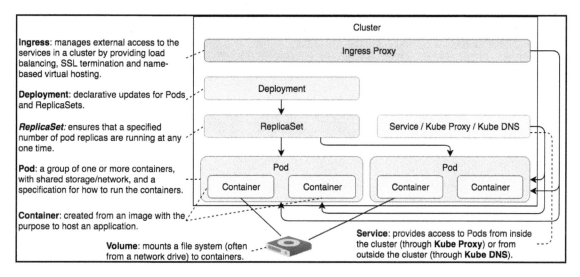

Figure 8-5: The components explored so far

Using ConfigMaps to Inject Configuration Files

9

ConfigMaps allow us to keep configurations separate from application images. Such separation is useful when other alternatives are not a good fit.

Almost every application can be fine-tuned through configuration. Traditional software deployment methods fostered the use of configuration files. However, we are not discussing traditional, but advanced, distributed, and immutable deployments through Kubernetes schedulers. Usage of fundamentally new technology often requires new processes and different architecture, if we are to leverage its potential to its maximum. On the other hand, we cannot just throw away everything we have and start anew.

We'll have to try to balance new principles and the legacy needs.

If we were to start developing a new application today, it would be, among other things, distributed, scalable, stateless, and fault tolerant. Those are some of the today's needs. While we might question how many of us know how to design an application with those quality attributes in mind, hardly anyone would argue against having any of them. What is often forgotten is the configuration. Which mechanism should your new application use to configure itself? How about environment variables?

Environment variables fit well into distributed systems. They are easy to define, and they are portable. They are the ideal choice for configuration mechanism of new applications.

However, in some cases, the configuration might be too complex for environment variables. In such situations, we might need to fall back to files (hopefully YAML). When those cases are combined with legacy applications which are almost exclusively using file-based configuration, it is evident that we cannot rely only on environment variables.

When a configuration is based on files, the best approach we can take is to bake the configuration into a Docker image. That way, we are going down the fully-immutable road. Still, that might not be possible when our application needs different configuration options for various clusters (for example, testing and production). I'll ignore my internal need to convert this into a discussion that ends with "you do NOT need a different configuration for different environments". Rather just assume that you might have an excellent reason for something like that. In such a case, baking config files into images will not do the trick. That's where ConfigMaps comes into play.

ConfigMap allows us to "inject" configuration into containers. The source of the configs can be files, directories, or literal values. The destination can be files or environment variables.

> ConfigMap takes a configuration from a source and mounts it into running containers as a volume.

That's all the theory you'll get up-front. Instead of a lengthy explanation, we'll run some examples, and comment on the features we experience. We'll be learning by doing, instead of learning by memorizing theory.

Let's prepare the cluster and see ConfigMaps in action.

Creating a cluster

It's still the same process as before, so let's get over with it silently.

> All the commands from this chapter are available in the `09-config-map.sh` (https://gist.github.com/vfarcic/717f8418982cc5ec1c755fcf7d4255dd) Gist.

```
cd k8s-specs
git pull
minikube start --vm-driver=virtualbox
minikube addons enable ingress
kubectl config current-context
```

Now we can try out the first variation of a ConfigMap.

Injecting configurations from files

In its purest, and probably the most common form, a ConfigMap takes a single file. For example, we can create one from the cm/prometheus-conf.yml file:

```
kubectl create cm my-config \
    --from-file=cm/prometheus-conf.yml
```

We created a **ConfigMap** (cm) called my-config. The data of the map is the content of the cm/prometheus-conf.yml file.

Let's describe it, and see what we'll get.

```
kubectl describe cm my-config
```

The output is as follows:

```
Name:         my-config
Namespace:    default
Labels:       <none>
Annotations:  <none>

Data
====
prometheus-conf.yml:
----
global:
  scrape_interval:      15s

scrape_configs:
  - job_name: Prometheus
    metrics_path: /prometheus/metrics
    static_configs:
      - targets:
        - localhost:9090

Events:  <none>
```

The important part is located below Data. We can see the key which, in this case, is the name of the file (prometheus-conf.yml). Further down you can see the content of the file. If you execute cat cm/prometheus-conf.yml, you'll see that it is the same as what we saw from the ConfigMap's description.

ConfigMap is useless by itself. It is yet another Volume which, like all the others, needs a mount.

Let's take a look at a Pod specification defined in `cm/alpine.yml`.

```
cat cm/alpine.yml
```

The output is as follows:

```
apiVersion: v1
kind: Pod
metadata:
  name: alpine
spec:
  containers:
  - name: alpine
    image: alpine
    command: ["sleep"]
    args: ["100000"]
    volumeMounts:
    - name: config-vol
      mountPath: /etc/config
  volumes:
  - name: config-vol
    configMap:
      name: my-config
```

The essential sections are `volumeMounts` and `volumes`. Since `volumeMounts` are the same no matter the type of the Volume, there's nothing special about it. We defined that it should be based on the volume called `config-vol` and that it should mount the path `/etc/config`. The `volumes` section uses `configMap` as the type and, in this case, has a single item `name`, that coincides with the name of the ConfigMap we created earlier.

Let's create the Pod and see what happens.

```
kubectl create -f cm/alpine.yml
kubectl get pods
```

Please confirm that the Pod is indeed running before moving on.

Let's see the content of the `/etc/config` directory inside the Pod's only container.

```
kubectl exec -it alpine -- \
    ls /etc/config
```

The output is as follows:

```
prometheus-conf.yml
```

The `/etc/config` now has a single file that coincides with the file we stored in the ConfigMap.

If you add `-l` to the `ls` command we executed a moment ago, you'll see that `prometheus-conf.yml` is a link to `..data/prometheus-conf.yml`. If you dig deeper, you'll see that `..data` is also a link to the directory named from a timestamp. And so on, and so forth. For now, the exact logic behind all the links and the actual files is not of great importance. From the functional point of view, there is `prometheus-conf.yml`, and our application can do whatever it needs to do with it.

Let's confirm that the content of the file inside the container is indeed the same as the source file we used to create the ConfigMap:

```
kubectl exec -it alpine -- \
    cat /etc/config/prometheus-conf.yml
```

The output should be the same as the contents of the `cm/prometheus-conf.yml` file.

We saw one combination of ConfigMap. Let's see what else we can do with it. We'll remove the objects we created thus far and start over:

```
kubectl delete -f cm/alpine.yml
kubectl delete cm my-config
```

We are not limited to a single `--from-file` argument. We can specify as many as we need.

Let's see what happens when we execute the commands that follow:

```
kubectl create cm my-config \
    --from-file=cm/prometheus-conf.yml \
    --from-file=cm/prometheus.yml
kubectl create -f cm/alpine.yml
kubectl exec -it alpine -- \
    ls /etc/config
```

We created a ConfigMap with two files, and we created the same Pod based on the `alpine.yml` definition. Finally, we output the list of files from the `/etc/config` directory inside the Pod's only container. The output of the latter command is as follows:

```
prometheus-conf.yml   prometheus.yml
```

We can see that both files are present in the container. That leads us to the conclusion that a ConfigMap can contain multiple files, and all will be created inside containers that mount it.

Let's delete the objects (again), and explore one more option behind the `--from-file` argument.

```
kubectl delete -f cm/alpine.yml
kubectl delete cm my-config
```

The `--from-file` argument might lead you to the conclusion that you can specify only a file path as its value. It works with directories as well. We can, for example, add all files from the cm directory to a ConfigMap.

```
kubectl create cm my-config \
    --from-file=cm
```

We created `my-config` ConfigMap with the directory cm. Let's describe it, and see what's inside.

```
kubectl describe cm my-config
```

The output is as follows (content of the files is removed for brevity).

```
Name:         my-config
Namespace:    default
Labels:       <none>
Annotations:  <none>
Data
====
alpine-env-all.yml:
----
. . .
alpine-env.yml:
----
. . .
alpine.yml:
----
. . .
my-env-file.yml:
----
. . .
prometheus-conf.yml:
----
. . .
prometheus.yml:
----
```

```
. . .
Events:   <none>
```

We can see that all six files from the `cm` directory are now inside the `my-config` ConfigMap.

I'm sure you already know what will happen if we create a Pod that mounts that ConfigMap. We'll check it out anyways:

```
kubectl create -f cm/alpine.yml
kubectl exec -it alpine -- \
    ls /etc/config
```

The output of the latter command is as follows:

```
alpine-env-all.yml alpine.yml       prometheus-conf.yml
alpine-env.yml      my-env-file.yml prometheus.yml
```

All the files are there, and the time has come to move away from files and directories. So, let's remove the objects first, and discuss the other sources.

```
kubectl delete -f cm/alpine.yml
kubectl delete cm my-config
```

Injecting configurations from key/value literals

Hopefully, even when our applications need different configs to work in distinct clusters, the differences are limited. Often, they should be limited to only a few key/value entries. In such cases, it might be easier to create ConfigMaps using `--from-literal`.

Let's take a look at an example:

```
kubectl create cm my-config \
    --from-literal=something=else \
    --from-literal=weather=sunny
kubectl get cm my-config -o yaml
```

The output of the latter command is as follows (`metadata` is removed for brevity):

```
apiVersion: v1
data:
  something: else
  weather: sunny
```

```
kind: ConfigMap
...
```

We can see that two entries were added, one for each literal.

Let's create a Pod with the ConfigMap mounted:

```
kubectl create -f cm/alpine.yml

kubectl exec -it alpine -- \
    ls /etc/config
```

The output of the latter command is as follows:

```
something  weather
Both files are there.
```

Finally, let's confirm that the content of one of the files is correct.

```
kubectl exec -it alpine -- \
    cat /etc/config/something
```

The output is as follows:

```
else
```

> The `--from-literal` argument is useful when we're in need to set a relatively small set of configuration entries in different clusters. It makes more sense to specify only the things that change, than all the configuration options.

The problem is that most of the existing applications are not designed to read separate configuration entries from different files. On the other hand, if you're sketching a new application, you might not choose this option either since you'd be able to develop it in a way that it reads environment variables. When faced with a choice between ConfigMap and environment variables, the latter wins most of the time.

All in all, I'm not sure how often you'll be using the `--from-literal` argument. Maybe a lot, more likely not at all.

There's one more config source left to explore, so let's delete the objects we're currently running, and move on.

```
kubectl delete -f cm/alpine.yml
kubectl delete cm my-config
```

Injecting configurations from environment files

Let's take a look at the cm/my-env-file.yml file:

```
cat cm/my-env-file.yml
```

The output is as follows:

```
something=else
weather=sunny
```

The file has the same key/value pairs as those we used in the example with --from-literal:

Let's see what happens if we create a ConfigMap using that file as the source.

```
kubectl create cm my-config \
    --from-env-file=cm/my-env-file.yml
kubectl get cm my-config -o yaml
```

We created the ConfigMap using the --from-env-file argument, and we retrieved the ConfigMap in yaml format.

The output of the latter command is as follows (metadata is removed for brevity):

```
apiVersion: v1
data:
  something: else
  weather: sunny
kind: ConfigMap
...
```

We can see that there are two entries, each corresponding to key/value pairs from the file. The result is the same as when we created a ConfigMap using --from-literal arguments. Two different sources produced the same outcome:

If we used --from-file argument, the result would be as follows:

```
apiVersion: v1
data:
  my-env-file.yml: |
    something=else
    weather=sunny
kind: ConfigMap
...
```

All in all, `--from-file` reads the content of a one or more files, and stores it using file names as keys. `--from-env-file`, assumes that content of a file is in key/value format, and stores each as a separate entry.

Converting ConfigMap output into environment variables

All the examples we've seen so far are differing only in the source. The destination is always the same. No matter whether ConfigMap is created from a file, from a directory, from literal values, or from an environment file, it perpetually resulted in one or more files being injected into a container.

This time we'll try something different. We'll see how we can convert a ConfigMap into environment variables.

Let's take a look at a sample definition:

```
cat cm/alpine-env.yml
```

The output is as follows.

```
apiVersion: v1
kind: Pod
metadata:
  name: alpine-env
spec:
  containers:
  - name: alpine
    image: alpine
    command: ["sleep"]
    args: ["100000"]
    env:
    - name: something
      valueFrom:
        configMapKeyRef:
          name: my-config
          key: something
    - name: weather
      valueFrom:
        configMapKeyRef:
          name: my-config
          key: weather
```

The major difference, when compared with `cm/alpine.yml`, is that `volumeMounts` and `volumes` sections are gone. This time we have `env` section.

Instead of a `value` field, we have `valueFrom`. Further on, we declared that it should get values from a ConfigMap (`configMapKeyRef`) named `my-config`. Since that ConfigMap has multiple values, we specified the `key` as well.

Let's create the Pod:

```
kubectl create \
    -f cm/alpine-env.yml
kubectl exec -it alpine-env -- env
```

We created the Pod and executed the `env` command inside its only container. The output of the latter command, limited to the relevant parts, is as follows:

```
...
weather=sunny
something=else
...
```

There's another, often more useful way to specify environment variables from a ConfigMap. Before we try it, we'll remove the currently running Pod:

```
kubectl delete \
    -f cm/alpine-env.yml
```

Let's take a look at yet another definition:

```
cat cm/alpine-env-all.yml
```

The output is as follows:

```
apiVersion: v1
kind: Pod
metadata:
  name: alpine-env
spec:
  containers:
  - name: alpine
    image: alpine
    command: ["sleep"]
    args: ["100000"]
    envFrom:
    - configMapRef:
        name: my-config
```

The difference is only in the way environment variables are defined. This time, the syntax is much shorter. We have `envFrom`, instead of the `env` section. It can be either `configMapRef` or `secretRef`. Since we did not yet explore Secrets, we'll stick with the prior. Inside `configMapRef` is the name reference to the `my-config` ConfigMap.

Let's see it in action.

```
kubectl create \
    -f cm/alpine-env-all.yml
kubectl exec -it alpine-env -- env
```

We created the Pod and retrieved all the environment variables from inside its only container. The output of the latter command, limited to the relevant parts, is as follows:

```
...
something=else
weather=sunny
...
```

The result is the same as before. The difference is only in the way we define environment variables. With `env.valueFrom.configMapKeyRef` syntax, we need to specify each ConfigMap key separately. That gives us control over the scope and the relation with the names of container variables.

The `envFrom.configMapRef` converts all ConfigMap's data into environment variables. That is often a better and simpler option if you don't need to use different names between ConfigMap and environment variable keys. The syntax is short, and we don't need to worry whether we forgot to include one of the ConfigMap's keys.

Defining ConfigMaps as YAML

All ConfigMaps we created so far were done through `kubectl create cm` commands. It would be a shame if we could not specify them through YAML definitions, just like other Kubernetes resources and objects. Fortunately, we can. Everything in Kubernetes can be defined as YAML, and that includes ConfigMaps as well.

Even though we have not yet specified ConfigMaps as YAML, we have seen the format quite a few times throughout this chapter. Since I cannot be sure whether you can create a ConfigMap YAML file from memory, let's make things easy on ourselves and use `kubectl` to output our existing `my-config` ConfigMap in YAML format.

```
kubectl get cm my-config -o yaml
```

The output is as follows:

```
apiVersion: v1
data:
  something: else
  weather: sunny
kind: ConfigMap
metadata:
  name: my-config
  ...
```

Just as with any other Kubernetes object, ConfigMap has `apiVersion`, `kind`, and `metadata`. The data is where the maps are defined. Each must have a key and a value. In this example, there's the key `weather` with the value `sunny`.

Let's try to translate that knowledge into the objects we'd need to deploy Prometheus.

cat cm/prometheus.yml

The output, limited to the relevant parts, is as follows:

```
apiVersion: apps/v1beta2
kind: Deployment
metadata:
  name: Prometheus
spec:
  ...
  template:
    ...
    spec:
      containers:
        ...
        volumeMounts:
        - mountPath: /etc/Prometheus
          name: prom-conf
      volumes:
      - name: prom-conf
        configMap:
          name: prom-conf
...
apiVersion: v1
kind: ConfigMap
metadata:
  name: prom-conf
data:
  prometheus.yml: |
    global:
      scrape_interval:    15s
```

```
scrape_configs:
  - job_name: Prometheus
    metrics_path: /prometheus/metrics
    static_configs:
      - targets:
        - localhost:9090
```

The `Deployment` object defines the `volumeMount` that references the `prom-conf` Volume, which is a `configMap`. We saw quite a few similar examples before.

The `ConfigMap` object's `data` section has only one key (`prometheus.yml`). Once this ConfigMap is mounted as a volume, the name of the file will be the same as the key (`prometheus.yml`). The value has a bit of "special" syntax. Unlike the previous example where the value was a single word written directly after the colon, the structure of the value is now a bit more complex. To be more precise, it contains multiple lines. When working with a large value, we can start with the pipe sign (`|`). Kubernetes will interpret the value as "everything that follows, as long as it is indented." You'll notice that all the lines of the value are at least two spaces to the right of the beginning of the key (`prometheus.yml`). If you'd like to insert an additional key, all you'd need to do is to add it on the same level (indentation), as the other `prometheus.yml`.

Let's create the application and confirm that everything works as expected.

```
cat cm/prometheus.yml | sed -e \
    "s/192.168.99.100/$(minikube ip)/g" \
    | kubectl create -f -
kubectl rollout status deploy prometheus
open "http://$(minikube ip)/prometheus/targets"
```

We created the objects (with the help of `sed` transformations), we waited until the Deployment rolled out, and, finally, we opened the Prometheus targets screen in a browser. The result should be a green target towards Prometheus internal metrics.

A plea NOT to use ConfigMaps!

ConfigMaps, in my experience, are overused.

If you have a configuration that is the same across multiple clusters, or if you have only one cluster, all you should do is include it in your Dockerfile and forget it ever existed. When there are no variations of a config, there's no need to have a configuration file. At least, not outside an immutable image. Unfortunately, that is not always the case. Heck, it's almost never the case. We tend to make things more complicated than they should be. That, among other things, often means an endless list configuration options hardly anyone ever uses. Still, some things usually do change, from one cluster to another, and we might need to look into alternatives to configurations baked into images.

Design your new applications to use a combination of configuration files and environment variables. Make sure that the default values in a configuration file are sensible and applicable in most use-cases. Bake it into the image. When running a container, declare only the environment variables that represent the differences of a specific cluster. That way, your configuration will be portable and simple at the same time.

What if your application is not new and it does not support configuration through environment variables? Refactor it so that it does. It shouldn't be hard to add the ability to read a few environment variables. Keep in mind that you don't need all the settings, but only those that differ from one cluster to another. It would be hard to imagine that such a trivial request would be complex or time-consuming. If it is, you might have more significant issues to fix before even thinking about putting your application into a container.

Still, configuration files will not disappear. No matter which strategy we choose, each image should have a copy of them with sensible default values. Maybe, we can put in an extra effort and change the application, so that configuration entries are loaded from two locations. That way, we can load the default values from one, and only the differences from the other. That would, at least, reduce the need to have to specify more than the minimum required for each cluster. In such a case, ConfigMap's `--from-literal` and `--from-env-file` sources are an excellent choice.

When everything else fails, the `--from-file` source is your friend. Just make sure that ConfigMap is not defined in the same file as the objects that mount it. If it is, it would mean that they could be used only inside one cluster. Otherwise, we'd be deploying the same config, and we should go back to the initial idea of having it baked into the image together with the application.

Do not let this pessimism discourage you from using ConfigMaps. They are very handy, and you should adopt them. My intent to discourage you from doing so had the intention of making you think of alternatives, not to tell you never to use ConfigMaps.

What now?

The next chapter will explore something very similar to ConfigMaps. The significant difference is that we'll be more secretive this time.

For now, we'll destroy the cluster we used in this chapter.

```
minikube delete
```

 If you'd like to know more about ConfigMaps, please explore ConfigMap v1 core (`https://v1-9.docs.kubernetes.io/docs/reference/ generated/kubernetes-api/v1.9/#configmap-v1-core`) API documentation.

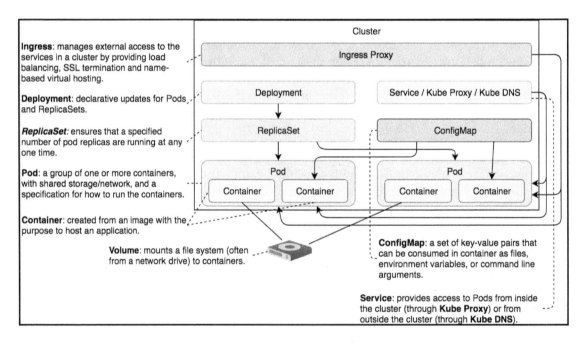

Figure 9-1: The components explored so far

Kubernetes ConfigMaps compared to Docker Swarm configs

The mechanisms behind Kubernetes ConfigMaps and Docker Swarm Configs are almost the same. At least, from the functional perspective. Both allow us to store some literal texts in the scheduler's internal data store, and both enable us to add them to containers. The syntax is equally simple and straightforward in both cases. Still, there are a few differences.

Docker is good at preventing people from doing silly things (the politically correct version of the word *stupid*). An example would be an attempt to delete a configuration. It cannot be deleted if there are Docker services that reference the configuration. Only after all the services that reference it are removed, are we allowed to remove the configuration source. Kubernetes, on the other hand, will let us delete a ConfigMap object without even a hint about the consequences.

Kubernetes ConfigMap, on the other hand, provides a wider variety of options. While a Docker Swarm configuration can be created only from a file or `stdin`, the Kubernetes equivalent can be generated from a file, from a directory, from a literal value, and from files with environment variables. Each of those sources can be used multiple times. We can even combine them. Further on, Kubernetes ConfigMaps can be converted not only to files, but also to environment variables. Flexibility and extra functionalities are available both at the source and the destination end-points.

Docker Swarm wins a user experience point. Kubernetes gains a star for providing more choices. Neither has a significant difference that would warrant a win, so I'm proclaiming it a *tie*.

There are many more features worthwhile comparing. We're not yet finished. Stay tuned for more.

10
Using Secrets to Hide Confidential Information

We cannot treat all information equally. Sensitive data needs to be handled with additional care. Kubernetes provides an additional level of protection through Secrets.

A Secret is a relatively small amount of sensitive data. Some of the typical candidates for Secrets would be passwords, tokens, and SSH keys.

Kubernetes Secrets are very similar to ConfigMaps. If you compare the differences in the syntax, you'll notice that there are only a few (if any). Conceptually, both ConfigMaps and Secrets are, more or less, the same. If you are familiar with ConfigMaps, you should have no trouble applying that knowledge to Secrets.

We already used Secrets without even knowing. Every Pod we created so far had a Secret mounted automatically by the system. We'll start by exploring auto-generated Secrets and proceed to produce some ourselves.

Creating a Cluster

We'll continue using Minikube, so the instructions for creating a cluster are still the same. They should be engraved in the back of your brain so we'll just execute them without any explanation.

All the commands from this chapter are available in the `10-secret.sh` (`https://gist.github.com/vfarcic/37b3ef7afeaf9237aeb2b9a8065b10c 3`) Gist.

```
cd k8s-specs
git pull
minikube start --vm-driver=virtualbox
minikube addons enable ingress
kubectl config current-context
```

We'll start by deploying an application without creating any user-defined Secret.

Exploring built-in Secrets

We'll create the same Jenkins objects we defined earlier:

```
kubectl create \
    -f secret/jenkins-unprotected.yml \
    --record --save-config
kubectl rollout status deploy jenkins
```

We created an Ingress, a Deployment, and a Service object. We also executed the `kubectl rollout status` command that will tell us when the deployment is finished.

The `secret/jenkins-unprotected.yml` definition does not use any new feature so we won't waste time going through the YAML file. Instead, we'll open Jenkins UI in a browser.

```
open "http://$(minikube ip)/jenkins"
```

Upon closer inspection, you'll notice that there is no login button. Jenkins is currently unprotected. The image does allow the option to define an initial administrative username and password. If the files `/etc/secrets/jenkins-user` and `/etc/secrets/jenkins-pass` are present, the init script will read them, and use the content inside those files to define the username and the password. Since we're already familiar with ConfigMaps, we could use them to generate those files. However, since the user and the password should be better protected than other configuration entries, we'll switch to Secrets.

If you're interested in details, please explore the `jenkins/Dockerfile` (https://github.com/vfarcic/docker-flow-stacks/blob/master/jenkins/Dockerfile) from the `vfarcic/docker-flow-stack` (https://github.com/vfarcic/docker-flow-stacks) repository. The important part is that it expects `/etc/secrets/jenkins-user` and `/etc/secrets/jenkins-pass` files. If we can provide them, in a relatively secure manner, our Jenkins will be (more) secured by default.

We'll start by checking whether we already have some Secrets in the cluster:

```
kubectl get secrets
```

The output is as follows:

```
NAME                     TYPE                                DATA AGE
default-token-19fhk kubernetes.io/service-account-token 3      32m
```

We did not create any Secret, and yet one is available in the system.

The `default-token-19fhk` Secret was created automatically by Kubernetes. It contains credentials that can be used to access the API. Moreover, Kubernetes automatically modifies the Pods to use this Secret. Unless we tweak Service Accounts, every Pod we create will have this Secret. Let's confirm that is indeed true.

```
kubectl describe pods
```

The output, limited to the relevant sections, is as follows:

```
. . .
    Mounts:
      /var/jenkins_home from jenkins-home (rw)
      /var/run/secrets/kubernetes.io/serviceaccount from default-
  token-19fhk (ro)
. . .
Volumes:
  jenkins-home:
    Type:      EmptyDir (a temporary directory that shares a pod's
  lifetime)
    Medium:
  default-token-19fhk:
    Type:        Secret (a volume populated by a Secret)
    SecretName:  default-token-19fhk
    Optional:    false
. . .
```

We can see that two volumes are mounted. The first one (`/var/jenkins_home`) was defined by us. It's the same mount volume we used in the previous chapter, and it is meant to preserve Jenkins' state by mounting its home directory.

The second mount is the more interesting one. We can see that it references the auto-generated Secret `default-token-19fhk` and that it mounts it as `/var/run/secrets/kubernetes.io/serviceaccount`. Let's take a look at that directory.

```
POD_NAME=$(kubectl get pods \
```

```
    -l service=jenkins,type=master \
    -o jsonpath="{.items[*].metadata.name}")
kubectl exec -it $POD_NAME -- ls \
    /var/run/secrets/kubernetes.io/serviceaccount
```

The output is as follows:

```
ca.crt   namespace   token
```

By auto-mounting that Secret, we got three files. They are required if we'd like to access the API server from within the containers. `ca.crt` is the certificate, the `namespace` contains the namespace the Pod is running in, and the last one is the token we'd need to establish communication with the API.

We won't go into examples that prove those files can be used to access the API server securely. Just remember that if you ever need to do that, Kubernetes has you covered through that auto-generated Secret.

Let's get back to the task at hand. We want to make Jenkins more secure by providing it with an initial username and password.

Creating and mounting generic Secrets

The commands to create Secrets are almost the same as those we used to create ConfigMaps. We can, for example, generate Secrets based on literal values.

```
kubectl create secret \
    generic my-creds \
    --from-literal=username=jdoe \
    --from-literal=password=incognito
```

The major difference is that we specified the type of the Secret as `generic`. It could also be `docker-registry` or `tls`. We won't explore those two, but only say that the former can be used to provide `kubelet` with credentials it needs to pull images from private registries. The latter is used for storing certificates. In this chapter, we'll focus on the `generic` type of secrets which happen to use the same syntax as ConfigMaps.

Just as with ConfigMaps, generic Secrets can use `--from-env-file`, `--from-file`, and `--from-literal` as sources. They can be mounted as files, or transformed into environment variables. Since creating Secrets is so similar to creating ConfigMaps, we won't go into all the permutations we can do. I expect that you'll consult the ConfigMaps chapter if you have already forgotten the arguments we can use.

For now, we created a Secret called `my-creds` which holds two literal values.

Let's take a look at the Secrets we now have in the cluster:

```
kubectl get secrets
```

The output is as follows:

```
NAME                TYPE                                     DATA AGE
default-token-n6fs4 kubernetes.io/service-account-token 3    33m
my-creds            Opaque                                   2    6s
```

We can see that the newly created Secret is available and that it has two pieces of data.

Let's see the `json` representation of the Secret and try to find out how to retrieve it.

```
kubectl get secret my-creds -o json
```

The output is as follows (`metadata` is removed for brevity):

```
{
    "apiVersion": "v1",
    "data": {
        "password": "aW5jb2duaXRv",
        "username": "amRvZQ=="
    },
    "kind": "Secret",
    "metadata": {
        . . .
    },
    "type": "Opaque"
}
```

We can see that the `data` field contains the `password` and the `username`. They coincide with the literal values we specified in the command that created the Secret.

You'll notice that the values are "strange". They are encoded. If we'd like to see the original values we stored as secrets, we'll need to decode them:

```
kubectl get secret my-creds \
    -o jsonpath="{.data.username}" \
    | base64 --decode
```

We used `jsonpath` to filter the output so that only the `username` data is retrieved. Since the value is encoded, we piped the output to `base64` command that decoded it for us. The result is `jdoe`.

Similarly, the command that will retrieve and decode the second Secret data is as follows:

```
kubectl get secret my-creds \
    -o jsonpath="{.data.password}" \
    | base64 --decode
```

The output is `incognito`:

Let's see how we could mount the Secret we created:

```
cat secret/jenkins.yml
```

The output, limited to the relevant parts, is as follows:

```
apiVersion: apps/v1beta2
kind: Deployment
metadata:
  name: Jenkins
spec:
  ...
  template:
    ...
    spec:
      containers:
      - name: Jenkins
        image: vfarcic/Jenkins
        env:
        - name: JENKINS_OPTS
          value: --prefix=/Jenkins
        volumeMounts:
        - name: jenkins-home
          mountPath: /var/jenkins_home
        - name: jenkins-creds
          mountPath: /run/secrets
      volumes:
      - name: jenkins-home
        emptyDir: {}
      - name: jenkins-creds
        secret:
          secretName: my-creds
          defaultMode: 0444
          items:
          - key: username
            path: jenkins-user
          - key: password
            path: jenkins-pass
  ...
```

We added `jenkins-creds` that mounts the `/etc/secrets` directory. The `jenkins-creds` Volume references the Secret named `my-creds`. Since we want the process inside the container to only read the Secret, we set the `defaultMode` to `0444`. That will give read permissions to everyone. Typically, we'd set it to `0400`, thus giving the read permissions only to the `root` user. However, since the Jenkins image uses the `jenkins` user, we gave read permissions to everyone instead of only to the `root` user.

Finally, since the image expected files named `jenkins-user` and `jenkins-pass`, we made explicit paths. Otherwise, Kubernetes would create files `username` and `password`.

Let's apply the new definition:

```
kubectl apply -f secret/jenkins.yml
kubectl rollout status deploy jenkins
```

We applied the definition and waited until the new objects were rolled out.

Now we can check whether the correct files are indeed stored in the `/etc/secrets` directory:

```
POD_NAME=$(kubectl get pods \
    -l service=jenkins,type=master \
    -o jsonpath="{.items[*].metadata.name}")
kubectl exec -it $POD_NAME \
    -- ls /etc/secrets
```

The output of the latter command is as follows:

```
jenkins-pass   jenkins-user
```

The files we need are indeed injected. To be on the safe side, we'll also check the content of one of them:

```
kubectl exec -it $POD_NAME \
    -- cat /etc/secrets/jenkins-user
```

The output is `jdoe`, the username of our newly deployed Jenkins.

Finally, let's confirm that the application is indeed secured.

```
open "http://$(minikube ip)/jenkins"
```

You'll see that, this time, the link to create new jobs is gone.

Please use `jdoe` and `incognito` if you'd like to login to your newly deployed and (more) secured Jenkins.

Secrets compared to ConfigMaps

So far, Kubernetes Secrets do not seem to differ from ConfigMaps. From a functional perspective, they are, indeed, the same. Both allow us to inject some content. Both can use files, literal values, and files with environment variables as data sources. Both can output data into containers as files or as environment variables. Even the syntax for using Secrets is almost the same as the one used for ConfigMaps.

The only significant difference between ConfigMaps and Secrets is that the latter creates files in a tmpfs. They are constructed as in-memory files, thus leaving no trace on the host's files system. That, in itself, is not enough to call Secrets secure, but it is a step towards it. We'd need to combine them with *Authorization Policies* to make the passwords, keys, tokens, and other never-to-be-seen-by-publicly types of data secure. Even then, we might want to turn our attention towards third-party Secret managers like HashiCorp Vault (`https://www.vaultproject.io/`).

 Secrets are almost the same as ConfigMaps. The main difference is that the secret files are created in tmpfs. Kubernetes secrets do not make your system secure. They are only a step towards such a system.

Not so secretive Secrets

Almost everything Kubernetes needs is stored in etcd (`https://github.com/coreos/etcd`). That includes Secrets. The problem is that they are stored as plain text. Anyone with access to etcd has access to Kubernetes Secrets. We can limit the access to etcd, but that's not the end of our troubles. *etcd* stores data to disk as plain text. Restricting the access to etcd still leaves the Secrets vulnerable to who has access to the file system. That, in a way, diminishes the advantage of storing Secrets in containers in tmpfs. There's not much benefit of having them in tmpfs used by containers, if those same Secrets are stored on disk by etcd.

Even after securing the access to etcd and making sure that unauthorized users do not have access to the file system partition used by etcd, we are still at risk. When multiple replicas of etcd are running, data is synchronized between them. By default, etcd communication between replicas is not secured. Anyone sniffing that communication could get a hold of our secrets.

Kubernetes Secrets are a step in the right direction. It is, without a doubt, better to use Secrets than to expose confidential information as environment variables or other less secure methods. Still, Secrets can give us a false sense of security.

We need to take additional precautions to protect ourselves. That might include, but is not limited to, the following actions:

- Secure the communication between etcd instances with SSL/TLS.
- Limit the access to etcd and wipe the disk or partitions that were used by it.
- Do not define Secrets in YAML files stored in a repository. Create Secrets through ad-hoc `kubectl create secret` commands. If possible, delete commands history afterward.
- Make sure that the applications using Secrets do not accidentally output them to logs or transmit them to other applications.
- Create policies that allow only trusted users to retrieve secrets. However, you should be aware that even with proper policies in place, any user with permissions to run a Pod could mount a Secret and read it.

We did not yet explore etcd configuration, nor did we learn how to set up authorization policies. For now, just remember that Secrets are not as secured as one might think. At least, not those provided by Kubernetes community. I do encourage you to use them, as long as you're aware of their shortcomings.

What now?

There isn't much left to say, so we'll enter into the destructive mode and eliminate the cluster we created:

```
minikube delete
```

 If you'd like to know more about Secrets, please explore Secret v1 core (`https://v1-9.docs.kubernetes.io/docs/reference/generated/kubernetes-api/v1.9/#secret-v1-core`) API documentation.

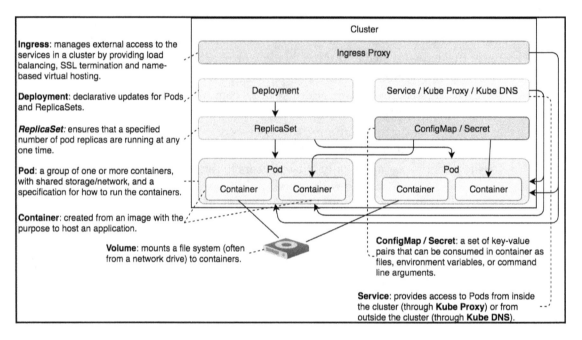

Figure 10-1: The components explored so far

Kubernetes Secrets compared to Docker Swarm Secrets

Secrets are very similar to Kubernetes ConfigMaps and Docker Swarm configs. Everything we said for configurations applies to Secrets, with a few additional features.

Both Kubernetes and Docker Swarm stores Secrets in tmpfs inside containers. From that aspect, they are equally secure. The significant difference is in the way Secrets are stored internally.

Kubernetes stores Secrets in etcd. By default, they are exposed, and we need to take extra precautions to protect them. Docker Swarm secrets are, on the other hand, more secure by default. They are synchronized between managers using SSL/TLS, and they are encrypted at rest. I prefer "secured by default" approach behind Docker Swarm secrets. In Kubernetes, we need to take extra steps to reach a similar level of security as with Docker Swarm.

On the other hand, Kubernetes integration with third-party solutions for secrets is much better. For example, plugging in HashiCorp Vault (`https://www.vaultproject.io/`) into a Kubernetes workflow is much smoother than if we'd try to integrate it with Docker Swarm. Using Vault is a better solution than what Kubernetes and Swarm offer.

Even though Kubernetes can be made more secure with Vault and similar products, for now, we are evaluating secrets management that comes with Kubernetes and Docker Swarm. If we exclude third-party solutions, Docker Swarm has a clear advantage over Kubernetes. Its secrets are more secure by default. Even after tweaking Kubernetes (especially etcd), Docker Swarm is still more secure. That does not mean that secrets management with both products does not have a lot to be desired. Both have their shortcomings. However, I must proclaim Docker Swarm as a winner in this round. Its secrets are more secretive.

11
Dividing a Cluster into Namespaces

Applications and corresponding objects often need to be separated from each other to avoid conflicts and other undesired effects.

We might need to separate objects created by different teams. We can, for example, give each team a separate cluster so that they can "experiment" without affecting others. In other cases, we might want to create different clusters that will be used for various purposes. For example, we could have a production and a testing cluster. There are many other problems that we tend to solve by creating different clusters. Most of them are based on the fear that some objects will produce adverse effects on others. We might be afraid that a team will accidentally replace a production release of an application with an untested beta. Or, we might be concerned that performance tests will slow down the whole cluster. Fear is one of the main reasons why we tend to be defensive and conservative. In some cases, it is founded on past experiences. In others, it might be produced by insufficient knowledge of the tools we adopted. More often than not, it is a combination of the two.

The problem with having many Kubernetes clusters is that each has an operational and resource overhead. Managing one cluster is often far from trivial. Having a few is complicated. Having many can become a nightmare and require quite a significant investment in hours dedicated to operations and maintenance. If that overhead is not enough, we must also be aware that each cluster needs resources dedicated to Kubernetes. The more clusters we have, the more resources (CPU, memory, IO) are spent. While that can be said for big clusters as well, the fact remains that the resource overhead of having many smaller clusters is higher than having a single big one.

I am not trying to discourage you from having multiple Kubernetes clusters. In many cases, that is a welcome, if not a required, strategy. However, there is the possibility of using Kubernetes Namespaces instead. In this chapter, we'll explore ways to split a cluster into different segments as an alternative to having multiple clusters.

Creating a Cluster

You know the drill, so let's get the cluster setup over and done with.

 All the commands from this chapter are available in the `11-ns.sh` (https://gist.github.com/vfarcic/6e0a03df4c64a9248fbb68673c1ab71 9) Gist.

```
cd k8s-specs
git pull
minikube start --vm-driver=virtualbox
minikube addons enable ingress
kubectl config current-context
```

Now that the cluster is created (again), we can start exploring Namespaces.

Deploying the first release

We'll start by deploying the `go-demo-2` application and use it to explore Namespaces.

```
cat ns/go-demo-2.yml
```

The definition is the same as the one we used before, so we'll skip the explanation of the YAML file. Instead, we'll jump right away into the deployment.

Unlike previous cases, we'll deploy a specific tag of the application. If this would be a Docker Swarm stack, we'd define the tag of the `vfarcic/go-demo-2` image as an environment variable with the default value set to `latest`. Unfortunately, Kubernetes does not have that option. Since I don't believe that it is a good idea to create a different version of the YAML file for each release, we'll use `sed` to modify the definition before passing it to `kubectl`.

Using `sed` to alter Kubernetes definitions is not a good solution. Heck, it's a terrible one. We should use a templating solution like, for example, Helm (`https://helm.sh/`). However, we are focusing purely on Kubernetes. Helm and other third-party products are out of the scope of this book. So, we'll have to do with a workaround in the form of `sed` commands:

```
IMG=vfarcic/go-demo-2
TAG=1.0
cat ns/go-demo-2.yml \
    | sed -e \
    "s@image: $IMG@image: $IMG:$TAG@g" \
    | kubectl create -f -
```

We declared environment variables `IMG` and `TAG`. Further on, we `cat` the YAML file and piped the output to `sed`. It, in return, replaced `image: vfarcic/go-demo-2` with `image: vfarcic/go-demo-2:1.0`. Finally, the modified definition was piped to `kubectl`. When the `-f` argument is followed with a dash (`-`), `kubectl` uses standard input (`stdin`) instead of a file. In our case, that input is the YAML definition altered by adding the specific `tag` (`1.0`) to the `vfarcic/go-demo-2` image.

Let's confirm that the deployment rolled out successfully:

```
kubectl rollout status \
    deploy go-demo-2-api
```

We'll check whether the application is deployed correctly by sending an HTTP request. Since the Ingress resource we just created has the `host` set to `go-demo-2.com`, we'll have to "fake" it by adding `Host: go-demo-2.com` header to the request:

```
curl -H "Host: go-demo-2.com" \
    "http://$(minikube ip)/demo/hello"
```

The output is as follows:

```
hello, release 1.0!
```

The reason we jumped through so many hoops to deploy a specific release will be revealed soon. For now, we'll assume that we're running the first release in production.

Exploring virtual clusters

Almost all of the system services are running as Kubernetes objects. Kube DNS is a deployment. Minikube Addon Manager, Dashboard, Storage Controller, and nginx Ingress are a few of the system Pods that are currently running in our Minikube cluster. Still, we haven't seen them yet. Even though we executed `kubectl get all` quite a few times, there was not a trace of any of those objects. How can that be? Will we see them now if we list all the objects? Let's check it out.

```
kubectl get all
```

The output shows only the objects we created. There are `go-demo-2` Deployments, ReplicaSets, Services, and Pods. The only system object we can observe is the `kubernetes` Service.

Judging from the current information, if we limit our observations to Pods, our cluster can be described through the *Figure 11-1*.

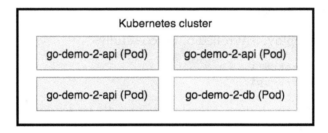

Figure 11-1: The cluster with go-demo-2 Pods

All in all, our cluster runs a mixture of system-level objects and the objects we created, but only the latter is visible. You might be compelled to execute `kubectl get --help` hoping that there is an argument that will allow you to retrieve the information about system level objects. You might think that they are hidden from you by default. That's not the case. They are not hidden. Instead, they do not live in the Namespace we're looking at.

Kubernetes uses Namespaces to create virtual clusters. When we created the Minikube cluster, we got three Namespaces. In a way, each Namespace is a cluster within the cluster. They provide scope for names.

So far our experience tells us that we cannot have two of the same types of objects with the same name. There cannot be, for example, two deployments named `go-demo-2-api`. However, that rule applies only within a Namespace. Inside a cluster, we can have many of same object types with the same name as long as they belong to different Namespaces.

So far, we had the impression that we are operating on the level of a Minikube Kubernetes cluster. That was a wrong assumption. All this time we were inside one Namespace of all the possible Namespaces in the cluster. To be more concrete, all the commands we executed thus far created objects in the `default` Namespace.

Namespaces are so much more than scopes for object names. They allow us to split a cluster among different groups of users. Each of those Namespaces can have different permissions and resources quotas. There are quite a few other things we can do if we combine Namespaces with other Kubernetes services and concepts. However, we'll ignore permissions, quotas, policies, and other things we did not yet explore. We'll focus on Namespaces alone.

We'll start by exploring the pre-defined Namespaces first.

Exploring the existing Namespaces

Now that we know that our cluster has multiple Namespaces, let's explore them a bit.

We can list all the Namespaces through the `kubectl get namespaces` command. As with the most of the other Kubernetes objects and resources, we can also use a shortcut `ns` instead of the full name.

```
kubectl get ns
```

The output is as follows:

```
NAME          STATUS    AGE
default       Active    3m
kube-public   Active    3m
kube-system   Active    3m
```

We can see that three Namespaces were set up automatically when we created the Minikube cluster.

The `default` Namespace is the one we used all this time. If we do not specify otherwise, all the `kubectl` commands will operate against the objects in the `default` Namespace. That's where our `go-demo-2` application is running. Even though we were not aware of its existence, we now know that's where the objects we created are placed.

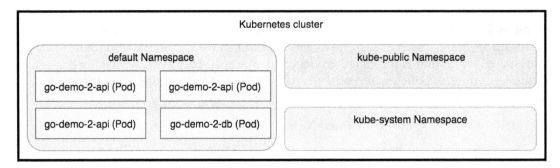

Figure 11-2: The Namespaces and the go-demo-2 Pods

There are quite a few ways to specify a Namespace. For now, we'll use the `--namespace` argument. It is one of the global options that is available for all `kubectl` commands.

The command that will retrieve all the objects from the `kube-public` Namespace is as follows:

```
kubectl --namespace kube-public get all
```

The output states that `No resources` were `found`. That's disappointing, isn't it? Kubernetes does not use the `kube-public` Namespace for its system-level object. All the objects we created are in the `default` Namespace.

The `kube-public` Namespace is readable by all users from all Namespaces. The primary reason for its existence is to provide space where we can create objects that should be visible throughout the whole cluster. A good example is ConfigMaps. When we create one in, let's say, the `default` Namespace, it is accessible only by the other objects in the same Namespace. Those residing somewhere else would be oblivious of its existence. If we'd like such a ConfigMap to be visible to all objects no matter where they are, we'd put it into the `kube-public` Namespace instead. We won't use this Namespace much (if at all).

The `kube-system` Namespace is critical. Almost all the objects and resources Kubernetes needs are running inside it. We can check that by executing the command that follows:

```
kubectl --namespace kube-system get all
```

We retrieved all the objects and resources running inside the `kube-system` Namespace. The output is as follows:

```
NAME                 DESIRED CURRENT UP-TO-DATE AVAILABLE AGE
deploy/kube-dns 1        1        1          1          3m
NAME                       DESIRED CURRENT READY AGE
rs/kube-dns-86f6f55dd5 1       1        1      3m
NAME                 DESIRED CURRENT UP-TO-DATE AVAILABLE AGE
deploy/kube-dns 1        1        1          1          3m
NAME                       DESIRED CURRENT READY AGE
rs/kube-dns-86f6f55dd5 1       1        1      3m
NAME                                   READY STATUS   RESTARTS AGE
po/default-http-backend-j7mlp          1/1   Running  0        3m
po/kube-addon-manager-minikube         1/1   Running  0        4m
po/kube-dns-86f6f55dd5-62dsn           3/3   Running  0        3m
po/kubernetes-dashboard-mtkrl          1/1   Running  1        3m
po/nginx-ingress-controller-fxrhn 1/1   Running  0        3m
po/storage-provisioner                 1/1   Running  0        3m
NAME                         DESIRED CURRENT READY AGE
rc/default-http-backend         1       1       1     3m
rc/kubernetes-dashboard         1       1       1     3m
rc/nginx-ingress-controller 1       1       1     3m
NAME                      TYPE      CLUSTER-IP      EXTERNAL-IP PORT
(S)        AGE
svc/default-http-backend NodePort  10.107.189.73 <none>      80:3
0001/TCP   3m
svc/kube-dns             ClusterIP 10.96.0.10      <none>      53/U
DP,53/TCP 3m
svc/kubernetes-dashboard NodePort  10.96.41.245  <none>      80:3
0000/TCP   3m
```

As we can see, quite a few things are running inside the `kube-system` Namespace. For example, we knew that there is an nginx Ingress controller, but this is the first time we saw its objects. It consists of a Replication Controller `nginx-ingress-controller`, and the Pod it created, `nginx-ingress-controller-fxrhn`.

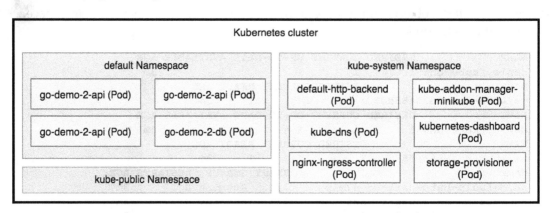

Figure 11-3: The Namespaces and the Pods

As long as the system works as expected, there isn't much need to do anything inside the `kube-system` Namespace. The real fun starts when we create new Namespaces.

Deploying to a new Namespace

Currently, we're running the release 1.0 of the `go-demo-2` application. We can consider it the production release. Now, let's say that the team in charge of the application just made a new release. They ran unit tests and built the binary. They produced a new Docker image and tagged it as `vfarcic/go-demo-2:2.0`. What they didn't do is run functional, performance, and other types of tests that require a running application. The new release is still not ready to be deployed to production so we cannot yet execute a rolling update and replace the production release with the new one. We need to finish running the tests, and for that we need the new release running in parallel with the old one.

We could, for example, create a new cluster that would be used only for testing purposes. While that is indeed a good option in some situations, in others it might be a waste of resources. Moreover, we'd face the same challenge in the testing cluster. There might be multiple new releases that need to be deployed and tested in parallel.

Another option could be to create a new cluster for each release that is to be tested. That would create the necessary separation and maintain the freedom we strive for. However, that is slow. Creating a cluster takes time. Even though it might not look like much, wasting ten minutes (if not more) only on that is too much time. Even if you disagree with me and you think that ten minutes is not that much, such an approach would be too expensive. Every cluster has a resource overhead that needs to be paid. While the overall size of a cluster affects the resource overhead, the number of clusters affects it even more. It's more expensive to have many smaller clusters than a big one. On top of all that, there is the operational cost. While it is often not proportional to the number of clusters, it still increases.

Having a separate cluster for all our testing needs is not a bad idea. We shouldn't discard it, just as we should consider creating (and destroying) a new cluster for each new release. However, before you start creating new Kubernetes clusters, we'll explore how we might accomplish the same goals with a single cluster and with the help of Namespaces.

First things first. We need to create a new Namespace before we can use it.

```
kubectl create ns testing
kubectl get ns
```

The output of the latter command is as follows:

```
NAME          STATUS    AGE
default       Active    5m
kube-public   Active    5m
kube-system   Active    5m
testing       Active    3s
```

We can see that the new Namespace `testing` was created.

We can continue using the `--namespace` argument to operate within the newly created Namespace. However, adding `--namespace` with every command is tedious. Instead, we'll create a new context.

```
kubectl config set-context testing \
    --namespace testing \
    --cluster minikube \
    --user minikube
```

We created a new context called `testing`. It is the same as the `minikube` context, except that it uses the `testing` Namespace.

```
kubectl config view
```

The output, limited to the relevant parts, is as follows:

```
...
contexts:
- context:
    cluster: minikube
    user: minikube
  name: minikube
- context:
    cluster: minikube
    Namespace: testing
    user: minikube
  name: testing
...
```

We can see that there are two contexts. Both are set to use the same `minikube` cluster with the same `minikube` user. The only difference is that one does not have the Namespace set, meaning that it will use the `default`. The other has it set to `testing`.

Now that we have two contexts, we can switch to `testing`.

```
kubectl config use-context testing
```

We switched to the `testing` context that uses the Namespace of the same name. From now on, all the `kubectl` commands will be executed within the context of the `testing` Namespace. That is, until we change the context again, or use the `--namespace` argument.

To be on the safe side, we'll confirm that nothing is running in the newly created Namespace.

```
kubectl get all
```

The output shows that `no resources` were `found`.

If we repeat the same command with the addition of the `--namespace=default` argument, we'll see that the `go-demo-2` objects we created earlier are still running.

Let's continue and deploy a new release. As we explained before, the main objective of the deployment is to provide a means to test the release. It should remain hidden from our users. They should be oblivious to the existence of the new Deployment and continue using the release 1.0 until we are confident that 2.0 works as expected:

```
TAG=2.0
DOM=go-demo-2.com
cat ns/go-demo-2.yml \
    | sed -e \
```

```
"s@image: $IMG@image: $IMG:$TAG@g" \
| sed -e \
"s@host: $DOM@host: $TAG\.$DOM@g" \
| kubectl create -f -
```

Just as before, we used `sed` to alter the image definition. This time, we're deploying the tag `2.0`.

Apart from changing the image tag, we also modified the host. This time, the Ingress resource will be configured with the host `2.0.go-demo-2.com`. That will allow us to test the new release using that domain while our users will continue seeing the production release 1.0 through the domain `go-demo-2.com`.

Let's confirm that the rollout finished.

```
kubectl rollout status \
    deploy go-demo-2-api
```

The output is as follows:

```
deployment "go-demo-2-api" successfully rolled out
```

As you can see, we rolled out the Deployment `go-demo-2-api`, along with some other resources. That means that we have two sets of the same objects with the same name. One is running in the `default` Namespace, while the other (release 2.0) is running in the `testing` Namespace.

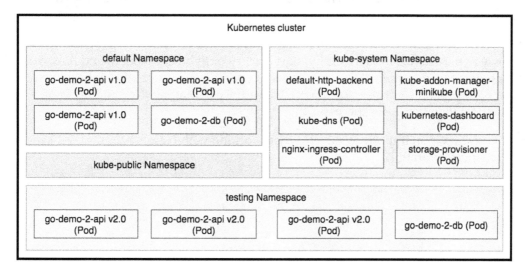

Figure 11-4: The cluster with the new Namespace testing

Before we open a new bottle of Champagne and celebrate the successful deployment of the new release without affecting production, we should verify that both are indeed working as expected.

If we send a request to go-demo-2.com, we should receive a response from the release 1.0 running in the default Namespace.

```
curl -H "Host: go-demo-2.com" \
    "http://$(minikube ip)/demo/hello"
```

The output is as follows:

```
hello, release 1.0!
```

If, on the other hand, we send a request to 2.0.go-demo-2.com, we should get a response from the release 2.0 running in the testing Namespace.

```
curl -H "Host: 2.0.go-demo-2.com" \
    "http://$(minikube ip)/demo/hello"
```

The output is as follows:

```
hello, release 2.0!
```

The result we accomplished through different Namespaces is very similar to what we'd expect by using separate clusters. The main difference is that we did not need to complicate things by creating a new cluster. We saved time and resources by using a new Namespace instead.

If this would be a "real world" situation, we'd run functional and other types of tests using the newly deployed release. Hopefully, those tests would be automated, and they would last for only a few minutes. We'll skip the testing part since it's not within the scope of this chapter (and probably not even the book). Instead, we'll imagine that the tests were executed and that they were successful.

Communication is an important subject when working with Namespaces, so we'll spend a few moments exploring it.

Communicating between Namespaces

We'll create an `alpine-based` Pod that we'll use to demonstrate communication between Namespaces.

```
kubectl config use-context minikube
kubectl run test --image=alpine \
    --restart=Never sleep 10000
```

We switched to the `minikube` context (`default` Namespace) and created a Pod with a container based on the `alpine` image. We let it `sleep` for a long time. Otherwise, the container would be without a process and would stop almost immediately.

Before we proceed, we should confirm that the Pod is indeed running.

```
kubectl get pod test
```

The output is as follows:

```
NAME READY STATUS   RESTARTS AGE
test 1/1    Running 0        10m
```

Please wait a few moments if, in your case, the Pod is not yet ready.

Before we proceed, we'll install `curl` inside the container in the `test` Pod.

```
kubectl exec -it test \
    -- apk add -U curl
```

We already explored communication between objects in the same Namespace. Since the `test` Pod is running in the `default` Namespace, we can, for example, reach the `go-demo-2-api` Service by using the Service name as a DNS name.

```
kubectl exec -it test -- curl \
    "http://go-demo-2-api:8080/demo/hello"
```

The output is as follows:

```
hello, release 1.0!
```

We got the response from the release 1.0 because that's the one running in the same Namespace. Does that mean that we cannot reach Services from other Namespaces?

When we create a Service, it creates a few DNS entries. One of them corresponds to the name of the Service. So, the `go-demo-2-api` Service created a DNS based on that name. Actually, the full DNS entry is `go-demo-2-api.svc.cluster.local`. Both resolve to the same service `go-demo-2-api` which, in this case, runs in the `default` Namespace.

The third DNS entry we got is in the format `<service-name>.<namespace-name>.svc.cluster.local`. In our case, that is `go-demo-2-api.default.svc.cluster.local`. Or, if we prefer a shorter version, we could use `go-demo-2-api.default`.

In most cases, there is no good reason to use the `<service-name>.<namespace-name>` format when communicating with Services within the same Namespace. The primary objective behind the existence of the DNSes with the Namespace name is when we want to reach services running in a different Namespace.

If we'd like to reach `go-demo-2-api` running in the `testing` Namespace from the `test` Pod in the `default` Namespace, we should use the `go-demo-2-api.testing.svc.cluster.local` DNS or, even better, the shorter version `go-demo-2-api.testing`.

```
kubectl exec -it test -- curl \
    "http://go-demo-2-api.testing:8080/demo/hello"
```

This time, the output is different:

```
hello, release 2.0!
```

Kube DNS used the DNS suffix `testing` to deduce that we want to reach the Service located in that Namespace. As a result, we got the response from the release 2.0 of the `go-demo-2` application.

Deleting a Namespace and all its Objects

Another handy feature of the Namespaces is their cascading effect. If, for example, we delete the `testing` Namespace, all the objects and the resources running inside it will be removed as well.

```
kubectl delete ns testing
kubectl -n testing get all
```

We deleted the `testing` Namespace and retrieved all the objects residing in it. The output is as follows:

```
NAME                              READY STATUS       RESTARTS AGE
po/go-demo-2-api-56dfb69dbd-8w6rf 0/1   Terminating  0        2m
po/go-demo-2-api-56dfb69dbd-hrr4b 0/1   Terminating  0        2m
po/go-demo-2-api-56dfb69dbd-ws855 0/1   Terminating  0        2m
po/go-demo-2-db-5b49cc946b-xdd6v  0/1   Terminating  0        2m
```

Please note that, in your case, the output might show more objects. If that's the case, you were too fast, and Kubernetes did not yet have time to remove them.

After a second or two, the only objects in the `testing` Namespace are the Pods with the status `terminating`. Once the grace period is over, they will be removed as well. The Namespace is gone, and everything we created in it was removed as well.

The ability to remove a Namespace and all the objects and the resources it hosts is especially useful when we want to create temporary objects. A good example would be **continuous deployment** (CDP) processes. We can create a Namespace to build, package, test, and do all the other tasks our pipeline requires. Once we're finished, we can simply remove the Namespace. Otherwise, we would need to keep track of all the objects we created and make sure that they are removed before we terminate the CDP pipeline.

Now that the Namespace hosting our release 2.0 is gone, we might want to double check that the production release (1.0) is still running.

```
kubectl get all
```

The output should show the `go-demo-2` Deployments, ReplicaSets, Pods, and Services since we are still using the `default` context.

To be on the safe side, we'll check that a request coming from the `go-demo-2.com` domain still returns a response from the release 1.0.

```
curl -H "Host: go-demo-2.com" \
    "http://$(minikube ip)/demo/hello"
```

As expected, the response is `hello, release 1.0!`.

If this were a continuous deployment pipeline, the only thing left would be to execute rolling updates that would change the image of the production release to `vfarcic/go-demo-2:2.0`. The command could be as follows:

```
kubectl set image \
    deployment/go-demo-2-api \
    api=vfarcic/go-demo-2:2.0 \
    --record
```

What now?

Deploying test releases as part of a continuous deployment process is not the only usage of Namespaces. There can be many other situations when they are useful. We could, for example, give a separate Namespace to each team in our organization. Or we could split the cluster into Namespaces based on the type of applications (for example, monitoring, continuous-deployment, back-end, and so on). All in all, Namespaces are a handy way to separate the cluster into different sections. Some of the Namespaces we'll create will be long-lasting while others, like testing Namespace from our examples, will be short-lived.

The real power behind Namespaces comes when they are combined with authorization policies and constraints. However, we did not yet explore those subjects so, for now, we'll need to limit our Namespaces experience to their basic form.

The chapter is finished, and that means that we are about to remove the cluster.

```
minikube delete
```

 If you'd like to know more about Namespaces, please explore Namespace v1 core (`https://v1-9.docs.kubernetes.io/docs/reference/generated/kubern etes-api/v1.9/#namespace-v1-core`) API documentation.

Kubernetes Namespaces compared to Docker Swarm equivalent (if there is any)

Docker Swarm does not have anything like Kubernetes Namespaces. We cannot split a Swarm cluster into sections. Therefore, we can finish this comparison by saying that Kubernetes is a clear winner regarding this feature since Docker Swarm doesn't have Namespaces. But, that would not be entirely accurate.

Docker Swarm stacks are, in a way, similar to Kubernetes Namespaces. All the services in a stack are uniquely identified through a combination of a stack name and the names of services inside it. By default, all services within a stack can communicate with each other through the stack's default network. Services can speak with those from other stacks only if they are explicitly attached to the same network. All in all, each Swarm stack is separated from other stacks. They are, in a way, similar to Kubernetes Namespaces.

Even though Docker Swarm stacks do provide a functionality similar to Kubernetes Namespaces, their usage is limited. If, for example, we'd like to split the cluster into production and testing, we'd need to create two potentially large Swarm stack files. That would be impractical. Moreover, Kubernetes Namespaces can be associated with resource quotas, policies, and quite a few other things. They do act as genuinely separate clusters. Swarm stacks, on the other hand, are meant to group services into logical entities. While some of the features in Kubernetes Namespaces and Docker Swarm stacks coincide, this is still a clear win for Kubernetes.

Some might argue that they are useful only for bigger clusters or organizations with many teams. I think that's an understatement. Namespaces can be applied to many other use-cases. For example, creating a new Namespace for every continuous integration, delivery, or deployment pipeline is a beneficial practice. We get a unique scope for names, we can mitigate potential problems through resource quotas, and we can increase security. At the end of the process, we can remove the Namespace and all the objects we created inside it.

Kubernetes Namespaces are one of the things that make Kubernetes a more likely candidate for teams that are in need of big clusters as well as those relying heavily on automation. Among the features we compared so far, this is the first real differentiator between the two platforms. Kubernetes is the winner of this round.

12
Securing Kubernetes Clusters

Security implementation is a game between a team with a total lock-down strategy and a team that plans to win by providing complete freedom to everyone. You can think of it as a battle between anarchists and totalitarians. The only way the game can be won is if both blend into something new. The only viable strategy is freedom without sacrificing security (too much).

Right now, our cluster is as secured as it can get. There is only one user (you). No one else can operate it. The others cannot even list the Pods in the cluster. You are the judge, the jury, and the executioner. You are the undisputed king with god-like powers that are not shared with anyone else.

The I-and-only-I-can-do-things strategy works well when simulating a cluster on a laptop. It serves the purpose when the only goal is to learn alone. The moment we create a "real" cluster where the whole company will collaborate (in some form or another), we'll need to define (and apply) an authentication and authorization strategy. If your business is small and there are only a few people who will ever operate the cluster, giving everyone the same cluster-wide administrative set of permissions is a simple and legitimate solution. More often than not, this will not be the case.

Your company probably has people with different levels of trust. Even if that's not the case, different people will require different levels of access. Some will be allowed to do anything they want, while others will not have any type of access. Most will be able to do something in between. We might choose to give everyone a separate Namespace and forbid them from accessing others. Some might be able to operate a production Namespace while others might have interest only in the one assigned for development and testing. The number of permutations we can apply is infinite. Still, one thing is certain. We will need to create an authentication and authorization mechanism. Most likely, we'll need to create permissions that are sometimes applied cluster-wide and, in other cases, limited to Namespaces.

Those and many other policies can be created by employing Kubernetes authorization and authentication.

Accessing Kubernetes API

Every interaction with Kubernetes goes through its API and needs to be authorized. That communication can be initiated through a user or a service account. All Kubernetes objects currently running inside our cluster are interacting with the API through service accounts. We won't go deep into those. Instead, we'll concentrate on the authorization of human users.

Typically, the Kubernetes API is served on a secured port. Our Minikube cluster is no exception. We can check the port from the `kubectl` config.

 All the commands from this chapter are available in the `12-auth.sh` (https://gist.github.com/vfarcic/f2c4a72a1e010f1237eea7283a9a0c11) Gist.

```
kubectl config view \
    -o jsonpath='{.clusters[?(@.name=="minikube")].cluster.server}'
```

We used `jsonpath` to output the `cluster.server` entry located in the cluster with the name `minikube`.

The output is as follows:

```
https://192.168.99.105:8443
```

We can see that `kubectl` accesses the Minikube Kubernetes API on the port `8443`. Since the access is secured, it requires certificates which are stored as the `certificate-authority` entry. Let's take a look.

```
kubectl config view \
    -o jsonpath='{.clusters[?(@.name=="minikube")].cluster.certif
icate-authority}'
```

The output is as follows:

```
/Users/vfarcic/.minikube/ca.crt
```

The `ca.crt` certificate was created with the Minikube cluster and, currently, provides the only way we can access the API.

If this was a "real" cluster, we'd need to enable access for other users as well. We could send them the certificate we already have, but that would be very insecure and would lead to a lot of potential problems. Soon, we'll explore how to enable other users to access the cluster securely. For now, we'll focus on the exploration of the process Kubernetes uses to authorize requests to its API.

Each request to the API goes through three stages. It needs to be authenticated, it needs to be authorized, and it needs to pass the admission control.

The authentication process is retrieving the username from the HTTP request. If the request cannot be authenticated, the operation is aborted with the status code 401.

Once the user is authenticated, the authorization validates whether it is allowed to execute the specified action. The authorization can be performed through ABAC, RBAC, or Webhook modes.

Finally, once a request is authorized, it passes through admission controllers. They intercept requests to the API before the objects are persisted and can modify them. They are advanced topics that we won't cover in this chapter.

Authentication is pretty standard, and there's not much to say about it. On the other hand, admission controllers are too advanced to be covered just yet. Therefore, we're left with authorization as the topic we'll explore in more detail.

Authorizing requests

Just like almost everything else in Kubernetes, authorization is modular. We can choose to use *Node*, *ABAC*, *Webhook*, or *RBAC* authorization. Node authorization is used for particular purposes. It grants permissions to kubelets based on the Pods they are scheduled to run. **Attribute-based access control** (**ABAC**) is based on attributes combined with policies and is considered deprecated in favor of RBAC. Webhooks are used for event notifications through HTTP POST requests. Finally, **Role-based access control** (**RBAC**) grants (or denies) access to resources based on roles of individual users or groups.

Among the four authorization methods, RBAC is the right choice for user-based authorization. Since we'll focus this chapter on the exploration of the means to authorize humans, RBAC will be our primary focus.

What can we do with RBAC? To begin with, we can use it to secure the cluster by allowing access only to authorized users. We can define roles that would grant different levels of access to users and groups. Some could have god-like permissions that would allow them to do almost anything, while others could be limited only to basic non-destructive operations. There can be many other roles in between. We can combine RBAC with Namespaces and allow users to operate only within specific segments of a cluster. There are many other combinations we could apply depending on particular use-cases.

Since I get uncomfortable with too much theory, we'll leave the rest for later and explore details through a few examples. As you might already suspect, we'll kick it off with a new Minikube cluster.

Creating a Cluster

The commands that will create a Minikube cluster are as follows:

```
cd k8s-specs
git pull
minikube start --vm-driver virtualbox

kubectl config current-context
```

 RBAC is installed by default starting from minikube v0.26. If your version is older than that, you'll need to add `--extra-config apiserver.Authorization.Mode=RBAC` argument. Or, better yet, upgrade your minikube binary.

It might come in handy to have a few objects in the cluster so we'll deploy the `go-demo-2` application. We'll use it to test different permutations of the authorization strategies we'll use soon.

The definition of the `go-demo-2` application is the same as the one we created in the previous chapters so we'll skip the explanation and just execute `kubectl create`:

```
kubectl create \
    -f auth/go-demo-2.yml \
    --record --save-config
```

Creating users

The word about Kubernetes awesomeness is spreading in your company. People are becoming curious and would like to try it out. Since you are the Kubernetes guru, it came as no surprise that you received a call from John Doe. He wants to "play" with Kubernetes, but he does not have time to set up his own cluster. Since he knows that you already have a cluster up and running, he'd appreciate if you would let him use yours.

Since you have no intention giving John your certificates, you decide to let him authenticate with his user.

You will have to create certificates for him, so the first step you'll need to do is to verify that OpenSSL is installed on your laptop.

```
openssl version
```

It shouldn't matter which version of OpenSSL is installed. We output the `version` only to verify that the software is working. If the output is something like `command not found: openssl`, you will have to install the binaries (`https://wiki.openssl.org/index.php/Binaries`).

The first thing we'll do is to create a private key for John. We'll assume that John Doe's username is `jdoe`.

```
mkdir keys
openssl genrsa \
    -out keys/jdoe.key 2048
```

We created the directory `keys` and generated a private key `jdoe.key`.

Next, we'll use the private key to generate a certificate:

```
openssl req -new \
    -key keys/jdoe.key \
    -out keys/jdoe.csr \
    -subj "/CN=jdoe/O=devs"
```

A note to Windows users
If you received an error like `Subject does not start with '/'. Problems making Certificate Request`, please replace `-subj "/CN=jdoe/O=devs"` with `-subj "//CN=jdoe\O=devs"` in the previous command and execute it again.

We created the certificate `jdoe.csr` with a specific subject that will help us identify John. `CN` is the username and `O` represents the organization he belongs. John is a developer, so `devs` should do.

For the final certificate, we'll need the cluster's **certificate authority (CA)**. It will be responsible for approving the request and for generating the necessary certificate John will use to access the cluster. Since we used Minikube, the authority is already produced for us as part of the cluster creation. It should be in the `.minikube` directory inside the OS user's home folder. Let's confirm it's there.

```
ls -1 ~/.minikube/ca.*
```

Minikube's directory might be somewhere else. If that's the case, please replace `~/.minikube` with the correct path.

The output is as follows:

```
/Users/vfarcic/.minikube/ca.crt
/Users/vfarcic/.minikube/ca.key
/Users/vfarcic/.minikube/ca.pem
```

Now we can generate the final certificate by approving the certificate sign request `jdoe.csr`.

```
openssl x509 -req \
    -in keys/jdoe.csr \
    -CA ~/.minikube/ca.crt \
    -CAkey ~/.minikube/ca.key \
    -CAcreateserial \
    -out keys/jdoe.crt \
    -days 365
```

Since we feel generous, we made the certificate `jdoe.crt` valid for a whole year (365 days).

To simplify the process, we'll copy the cluster's certificate authority to the `keys` directory.

```
cp ~/.minikube/ca.crt keys/ca.crt
```

Let's check what we generated:

```
ls -1 keys
```

The output is as follows:

```
ca.crt
jdoe.crt
jdoe.csr
jdoe.key
```

John does not need the `jdoe.csr` file. We used it only to generate the final certificate `jdoe.crt`. He will need all the others though.

Apart from the keys, John will need to know the address of the cluster. At the beginning of the chapter, we already created the `jsonpath` that retrieves the server so that part should be easy.

```
SERVER=$(kubectl config view \
    -o jsonpath='{.clusters[?(@.name=="minikube")].cluster.server
}')
echo $SERVER
```

The output is as follows:

```
https://192.168.99.106:8443
```

Equipped with the new certificate, the key, the cluster authority, and the address of the server, John can configure his `kubectl` installation.

Since John is not around, we'll do some role playing and impersonate him.

John will first have to set the cluster using the address and the certificate authority we sent him.

```
kubectl config set-cluster jdoe \
    --certificate-authority \
    keys/ca.crt \
    --server $SERVER
```

We created a new cluster called `jdoe`.

Next, he'll have to set the credentials using the certificate and the key we created for him.

```
kubectl config set-credentials jdoe \
    --client-certificate keys/jdoe.crt \
    --client-key keys/jdoe.key
```

We created a new set of credentials called `jdoe`.

Finally, John will have to create a new context:

```
kubectl config set-context jdoe \
    --cluster jdoe \
    --user jdoe
kubectl config use-context jdoe
```

We created the context `jdoe` that uses the newly created cluster and the user. We also made sure that we're using the newly created context.

Let's take a look at the config:

```
kubectl config view
```

The output, limited to John's settings, is as follows:

```
...
clusters:
- cluster:
    certificate-authority: /Users/vfarcic/IdeaProjects/k8s-specs/
keys/ca.crt
    server: https://192.168.99.106:8443
  name: jdoe
...
contexts:
- context:
    cluster: jdoe
    user: jdoe
  name: jdoe
...
current-context: jdoe
...
users:
- name: jdoe
  user:
    client-certificate: /Users/vfarcic/IdeaProjects/k8s-specs/key
s/jdoe.crt
    client-key: /Users/vfarcic/IdeaProjects/k8s-specs/keys/jdoe.k
ey
...
```

John should be happy thinking that he can access our cluster. Since he's a curious person, he'll want to see the Pods we're running.

```
kubectl get pods
```

The output is as follows:

```
Error from server (Forbidden): pods is forbidden: User "jdoe" can
not list pods in the namespace "default"
```

That's frustrating. John can reach our cluster, but he cannot retrieve the list of Pods. Since hope dies last, John might check whether he is forbidden from seeing other types of objects.

```
kubectl get all
```

The output is a long list of all the objects he's forbidden from seeing.

John picks up his phone to beg not only that you give him the access to the cluster, but also the permissions to "play" with it.

Before we change John's permission, we should explore the components involved in the RBAC authorization process.

Exploring RBAC authorization

Managing Kubernetes RBAC requires knowledge of a few elements. Specifically, we should learn about Rules, Roles, Subjects, and RoleBindings.

A *Rule* is a set of operations (verbs), resources, and API groups. Verbs describe activities that can be performed on resources which belong to different API Groups.

Permissions defined through Rules are additive. We cannot deny access to some resources.

Currently supported verbs are as follows:

Verb	Description
get	Retrieves information about a specific object
list	Retrieves information about a collection of objects
create	Creates a specific object
update	Updates a specific object
patch	Patches a specific object
watch	Watches for changes to an object
proxy	Proxies requests
redirect	Redirects requests
delete	Deletes a specific object
deletecollection	Deletes a collection of objects

If, for example, we'd like to allow a user only to create objects and retrieve their information, we'd use the verbs `get`, `list` and `create`. A verb can be an asterisk (*), thus allowing all verbs (operations).

Verbs are combined with Kubernetes resources. For example, if we'd like to allow a user only to create Pods and retrieve their information, we'd mix `get`, `list` and `create` verbs with the `pods` resource.

The last element of a Rule is the API Group. RBAC uses the `rbac.authorization.k8s.io` group. If we'd switch to a different authorization method, we'd need to change the group as well.

A *Role* is a collection of Rules. It defines one or more Rules that can be bound to a user or a group of users. The vital aspect of Roles is that they are applied to a Namespace. If we'd like to create a role that refers to a whole cluster, we'd use *ClusterRole* instead. Both are defined in the same way, and the only difference is in the scope (Namespace or an entire cluster).

The next piece of the authorization mechanism is *Subjects*. They define entities that are executing operations. A Subject can be a *User*, a *Group*, or a *Service Account*. A User is a person or a process residing outside a cluster. A Service Account is used for processes running inside Pods that want to use the API. Since this chapter focuses on human authentication, we won't explore them right now. Finally, Groups are collections of Users or Service Accounts. Some Groups are created by default (for example, `cluster-admin`).

Finally, we need *RoleBindings*. As the name suggests, they bind Subjects to Roles. Since Subjects define users, RoleBindings effectively bind users (or Groups or Service Accounts) to Roles, thus giving them permissions to perform certain operations on specific objects within a Namespace. Just like roles, RoleBindings have a cluster-wide alternative called *ClusterRoleBindings*. The only difference is that their scope is not limited to a Namespace, but applied to a whole cluster.

All that might seem confusing and overwhelming. You might even say that you did not understand anything. Fear not. We'll explore each of the RBAC components in more details through practical examples. We went through the explanation because people say that things should be explained first, and demonstrated later. I don't think that's a right approach, but I didn't want you to say that I did not provide the theory. In any case, the examples that follow will clarify everything.

Let's go back to John's issue and try to solve it.

Peeking into pre-defined Cluster roles

John is frustrated. He can access the cluster, but he is not permitted to perform any operation. He cannot even list the Pods. Naturally, he asked us to be more generous and allow him to "play" with our cluster.

Since we are not taking anything for granted, we decided that the first action should be to verify John's claim. Is it true that he cannot even retrieve the Pods running inside the cluster?

Before we move further, we'll stop impersonating John and go back to using the cluster with god-like administrative privileges granted to the `minikube` user.

```
kubectl config use-context minikube
kubectl get all
```

Now that we switched to the `minikube` context (and the `minikube` user), we regained full permissions, and `kubectl get all` returned all the objects from the `default` Namespace.

Let's verify that John indeed cannot list Pods in the `default` Namespace.

We could configure the same certificates as those he's using, but that would complicate the process. Instead, we'll use a `kubectl` command that will allow us to check whether we could perform an action if we would be a specific user.

```
kubectl auth can-i get pods --as jdoe
```

The response is `no`, indicating that `jdoe` cannot `get pods`. The `--as` argument is a global option that can be applied to any command. The `kubectl auth can-i` is a "special" command. It does not perform any action but only validates whether an operation could be performed. Without the `--as` argument, it would verify whether the current user (in this case `minikube`) could do something.

We already discussed Roles and ClusterRoles briefly. Let's see whether there are any already configured in the cluster or the `default` namespace.

```
kubectl get roles
```

The output reveals that `no resources` were `found`. We do not have any Roles in the `default` Namespace. That was the expected outcome since a Kubernetes cluster comes with no pre-defined Roles. We'd need to create those we need ourselves.

How about Cluster Roles? Let's check them out.

```
kubectl get clusterroles
```

This time we got quite a few resources. Our cluster already has some Cluster Roles defined by default. Those prefixed with `system:` are Cluster Roles reserved for Kubernetes system use. Modifications to those roles can result in non-functional clusters, so we should not update them. Instead, we'll skip system Roles and focus on those that should be assigned to users.

The output, limited to Cluster Roles that are meant to be bound to users, is as follows:

```
NAME            AGE
admin           1h
cluster-admin   1h
edit            1h
view            1h
```

The Cluster Role with the least permissions is `view`. Let's take a closer look at it:

```
kubectl describe clusterrole view
```

The output, limited to the first few rows, is as follows:

```
Name:          view
Labels:        kubernetes.io/bootstrapping=rbac-defaults
Annotations:   rbac.authorization.kubernetes.io/autoupdate=true
PolicyRule:
  Resources                  Non-Resource URLs Resource Names Verbs
  ---------                  ----------------- -------------- -----
  bindings                   []                []             [get li
st watch]
  configmaps                 []                []             [get li
st watch]
  cronjobs.batch             []                []             [get li
st watch]
  daemonsets.extensions      []                []             [get li
st watch]
  deployments.apps           []                []             [get li
st watch]
  ...
```

It contains a long list of resources, all of them with the get, list, and watch verbs. It looks like it would allow users bound to it to retrieve all the resources. We have yet to validate whether the list of resources is truly complete. For now, it looks like an excellent candidate to assign to users that should have very limited permissions. Unlike Roles that are tied to a specific Namespace, Cluster Roles are available across the whole cluster. That is a significant difference that we'll exploit later on.

Let's explore another pre-defined Cluster Role.

```
kubectl describe clusterrole edit
```

The output, limited to Pods, is as follows:

```
...
pods              [] [] [create delete deletecollection get list p
atch update watch]
pods/attach       [] [] [create delete deletecollection get list p
atch update watch]
pods/exec         [] [] [create delete deletecollection get list p
atch update watch]
pods/log          [] [] [get list watch]
pods/portforward  [] [] [create delete deletecollection get list p
atch update watch]
pods/proxy        [] [] [create delete deletecollection get list p
atch update watch]
pods/status       [] [] [get list watch]
...
```

As we can see, the `edit` Cluster Role allows us to perform any action on Pods. If we go through the whole list, we'd see that the `edit` role allows us to execute almost any operation on any Kubernetes object. It seems like it gives us unlimited permissions. However, there are a few resources that are not listed. We can observe those differences through the Cluster Role `admin`.

```
kubectl describe clusterrole admin
```

If you pay close attention, you'll notice that the Cluster Role `admin` has a few additional entries.

The output, limited to the records not present in the Cluster Role `edit`, is as follows:

```
. . .
localsubjectaccessreviews.authorization.k8s.io [] [] [create]
rolebindings.rbac.authorization.k8s.io          [] [] [create dele
te deletecollection get list patch update watch]
roles.rbac.authorization.k8s.io                 [] [] [create dele
te deletecollection get list patch update watch]
. . .
```

The main difference between `edit` and `admin` is that the latter allows us to manipulate Roles and RoleBindings. While `edit` permits us to do almost any operation related to Kubernetes objects like Pods and Deployments, `admin` goes a bit further and provides an additional capability that allows us to define permissions for other users by modifying existing or creating new Roles and Role Bindings. The major restriction of the `admin` role is that it cannot alter the Namespace itself, nor it can update Resource Quotas (we haven't explored them yet).

There is only one more pre-defined non-system Cluster Role left.

```
kubectl describe clusterrole \
    cluster-admin
```

The output is as follows:

```
Name:          cluster-admin
Labels:        kubernetes.io/bootstrapping=rbac-defaults
Annotations:   rbac.authorization.kubernetes.io/autoupdate=true
PolicyRule:
  Resources Non-Resource URLs Resource Names Verbs
  --------- ------------------ -------------- -----
            [*]                []             [*]
  *.*       []                 []             [*]
```

The Cluster Role `cluster-admin` holds nothing back. An asterisk (*) means everything. It provides god-like powers. A user bound to this role can do anything, without any restrictions. The `cluster-admin` role is the one bound to the `minikube` user. We can confirm that easily by executing:

```
kubectl auth can-i "*" "*"
```

The output is `yes`. Even though we did not really confirm that the `cluster-admin` role is bound to `minikube`, we did verify that it can do anything.

Creating Role bindings and Cluster Role bindings

Role Bindings bind a User (or a Group, or a Service Account) to a Role (or a Cluster Role). Since John wants more visibility to our cluster, we'll create a Role Binding that will allow him to view (almost) all the objects in the `default` namespace. That should be a good start of our quest to give John just the right amount of privileges:

```
kubectl create rolebinding jdoe \
    --clusterrole view \
    --user jdoe \
    --namespace default \
    --save-config
kubectl get rolebindings
```

We created a Role Binding called `jdoe`. Since the Cluster Role `view` already provides, more or less, what we need, we used it instead of creating a whole new Role.

The output of the latter command proved that the new Role Binding `jdoe` was indeed created.

This is a good moment to clarify that a Role Binding does not need to be used only with a Role, but that it can also be combined with a Cluster Role (as in our example). As the rule of thumb, we define Cluster Roles when we think that they might be used cluster-wide (with Cluster Role Bindings) or in multiple Namespaces (with Role Bindings). The scope of the permissions is defined with the type of binding, not with the type of role. Since we used Role Binding, the scope is limited to a single Namespace which, in our case, is the `default`.

Let's take a look at the details of the newly created Role Binding:

```
kubectl describe rolebinding jdoe
Name:        jdoe
Labels:      <none>
Annotations: <none>
Role:
  Kind: ClusterRole
  Name: view
Subjects:
  Kind Name Namespace
  ---- ---- ---------
  User jdoe
```

We can see that the Role Binding `jdoe` has a single subject with the User `jdoe`. It might be a bit confusing that the Namespace is empty and you might think that the Role Binding applies to all Namespaces. Such an assumption would be false. Remember, a Role Binding is always tied to a specific Namespace, and we just described the one created in the `default` Namespace. The same Role Binding should not be available anywhere else. Let's confirm that:

```
kubectl --namespace kube-system \
    describe rolebinding jdoe
```

We described the Role Binding `jdoe` in the Namespace `kube-system`.

The output is as follows:

```
Error from server (NotFound): rolebindings.rbac.authorization.k8s
.io "jdoe" not found
```

The Namespace `kube-system` does not have that Role Binding. We never created it.

It might be easier to verify that our permissions are set correctly through the `kubectl auth can-i` command:

```
kubectl auth can-i get pods \
    --as jdoe
kubectl auth can-i get pods \
    --as jdoe --all-namespaces
```

The first command validated whether the user `jdoe` can `get pods` from the `default` Namespace. The answer was `yes`. The second checked whether the Pods could be retrieved from all the Namespaces and the answer was `no`. Currently, John can only see the Pods from the `default` Namespace, and he is forbidden from exploring those from the other Namespaces.

From now on, John should be able to view the Pods in the default Namespace. However, he works in the same company as we do and we should have more trust in him. Why don't we give him permissions to view Pods in any Namespace? Why not apply the same permissions cluster-wide? Before we do that, we'll delete the Role Binding we created and start over:

```
kubectl delete rolebinding jdoe
```

We'll change John's view permissions so that they are applied across the whole cluster. Instead of executing yet another ad-hoc kubectl commands, we'll define ClusterRoleBinding resource in YAML format so that the change is documented.

Let's take a look at the definition in the auth/crb-view.yml file.

```
cat auth/crb-view.yml
```

The output is as follows:

```
apiVersion: rbac.authorization.k8s.io/v1
kind: ClusterRoleBinding
metadata:
  name: view
subjects:
- kind: User
  name: jdoe
  apiGroup: rbac.authorization.k8s.io
roleRef:
  kind: ClusterRole
  name: view
  apiGroup: rbac.authorization.k8s.io
```

Functionally, the difference is that, this time, we're creating ClusterRoleBinding instead of RoleBinding. Also, we specified the apiGroup explicitly thus making it clear that the ClusterRole is RBAC.

```
kubectl create -f auth/crb-view.yml \
    --record --save-config
```

We created the role defined in the YAML file, and the output confirmed that clusterrolebinding "view" was created.

We can further validate that everything looks correct by describing the newly created role.

```
kubectl describe clusterrolebinding \
    view
```

The output is as follows:

```
Name:           view
Labels:         <none>
Annotations:    <none>
Role:
  Kind:   ClusterRole
  Name:   view
Subjects:
  Kind   Name   Namespace
  ----   ----   ---------
  User   jdoe
```

Finally, we'll impersonate John and validate that he can indeed retrieve the Pods from any Namespace:

```
kubectl auth can-i get pods \
    --as jdoe --all-namespaces
```

The output is `yes`, thus confirming that `jdoe` can view the Pods.

We're so excited that we cannot wait to let John know that he was granted permissions. However, a minute into the phone call, he raises a concern. While being able to view Pods across the cluster is a good start, he will need a place where he and other developers will have more freedom. They will need to be able to deploy, update, delete, and access their applications. They will probably need to do more, but they can't give you more information. They are not yet very experienced with Kubernetes, so they don't know what to expect. He's asking you to find a solution that will allow them to perform actions that will help them develop and test their software without affecting other users of the cluster.

The new request provides an excellent opportunity to combine Namespaces with Role Bindings. We can create a `dev` Namespace and allow a selected group of users to do almost anything in it. That should give developers enough freedom within the `dev` Namespace while avoiding the risks of negatively impacting the resources running in others.

Let's take a look at the `auth/rb-dev.yml` definition:

```
cat auth/rb-dev.yml
```

The output is as follows:

```
apiVersion: v1
kind: Namespace
metadata:
  name: dev
---
```

```
apiVersion: rbac.authorization.k8s.io/v1
kind: RoleBinding
metadata:
  name: dev
  namespace: dev
subjects:
- kind: User
  name: jdoe
  apiGroup: rbac.authorization.k8s.io
roleRef:
  kind: ClusterRole
  name: admin
  apiGroup: rbac.authorization.k8s.io
```

The first section defines the dev Namespace, while the second specifies the binding with the same name. Since we're using RoleBinding (not ClusterRoleBinding), the effects will be limited to the dev Namespace. At the moment, there is only one subject (the User jdoe). We can expect the list to grow with time.

Finally, roleRef uses ClusterRole (not Role) kind. Even though the Cluster Role is available across the whole cluster, the fact that we are combining it with RoleBinding will limit it to the specified Namespace.

The Cluster Role admin has an extensive set of resources and verbs, and the Users (at the moment only jdoe) will be able to do almost anything within the dev Namespace.

Let's create the new resources:

```
ubectl create -f auth/rb-dev.yml \
    --record --save-config
```

The output is as follows:

```
namespace "dev" created
rolebinding "dev" created
```

We can see that the Namespace and the Role Binding were created.

Let's verify that, for example, jdoe can create and delete Deployments:

```
kubectl --namespace dev auth can-i \
    create deployments --as jdoe
kubectl --namespace dev auth can-i \
    delete deployments --as jdoe
```

In both cases, the output was `yes`, confirming that `jdoe` can perform at least `create` and `delete` actions with Deployments. Since we already explored the list of resources defined in the Cluster Role `admin`, we can assume that we'd get the same response if we'd check other operations.

Still, there are a few permissions that are not granted to John. Only the `cluster-admin` role covers all the permissions. The Cluster Role `admin` is very wide, but it does not include all the resources and verbs. We can confirm that with the command that follows:

```
kubectl --namespace dev auth can-i \
    "*" "*" --as jdoe
```

The output is `no`, indicating that there are still a few operations forbidden to John within the `dev` Namespace. Those operations are mostly related to cluster administration that is still in our control.

John is happy. He and his fellow developers have a segment of the cluster where they can do almost anything without affecting other Namespaces.

John is a team player, but he'd also like to have space for himself. Now that he knows how easy it was to create a Namespace for developers, he's wondering whether we could generate one only for him. You are starting to feel like he's an ungrateful guy that will always be asking for more, but you cannot deny the fact that his new request makes sense. It should be easy to create his personal Namespace, so why not grant him that wish.

Let's take a look at yet another YAML definition:

```
cat auth/rb-jdoe.yml
```

The output is as follows:

```
apiVersion: v1
kind: Namespace
metadata:
    name: jdoe
---
apiVersion: rbac.authorization.k8s.io/v1
kind: RoleBinding
metadata:
  name: jdoe
  namespace: jdoe
subjects:
- kind: User
  name: jdoe
  apiGroup: rbac.authorization.k8s.io
roleRef:
```

```
kind: ClusterRole
name: cluster-admin
apiGroup: rbac.authorization.k8s.io
```

This definition is not much different from the previous one. The important change is that the Namespace is `jdoe`, and that John is likely to be its only user, at least until he decides to add someone else. By referencing the role `cluster-admin`, he's given full permissions to do whatever he wants within that Namespace. He might deploy something cool and give others permissions to see it. Everyone likes to show off every once in a while. In any case, that would be his decision. It's his Namespace, and he should be able to do anything he likes inside it.

Let's create the new resources:

```
kubectl create -f auth/rb-jdoe.yml \
    --record --save-config
```

Before we move on, we'll confirm that John can indeed do anything he likes in the `jdoe` Namespace.

```
kubectl --namespace jdoe auth can-i \
    "*" "*" --as jdoe
```

As expected, the response is `yes`, indicating that John is a god-like figure in his own little galaxy.

John loves the idea of having his own Namespace. He'll use it as his playground. However, there's one more thing he's missing. He happens to be a release manager. Unlike his other fellow developers, he's in charge of deploying new releases to production. He's planning to automate that process with Jenkins. However, that will require a bit of time, and until then he should be allowed to perform deployments manually. We already decided that production releases should be deployed to the `default` Namespace, so he'll need additional permissions.

After a short discussion, we decided that the minimum permissions required for the release manager is to perform actions on Pods, Deployments, and ReplicaSets. People with that role should be able to do almost anything related to Pods, while the allowed actions for the Deployments and ReplicaSets should be restricted to `create`, `get`, `list`, `update`, and `watch`. We don't think that they should be able to delete them.

We're not entirely confident that those are all the permissions release managers will need, but it's a good start. We can always update the role later on if the need arises.

John will be the only release manager for now. We'll add more users once we're confident that the role is working as expected.

Now that we have a plan, we can proceed to create a role and a binding that will define the permissions for release managers. The first thing we need to do is to figure out the resources, the Verbs, and the API Groups we'll use. We might want to take a look at the Cluster Role `admin` for inspiration:

```
kubectl describe clusterrole admin
```

The output, limited to Pods, is as follows:

```
. . .
pods              [] [] [create delete deletecollection get list p
atch update watch]
pods/attach       [] [] [create delete deletecollection get list p
atch update watch]
pods/exec         [] [] [create delete deletecollection get list p
atch update watch]
pods/log          [] [] [get list watch]
pods/portforward [] [] [create delete deletecollection get list p
atch update watch]
pods/proxy        [] [] [create delete deletecollection get list p
atch update watch]
pods/status       [] [] [get list watch]
. . .
```

If we'd specify only `pods` as a Rule resource, we would probably not create all the Pods-related permissions we need. Even though most of the operations we can perform on Pods are covered with the `pods` resource, we might need to add a few sub-resources as well. For example, if we'd like to be able to retrieve the logs, we'll need `pods/log` resource. In that case, `pods` would be a namespaced resource, and `log` would be a sub-resource of `pods`.

Deployment and ReplicaSet objects present a different challenge. If we go back to the output of the `kubectl describe clusterrole admin` command, we'll notice that the `deployments` have API Groups. Unlike sub-resources that are separated from resources with a slash (`/`), API Groups are separated with a dot (`.`). So, when we see a resource like `deployments.apps`, it means that it is a Deployment through the API Group `apps`. Core API Groups are omitted.

It'll probably be easier to understand sub-resources and API Groups by exploring the definition in `auth/crb-release-manager.yml`:

```
cat auth/crb-release-manager.yml
```

Most of that definition follows the same formula we already used a few times. We'll focus only on the `rules` section of the `ClusterRole`. It is as follows:

```
...
rules:
- resources: ["pods", "pods/attach", "pods/exec", "pods/log", "po
ds/status"]
  verbs: ["*"]
  apiGroups: [""]
- resources: ["deployments", "replicasets"]
  verbs: ["create", "get", "list", "watch"]
  apiGroups: ["", "apps", "extensions"]
...
```

The level of access release managers' need differs between Pods on the one hand and Deployments and ReplicaSets on the other. Therefore, we split them into two groups.

The first group specifies the `pods` resource together with a few sub-resources (`attach`, `exec`, `log`, and `status`). That should cover all the use cases we explored so far. Since we did not create Pod proxies nor port forwarding, they are not included.

We already said that release managers should be able to perform any operation on Pods, so the `verbs` consist of a single entry with an asterisk (`*`). On the other hand, all Pod resources belong to the same Core group, so we did not have to specify any in the `apiGroups` field.

The second group of rules is set for `deployments` and `replicasets` resources. Considering we decided that we'll be more restrictive with them, we specified more specific `verbs`, allowing release managers only to `create`, `get`, `list`, and `watch`. Since we did not specify `delete`, `deletecollection`, `patch`, and `update` Verbs, release managers will not be able to perform related actions.

As you can see, RBAC Rules can be anything from being very simple to finely tuned to particular needs. It's up to us to decide the level granularity we'd like to accomplish.

Let's create the role and the binding related to release managers.

```
kubectl create \
    -f auth/crb-release-manager.yml \
    --record --save-config
```

To be on the safe side, we'll describe the newly created Cluster Role, and confirm that it has the permissions we need.

```
kubectl describe \
    clusterrole release-manager
```

The output is as follows:

```
Name:           release-manager
Labels:         <none>
Annotations:    kubectl.kubernetes.io/last-applied-configuration={"
apiVersion":"rbac.authorization.k8s.io/v1","kind":"ClusterRole","
metadata":{"annotations":{},"name":"release-manager","namespace":
""},"rules":[{"apiG...
                kubernetes.io/change-cause=kubectl create --filenam
e=auth/crb-release-manager.yml --record=true --save-config=true
PolicyRule:
  Resources              Non-Resource URLs Resource Names Verbs
  ---------              ----------------- -------------- -----
  deployments            []                []             [create
get list update watch]
  deployments.apps       []                []             [create
get list update watch]
  deployments.extensions []                []             [create
get list update watch]
  pods                   []                []             [*]
  pods/attach            []                []             [*]
  pods/exec              []                []             [*]
  pods/log               []                []             [*]
  pods/status            []                []             [*]
  replicasets            []                []             [create
get list update watch]
  replicasets.apps       []                []             [create
get list update watch]
  replicasets.extensions []                []             [create
get list update watch]
```

As you can see, the users assigned to the role can do (almost) anything with Pods, while their permissions with Deployments and ReplicaSets are limited to creation and viewing. They will not be able to update or delete them. Access to any other resource is forbidden.

At the moment, John is the only User bound to the `release-manager` role. We'll impersonate him, and verify that he can, for example, do anything related to Pods:

```
kubectl --namespace default auth \
    can-i "*" pods --as jdoe
```

We'll do a similar type of verification but limited to creation of Deployments.

```
kubectl --namespace default auth \
    can-i create deployments --as jdoe
```

In both cases, we got the answer `yes`, thus confirming that John can perform those actions.

The last verification we'll do, before letting John know about his new permissions, is to verify that he cannot delete Deployments.

```
kubectl --namespace default auth can-i \
    delete deployments --as jdoe
```

The output is `no`, clearly indicating that such action is forbidden.

We phone John to tell him all the things he's now permitted to do within the cluster in his role as release manager.

Let's see a few of the things John would do with his newly generated permissions. We'll simulate that we are him by switching to the `jdoe` context.

```
kubectl config use-context jdoe
```

A quick validation that John can create Deployments could be done with Mongo DB.

```
kubectl --namespace default \
    run db --image mongo:3.3
```

John managed to create the Deployment in the `default` Namespace.

```
kubectl --namespace default \
    delete deployment db
```

The output is as follows:

```
Error from server (Forbidden): replicasets.extensions "db-649df9d
899" is forbidden: User "jdoe" cannot delete replicasets.extensio
ns in the namespace "default"
```

We can see that John cannot delete the ReplicaSet created by the Deployment.

Let's check whether John can perform any action in his own Namespace:

```
kubectl config set-context jdoe \
    --cluster jdoe \
    --user jdoe \
    --namespace jdoe
kubectl config use-context jdoe
kubectl run db --image mongo:3.3
```

We updated the `jdoe` context so that it uses the Namespace with the same name as default. Further on, we made sure that the context is used, and created a new Deployment based on the `mongo` image.

Since John should be able to do anything within his Namespace, he should be able to delete the Deployment as well.

```
kubectl delete deployment db
```

Finally, let's try something that requires a truly high level of permissions:

```
kubectl create rolebinding mgandhi \
    --clusterrole=view \
    --user=mgandhi \
    --namespace=jdoe
```

The output is as follows:

```
rolebinding "mgandhi" created
```

John is even able to add new users to his Namespace and bind them to any role (as long as it does not exceed his permissions).

Replacing Users with Groups

Defining a single user that can access the `jdoe` Namespace was probably the best approach. We expect that only John will want to access it. He is the owner of that Namespace. It's his private playground. Even if he chooses to add more users to it, he'll probably do it independently from our YAML definitions. After all, what's the point of giving him god-like privileges if not to let him do things without asking for our permission or involvement? From our perspective, that Namespace has, and will continue having only one User.

We cannot apply the same logic to the permissions in `default` and `dev` Namespaces. We might choose to give everyone in our organization the `view` role in the `default` Namespace. Similarly, developers in our company should be able to `deploy`, `update`, and `delete` resources from the `dev` Namespace. All in all, we can expect that the number of users in the `view` and `dev` bindings will increase with time. Continually adding new users is repetitive, boring, and error-prone process you probably don't want to do. Instead of becoming a person who hates his tedious job, we can create a system that groups users based on their roles. We already did a step in that direction when we created John's certificate.

Let's take another look at the subject of the certificate we created earlier.

```
openssl req -in keys/jdoe.csr \
    -noout -subject
```

The output is as follows:

```
subject=/CN=jdoe/O=devs
```

We can see that the name is jdoe and that he belongs to the organization devs. We'll ignore the fact that he should probably belong to at least one more organization (release-manager).

If you paid close attention, you probably remember that I mentioned a few times that RBAC can be used with Users, Groups, and Service Accounts. Groups are the same as Users, except that they are validating whether the certificate attached to a request to the API belongs to a specified group (O), instead of a name (CN).

Let's take a quick look at yet another YAML definition.

```
cat auth/groups.yml
```

The output is as follows:

```
apiVersion: v1
kind: Namespace
metadata:
  name: dev
---
apiVersion: rbac.authorization.k8s.io/v1
kind: RoleBinding
metadata:
  name: dev
  namespace: dev
subjects:
- kind: Group
  name: devs
  apiGroup: rbac.authorization.k8s.io
roleRef:
  kind: ClusterRole
  name: admin
  apiGroup: rbac.authorization.k8s.io
---
apiVersion: rbac.authorization.k8s.io/v1
kind: ClusterRoleBinding
metadata:
  name: view
```

```
subjects:
- kind: Group
  name: devs
  apiGroup: rbac.authorization.k8s.io
roleRef:
  kind: ClusterRole
  name: view
  apiGroup: rbac.authorization.k8s.io
```

You'll notice that the Role Binding `dev` and the Cluster Role Binding `view` are almost the same as those we used before. The only difference is in the `subjects.kind` field. This time, we're using `Group` as the value. As a result, we'll grant permissions to all users that belong to the organization `devs`.

We'll need to switch the context back to `minikube` before we apply the changes.

```
kubectl config use-context minikube
kubectl apply -f auth/groups.yml \
    --record
```

The output is as follows:

```
namespace "dev" configured
rolebinding "dev" configured
clusterrolebinding "view" configured
```

We can see that the new definition reconfigured a few resources.

Now that the new definition is applied, we can validate whether John can still create objects inside the `dev` Namespace.

```
kubectl --namespace dev auth \
    can-i create deployments --as jdoe
```

The output is `no`, indicating that `jdoe` cannot `create deployments`. Before you start wondering what's wrong, I should inform you that the response is expected and correct. The `--as` argument is impersonating John, but the certificate is still from `minikube`. Kubernetes has no way of knowing that `jdoe` belongs to the group `devs`. At least, not until John issues a request with his own certificate.

Instead of using the `--as` argument, we'll switch back to the `jdoe` context and try to create a Deployment.

```
kubectl config use-context jdoe
kubectl --namespace dev \
    run new-db --image mongo:3.3
```

This time the output is `deployment "new-db" created`, clearly indicating that the John as a member of the `devs` group can `create deployments`.

From now on, any user with a certificate that has `/O=devs` in the subject will have the same permissions as John within the `dev` Namespace as well as `view` permissions everywhere else. We just saved ourselves from constantly modifying YAML files and applying changes.

What now?

Authorization and authentication are critical security components. Without a proper set of permissions, we are risking exposure with potentially devastating results. Moreover, with appropriate Rules, Roles, and RoleBindings, we can make a cluster not only more secure but also increase collaboration between different members of our organization. The only trick is to find a right balance between tight security and freedom. It takes time until that equilibrium is established.

RBAC combined with Namespaces provides an excellent separation. Without Namespaces, we'd need to create multiple clusters. Without RBAC, those clusters would be exposed or locked down to only a handful of users. The two combined provide an excellent way to increase collaboration without sacrificing security.

We did not explore Service Accounts. They are the third kind of Subjects, besides Users and Groups. We'll leave that for some other time and place since they are used primarily for Pods that need to access the Kubernetes API. This chapter focused on humans and the ways we can enable them to reach a cluster in a safe and controlled manner.

We are still missing one important restriction. By combining Namespaces and RBAC, we can restrict what users can do. However, that will not prevent them from deploying applications that could potentially bring down the whole cluster. We need to add Resource Quotas to the mix. That will be the subject of the next chapter.

For now, we'll destroy the cluster and take a rest. We covered a lot of ground in this chapter. We deserve a break.

```
minikube delete
```

If you'd like to know more about Roles, please explore the Role v1 rbac (`https://v1-9.docs.kubernetes.io/docs/reference/generated/kubern etes-api/v1.9/#role-v1-rbac`) and ClusterRole v1 rbac (`https://v1-9.docs.kubernetes.io/docs/reference/generated/kubern etes-api/v1.9/#clusterrole-v1-rbac`) API documentation. Similarly, you might want to visit the RoleBinding v1 rbac (`https://v1-9.docs.kubernetes.io/docs/reference/generated/kubern etes-api/v1.9/#rolebinding-v1-rbac`) and ClusterRoleBinding v1 rbac (`https://v1-9.docs.kubernetes.io/docs/reference/generated/kubern etes-api/v1.9/#clusterrolebinding-v1-rbac`) API documentation as well.

Kubernetes RBAC compared to Docker Swarm RBAC

Docker has RBAC. Just as Kubernetes, it is organized around subjects, roles, and resource collections. In many aspects, both provide a very similar set of features. Should we quickly declare it a tie?

There is one crucial difference between Kubernetes RBAC and the one provided by Docker. The latter is not free. You'd need to purchase Docker **Enterprise Edition** (**EE**) to secure your cluster beyond "only those with the certificate can access it." If you do have Docker EE, you already made up your mind, and the discussion whether to use one or the other is over. Docker EE is great, and soon it will work not only with Swarm but also with Kubernetes. You bought it, and there's not much reason to switch to something else. However, this comparison focuses on what open source core versions can offer. It ignores third party and enterprise additions.

If we stick with an "only what's in the box" comparison, Kubernetes is a clear winner. It has RBAC, and Docker Swarm doesn't. The problem is not that Swarm doesn't have RBAC, but that it doesn't have any user-based authentication baked in. Therefore, this is a very short comparison. If you don't want to purchase enterprise products, and you do need an authorization and authentication mechanism, Kubernetes is the only option. Just as with Namespaces, Kubernetes shows its strength by the sheer number of features that do not exist in Swarm.

13
Managing Resources

Without an indication how much CPU and memory a container needs, Kubernetes has no other option than to treat all containers equally. That often produces a very uneven distribution of resource usage. Asking Kubernetes to schedule containers without resource specifications is like entering a taxi driven by a blind person.

We have come a long way, from humble beginnings, towards understanding many of the essential Kubernetes object types and principles. One of the most important things we're missing is resource management. Kubernetes was blindly scheduling the applications we deployed so far. We never gave it any indication how much resources we expect those applications to use, nor established any limits. Without them, Kubernetes was carrying out its tasks in a very myopic fashion. Kubernetes could see a lot, but not enough. We'll change that soon. We'll give Kubernetes a pair of glasses that will provide it a much better vision.

Once we learn how to define resources, we'll go further and make sure that certain limitations are set, that some defaults are determined, and that there are quotas that will prevent applications from overloading the cluster.

This chapter is the last piece of the puzzle. Once we solve it, we'll be ready to start thinking about using Kubernetes in production. You won't know everything you should know about operating Kubernetes. No one does. But, you will know just enough to get you going in the right direction.

Creating a cluster

We'll go through almost the same routine as we did in the previous chapters. We'll enter the directory where we cloned the `vfarcic/k8s-specs` repository, pull the latest code, start a Minikube cluster, and so on and so forth. The only new thing we'll do this time is to enable one more addon. We'll add Heapster to the cluster. It's too soon to explain what it does and why we'll need it. That will come later. For now, just remember that there will soon be something in your cluster called Heapster. If you do not already know what it is, consider this a teaser meant to build suspense.

 All the commands from this chapter are available in the `13-resource.sh` (`https://gist.github.com/vfarcic/cc8c44e1e84446dccde3d377c131a5cd`) Gist.

```
cd k8s-specs
git pull
minikube start --vm-driver=virtualbox
kubectl config current-context
minikube addons enable ingress
minikube addons enable heapster
```

Now that the latest code is pulled, the cluster is running, and the add-ons are enabled, we can proceed and explore how to define container memory and CPU resources.

Defining container memory and CPU resources

So far, we did not specify how much memory and CPU containers should use, nor what their limits should be. If we do that, Kubernetes' scheduler will have a much better idea about the needs of those containers, and it'll make much better decisions on which nodes to place the Pods and what to do if they start "misbehaving".

Let's take a look at a modified `go-demo-2` definition:

```
cat res/go-demo-2-random.yml
```

The specification is almost the same as those we used before. The only new entries are in the `resources` section.

The output, limited to the relevant parts, is as follows:

```
...
apiVersion: apps/v1beta2
kind: Deployment
metadata:
  name: go-demo-2-db
spec:
  ...
  template:
    ...
    spec:
      containers:
      - name: db
        image: mongo:3.3
        resources:
          limits:
            memory: 200Mi
            cpu: 0.5
          requests:
            memory: 100Mi
            cpu: 0.3
...
apiVersion: apps/v1beta2
kind: Deployment
metadata:
  name: go-demo-2-api
spec:
  ...
  template:
    ...
    spec:
      containers:
      - name: api
        image: vfarcic/go-demo-2
        ...
        resources:
          limits:
            memory: 100Mi
            cpu: 200m
          requests:
            memory: 50Mi
            cpu: 100m
...
```

We specified `limits` and `requests` entries in the `resources` section.

CPU resources are measured in `cpu` units. The exact meaning of a `cpu` unit depends on where we host our cluster. If servers are virtualized, one `cpu` unit is equivalent to one **virtualized processor** (**vCPU**). When running on bare-metal with Hyperthreading, one `cpu` equals one Hyperthread. For the sake of simplification, we'll assume that one `cpu` resource is one CPU processor (even though that is not entirely true).

If one container is set to use `two` CPU, and the other is set to `one` CPU, the later is guaranteed half as much processing power.

CPU values can be fractioned. In our example, the `db` container has the CPU requests set to `0.5` which is equivalent to half CPU. The same value could be expressed as `500m`, which translates to five hundred millicpu. If you take another look at the CPU specs of the `api` container, you'll see that its CPU limit is set to `400m` and the requests to `200m`. They are equivalent to `0.4` and `0.2` CPUs.

Memory resources follow a similar pattern as CPU. The significant difference is in the units. Memory can be expressed as **K** (**kilobyte**), **M** (**Megabyte**), **G** (**Gigabyte**), **T** (**Terabyte**), **P** (**Petabyte**), and **E** (**Exabyte**). We can also use the power-of-two equivalents `Ki`, `Mi`, `Gi`, `Ti`, `Pi`, and `Ei`.

If we go back to the `go-demo-2-random.yml` definition, we'll see that the `db` container has the limit set to **200Mi** (**two hundred megabytes**) and the requests to **100Mi** (**one hundred megabytes**).

We have already mentioned `limits` and `requests` quite a few times and yet we have not explained what each of them mean.

A limit represents the amount of resources that a container should not pass. The assumption is that we define limits as upper boundaries which, when reached, indicate that something went wrong, as well as a way to guard our resources from being overtaken by a single rouge container due to memory leaks or similar problems.

If a container is restartable, Kubernetes will restart a container that exceeds its memory limit. Otherwise, it might terminate it. Bear in mind that a terminated container will be recreated if it belongs to a Pod (as all Kubernetes-controlled containers do).

Unlike memory, CPU limits never result in termination or restarts. Instead, a container will not be allowed to consume more than the CPU limit for an extended period.

Requests represent the expected resource utilization. They are used by Kubernetes to decide where to place Pods depending on actual resource utilization of the nodes that form the cluster.

If a container exceeds its memory requests, the Pod it resides in might be evicted if a node runs out of memory. Such eviction usually results in the Pod being scheduled on a different node, as long as there is one with enough available memory. If a Pod cannot be scheduled to any of the nodes due to lack of available resources, it enters the pending state waiting until resources on one of the nodes are freed, or a new node is added to the cluster.

Simply discussing the theory of `resources` might be confusing if not followed by practical examples. Therefore, we'll move on and create the resources defined in the `go-demo-2-random.yml` file:

```
kubectl create \
    -f res/go-demo-2-random.yml \
    --record --save-config
kubectl rollout status \
    deployment go-demo-2-api
```

We created the resources and waited until the `go-demo-2-api` Deployment was rolled out. The output of the later command should be as follows:

```
deployment "go-demo-2-api" successfully rolled out
```

Let's describe the `go-demo-2-api` Deployment and see its `limits` and `requests`:

```
kubectl describe deploy go-demo-2-api
```

The output, limited to the `limits` and the `requests`, is as follows:

```
...
Pod Template:
  ...
  Containers:
    ...
    Limits:
        cpu:      200m
        memory:  100Mi
     Requests:
        cpu:      100m
        memory:  50Mi
  ...
```

We can see that the `limits` and the `requests` correspond to those we defined in the `go-demo-2-random.yml` file. That should come as no surprise.

Let's describe the nodes that form the cluster (even though there's only one).

```
kubectl describe nodes
```

The output, limited to the resource-related entries, is as follows:

```
. . .
Capacity:
 cpu:     2
 memory:  2048052Ki
 pods:    110
. . .
Non-terminated Pods: (12 in total)
  Namespace            Name                          CPU Requests CPU Limits
Memory Requests Memory Limits
  ---------            ----                          ------------ ---------- -
--------------- --------------
  default              go-demo-2-api-...             100m (5%)    200m (10%)
50Mi (2%)        100Mi (5%)
  default              go-demo-2-api-...             100m (5%)    200m (10%)
50Mi (2%)        100Mi (5%)
  default              go-demo-2-api-...             100m (5%)    200m (10%)
50Mi (2%)        100Mi (5%)
  default              go-demo-2-db-...              300m (15%)   500m (25%)
100Mi (5%)       200Mi (10%)
  kube-system          default-http-...             10m (0%)     10m (0%)
20Mi (1%)        20Mi (1%)
  kube-system          heapster-...                 0 (0%)       0 (0%)      0
(0%)             0 (0%)
  kube-system          influxdb-grafana-...         0 (0%)       0 (0%)      0
(0%)             0 (0%)
  kube-system          kube-addon-manager-minikube  5m (0%)      0 (0%)
50Mi (2%)        0 (0%)
  kube-system          kube-dns-54cccfbdf8-...      260m (13%)   0 (0%)
110Mi (5%)       170Mi (8%)
  kube-system          kubernetes-dashboard-...     0 (0%)       0 (0%)      0
(0%)             0 (0%)
  kube-system          nginx-ingress-controller-... 0 (0%)       0 (0%)      0
(0%)             0 (0%)
  kube-system          storage-provisioner          0 (0%)       0 (0%)      0
(0%)             0 (0%)
Allocated resources:
  (Total limits may be over 100 percent, i.e., overcommitted.)
  CPU Requests CPU Limits  Memory Requests Memory Limits
  ------------ ----------  --------------- --------------
  875m (43%)   1110m (55%) 430Mi (22%)     690Mi (36%)
. . .
```

The `Capacity` represents the overall capacity of a node. In our case, the `minikube` node has 2 CPUs, 2GB of RAM, and can run up to one hundred and ten Pods. Those are the upper limits imposed by the hardware or, in our case, the size of the VM created by Minikube.

Further down is the `Non-terminated Pods` section. It lists all the Pods with the CPU and memory limits and requests. We can, for example, see that the `go-demo-2-db` Pod has the memory limit set to `100Mi`, which is `5%` of the capacity. Similarly, we can see that not all Pods have specified resources. For example, the `heapster-snq2f` Pod has all the values set to `0`. Kubernetes will not be able to handle those Pods appropriately. However, since this is a demo cluster, we'll give the Minikube authors a pass and ignore the lack of resource specification.

Finally, the `Allocated resources` section provides summed values from all the Pods. We can, for example, see that the CPU limits are `55%`. Limits can be even higher than `100%`, and that would not necessarily be a thing to worry about. Not all the containers will have memory and CPU bursts over the requested values. Even if that happens, Kubernetes will know what to do.

What truly matters is that the total amount of requested memory and CPU is within the limits of the capacity. That, however, leads us to an interesting question. What is the basis for the resources we defined so far?

Measuring actual memory and CPU consumption

How did we come up with the current memory and CPU values? Why did we set the memory of the MongoDB to `100Mi`? Why not `50Mi` or `1Gi`? It is embarrassing to admit that the values we have right now are random. I guessed that the containers based on the `vfarcic/go-demo-2` image require less resources than Mongo database, so their values are comparatively smaller. That was the only criteria I used to define the resources.

Before you frown upon my decision to put random values for resources, you should know that we do not have any metrics to back us up. Anybody's guess is as good as mine.

The only way to truly know how much memory and CPU an application uses is by retrieving metrics. We'll use Heapster (`https://github.com/kubernetes/heapster`) for that purpose.

Heapster collects and interprets various signals like compute resource usage, lifecycle events, and so on. In our case, we're interested only in CPU and memory consumption of the containers we're running in our cluster.

When we created the cluster, we enabled the `heapster` addon and Minikube deployed it as a system application. Not only that, but it also deployed InfluxDB (`https://github.com/influxdata/influxdb`) and Grafana (`https://grafana.com/`). The former is the database where Heapster stores data and the latter can be used to visualize it through dashboards.

You might be inclined to think that Heapster, InfluxDB, and Grafana might be the solution for your monitoring needs. I advise against such a decision. We're using Heapster only because it's readily available as a Minikube addon. The idea to develop Heapster as a tool for monitoring needs is mostly abandoned. Its primary focus is to serve as an internal tool required for some of the Kubernetes features. Instead, I'd suggest a combination of Prometheus (`https://prometheus.io/`) combined with the Kubernetes API as the source of metrics and Alertmanager (`https://prometheus.io/docs/alerting/alertmanager/`) for your alerting needs. However, those tools are not in the scope of this chapter, so you might need to educate yourself from their documentation, or wait until the sequel to this book is published (the tentative name is *Advanced Kubernetes*).

 Use Heapster only as a quick-and-dirty way to retrieve metrics. Explore the combination of Prometheus and Alertmanager for your monitoring and alerting needs.

Now that we clarified what Heapster is good for, as well as what it isn't, we can proceed and confirm that it is indeed running inside our cluster.

```
kubectl --namespace kube-system \
    get pods
```

The output is as follows:

NAME	READY	STATUS	RESTARTS	AGE
default-http-backend-...	1/1	Running	0	59m
heapster-...	1/1	Running	0	59m
influxdb-grafana-...	2/2	Running	0	59m
kube-addon-manager-minikube	1/1	Running	0	59m
kube-dns-54cccfbdf8-...	3/3	Running	0	59m
kubernetes-dashboard-...	1/1	Running	0	59m
nginx-ingress-controller-...	1/1	Running	0	59m
storage-provisioner	1/1	Running	0	59m

As you can see, the `heapster` and `influxdb-grafana` Pods are running.

We'll explore Heapster just enough to retrieve the data we need. For that, we'll need access to its API. However, Minikube didn't expose its port so that'll be the first thing we'll do:

```
kubectl --namespace kube-system \
    expose rc heapster \
    --name heapster-api \
    --port 8082 \
    --type NodePort
```

We'll need to find out which `NodePort` was created for us. To do that, we need to get familiar with the JSON definition of the service:

```
kubectl --namespace kube-system \
    get svc heapster-api \
    -o json
```

We are looking for the `nodePort` entry inside the `spec.ports` array. The command that retrieves it and assigns the output to the `PORT` variable is as follows:

```
PORT=$(kubectl --namespace kube-system \
    get svc heapster-api \
    -o jsonpath="{.spec.ports[0].nodePort}")
```

We used the `jsonpath` output to retrieve only `nodePort` of the first (and the only) entry of the `spec.ports` array.

Let's try a very simple query of the Heapster API.

```
BASE_URL="http://$(minikube ip):$PORT/api/v1/model/namespaces/default/pods"

curl "$BASE_URL"
```

The output of the `curl` request is as follows:

```
[
  "go-demo-2-api-796db5987d-dm69g",
  "go-demo-2-db-bf6f5b486-p9vhj",
  "go-demo-2-api-796db5987d-5t84b",
  "go-demo-2-api-796db5987d-99nh6"
]
```

We don't really need Heapster to retrieve the list of Pods. What we do need are metrics of one of the Pods. For that, we need it's name.

We'll use a similar command we used to retrieve Heapster's service port.

```
DB_POD_NAME=$(kubectl get pods \
    -l service=go-demo-2 \
    -l type=db \
    -o jsonpath="{.items[0].metadata.name}")
```

We retrieved all the Pods with the labels `service=go-demo-2` and `type=db`, and formatted the output so that `metadata.name` from the first item is retrieved. The value is stored as the `DB_POD_NAME` variable.

Now we can take a look at the available metrics of the `db` container inside the Pod.

```
curl "$BASE_URL/$DB_POD_NAME/containers/db/metrics"
```

The output is as follows:

```
[
  "memory/rss",
  "cpu/usage_rate",
  "cpu/request",
  "memory/usage",
  "memory/major_page_faults_rate",
  "cpu/limit",
  "memory/page_faults",
  "memory/major_page_faults",
  "uptime",
  "memory/limit",
  "cpu/usage",
  "memory/page_faults_rate",
  "memory/working_set",
  "restart_count",
  "memory/request"
]
```

As you can see, most of the available metrics are related to memory and CPU.

Let's see whether memory usage indeed corresponds with the memory resources we defined for the `go-demo-2-db` Deployment. As a reminder, we set memory request to `100Mi` and memory limit to `200Mi`.

A request that retrieves memory usage of the `db` container is as follows.

```
curl "$BASE_URL/$DB_POD_NAME/containers/db/metrics/memory/usage"
```

The output, limited only to a few entries, is as follows:

```
{
  "metrics": [
    ...
    {
      "timestamp": "2018-02-01T20:24:00Z",
      "value": 38334464
    },
    {
      "timestamp": "2018-02-01T20:25:00Z",
      "value": 38342656
    }
  ],
  "latestTimestamp": "2018-02-01T20:25:00Z"
}
```

We can see that memory usage is somewhere around 38 megabytes. That's quite a big difference from `100Mi` we set. Sure, this service is not under real production load but, since we're simulating a "real" cluster, we'll pretend that `38Mi` is indeed memory usage under "real" conditions. That means that we overestimated the requests by assigning a value almost three times larger than the actual usage.

How about CPU? Did we make such a colossal mistake with it as well? As a reminder, we set the CPU request to `0.3` and the limit to `0.5`.

```
curl "$BASE_URL/$DB_POD_NAME/containers/db/metrics/cpu/usage_rate"
```

The output, limited to only a few entries, is as follows.

```
{
  "metrics": [
    ...
    {
      "timestamp": "2018-02-01T20:25:00Z",
      "value": 5
    },
    {
      "timestamp": "2018-02-01T20:26:00Z",
      "value": 4
    }
  ],
  "latestTimestamp": "2018-02-01T20:26:00Z"
}
```

As we can see, the CPU usage is around 5m or 0.005 CPU. We, again, made a huge mistake with resource specification. Our value is around sixty times higher.

Such deviations between our expectations (resource requests and limits) and the actual usage can lead to very unbalanced scheduling with undesirable effects. We'll correct the resources soon. For now, we'll explore what happens if the amount of resources is below the actual usage.

Exploring the effects of discrepancies between resource specifications and resource usage

Let's take a look at a slightly modified version of the go-demo-2 definition:

```
cat res/go-demo-2-insuf-mem.yml
```

When compared with the previous definition, the difference is only in resources of the db container in the go-demo-2-db Deployment.

The output, limited to the relevant parts, is as follows:

```
apiVersion: apps/v1beta2
kind: Deployment
metadata:
  name: go-demo-2-db
spec:
  ...
  template:
    ...
    spec:
      containers:
      - name: db
        image: mongo:3.3
        resources:
          limits:
            memory: 10Mi
            cpu: 0.5
          requests:
            memory: 5Mi
            cpu: 0.3
```

The memory limit is set to 10Mi and the request to 5Mi. Since we already know from Heapster's data that MongoDB requires around 38Mi, memory resources are, this time, much lower than the actual usage.

Let's see what will happen when we apply the new configuration:

```
kubectl apply \
    -f res/go-demo-2-insuf-mem.yml \
    --record

kubectl get pods
```

We applied the new configuration and retrieved the Pods. The output is as follows:

```
NAME               READY STATUS     RESTARTS AGE
go-demo-2-api-...  1/1   Running    0        1m
go-demo-2-api-...  1/1   Running    0        1m
go-demo-2-api-...  1/1   Running    0        1m
go-demo-2-db-...   0/1   OOMKilled  2        17s
```

In your case, the status might not be OOMKilled. If so, wait for a while longer and retrieve the Pods again. The status should eventually change to CrashLoopBackOff.

As you can see, the status of the go-demo-2-db Pod is OOMKilled (**Out Of Memory Killed**). Kubernetes detected that the actual usage is way above the limit and it declared the Pod as a candidate for termination. The container was terminated shortly afterwards. Kubernetes will recreate the terminated container a while later only to discover that the memory usage is still above the limit. And so on, and so forth. The loop will continue.

> A container can exceed its memory request if the node has enough available memory. On the other hand, a container is not allowed to use more memory than the limit. When that happens, it becomes a candidate for termination.

Let's describe the Deployment and see the status of the db container:

```
kubectl describe pod go-demo-2-db
```

The output, limited to relevant parts, is as follows:

```
...
Containers:
  db:
    ...
    Last State:    Terminated
      Reason:      OOMKilled
```

```
        Exit Code:    137
        ...
Events:
  Type      Reason  Age           From          Message
  ----      ------  ----          ----          -------
  ...
  Warning BackOff 3s (x8 over 1m) kubelet, minikube Back-off restarting
failed container
```

We can see that the last state of the db container is OOMKilled. When we explore the events, we can see that, so far, the container was restarted eight times with the reason BackOff.

Let's explore another possible situation through yet another updated definition:

`cat res/go-demo-2-insuf-node.yml`

Just as before, the change is only in the resources of the go-demo-2-db Deployment. The output, limited to the relevant parts, is as follows:

```
apiVersion: apps/v1beta2
kind: Deployment
metadata:
  name: go-demo-2-db
spec:
  ...
  template:
    ...
    spec:
      containers:
      - name: db
        image: mongo:3.3
        resources:
          limits:
            memory: 8Gi
            cpu: 0.5
          requests:
            memory: 4Gi
            cpu: 0.3
```

This time, we specified that the requested memory is twice as much as the total memory of the node (2GB). The memory limit is even higher.

Let's apply the change and observe what happens:

```
kubectl apply \
    -f res/go-demo-2-insuf-node.yml \
    --record
```

```
kubectl get pods
```

The output of the latter command is as follows:

```
NAME                             READY STATUS  RESTARTS AGE
go-demo-2-api-796db5987d-8wbk4 1/1   Running 0        8m
go-demo-2-api-796db5987d-w6mnx 1/1   Running 0        8m
go-demo-2-api-796db5987d-wtz4q 1/1   Running 0        9m
go-demo-2-db-5d5c46bc7c-d676j  0/1   Pending 0        13s
```

This time, the status of the Pod is `Pending`. Kubernetes could not place it anywhere in the cluster and is waiting until the situation changes.

Even though memory requests are associated with containers, it often makes sense to translate them into Pods requirements. We can say that the requested memory of a Pod is the sum of the requests of all the containers that form it. In our case, the Pod has only one container, so the requests of the two are equal. The same can be said for limits.

During the scheduling process, Kubernetes sums the requests of a Pod and looks for a node that has enough available memory and CPU. If Pod's request cannot be satisfied, it is placed in the pending state in the hope that resources will be freed on one of the nodes, or that a new server will be added to the cluster. Since such a thing will not happen in our case, the Pod created through the `go-demo-2-db` Deployment will be pending forever, unless we change the memory request again.

 When Kubernetes cannot find enough free resources to satisfy the resource requests of all the containers that form a Pod, it changes its state to `Pending`. Such Pods will remain in this state until requested resources become available.

Let's describe the `go-demo-2-db` Deployment and see whether there is some additional useful information in it.

```
kubectl describe pod go-demo-2-db
```

The output, limited to the events section, is as follows:

```
. . .
Events:
  Type     Reason          Age                From              Message
  ----     ------          ----               ----              -------
  Warning FailedScheduling 11s (x7 over 42s) default-scheduler 0/
1 nodes are available: 1 Insufficient memory.
```

We can see that it has already `FailedScheduling` seven times and that the message clearly indicates that there is `Insufficient memory`.

We'll revert to the initial definition. Even though we know that its resources are incorrect, we know that it satisfies all the requirements and that all the Pods will be scheduled successfully:

```
kubectl apply \
    -f res/go-demo-2-random.yml \
    --record

kubectl rollout status \
    deployment go-demo-2-db

kubectl rollout status \
    deployment go-demo-2-api
```

Now that all the Pods are running, we should try to write a better definition. For that, we need to observe memory and CPU usage and use that information to decide the requests and the limits.

Adjusting resources based on actual usage

We saw some of the effects that can be caused by a discrepancy between resource usage and resource specification. It's only natural that we should adjust our specification to reflect the actual memory and CPU usage better.

Let's start with the database:

```
DB_POD_NAME=$(kubectl get pods \
    -l service=go-demo-2 \
    -l type=db \
    -o jsonpath="{.items[0].metadata.name}")

curl "$BASE_URL/$DB_POD_NAME/containers/db/metrics/memory/usage"

curl "$BASE_URL/$DB_POD_NAME/containers/db/metrics/cpu/usage_rate"
```

We retrieved the name of the database Pod and used it to obtain memory and CPU usage of the `db` container. As a result, we now know that memory usage is somewhere between `30Mi` and `40Mi`. Similarly, we know that the CPU consumption is somewhere around `5m`

Let's take the same metrics for the `api` container.

```
API_POD_NAME=$(kubectl get pods \
    -l service=go-demo-2 \
    -l type=api \
    -o jsonpath="{.items[0].metadata.name}")

curl "$BASE_URL/$API_POD_NAME/containers/api/metrics/memory/usage"

curl
  "$BASE_URL/$API_POD_NAME/containers/api/metrics/cpu/usage_rate"
```

As expected, an `api` container uses even less resources than MongoDB. Its memory is somewhere between `3Mi` and `7Mi`. Its CPU usage is so low that Heapster rounded it to `0m`.

Equipped with this knowledge, we can proceed to update our YAML definition. Still, before we do that, I need to clarify a few things.

The metrics we collected are based on applications that do nothing. Once they start getting real load and start hosting production size data, the metrics would change drastically. What you need is a way to predict how much resources an application will use in production, not in a simple test environment. You might be inclined to run stress tests that would simulate production setup. Do that. It's significant, but it does not necessarily result in real production-like behavior.

Replicating production and behavior of real users is tough. Stress tests will get you half-way. For the other half, you'll have to monitor your applications in production and, among other things, adjust resources accordingly. There are many additional things you should take into account but, for now, I wanted to stress that applications that do nothing are not a good measure of resource usage. Still, we're going to imagine that the applications we're currently running are under production-like load and that the metrics we retrieved represent how the applications would behave in production.

 Simple test environments do not reflect production usage of resources. Stress tests are a good start, but not a complete solution. Only production provides real metrics.

Let's take a look at a new definition that better represents resource usage of the applications.

```
cat res/go-demo-2.yml
```

The output, limited to the relevant parts, is as follows:

```
apiVersion: apps/v1beta2
kind: Deployment
metadata:
  name: go-demo-2-db
spec:
  ...
  template:
    ...
    spec:
      containers:
      - name: db
        image: mongo:3.3
        resources:
          limits:
            memory: "100Mi"
            cpu: 0.1
          requests:
            memory: "50Mi"
            cpu: 0.01
...
apiVersion: apps/v1beta2
kind: Deployment
metadata:
  name: go-demo-2-api
spec:
  ...
  template:
    ...
    spec:
      containers:
      - name: api
        image: vfarcic/go-demo-2
        ...
        resources:
          limits:
            memory: "10Mi"
            cpu: 0.1
          requests:
            memory: "5Mi"
            cpu: 0.01
```

That is much better. The resource requests are only slightly higher than the current usage. We set the memory limits value to double that of the requests so that the applications have ample resources for occasional (and short-lived) bursts of additional memory consumption. CPU limits are much higher than requests mostly because I was too embarrassed to put anything less than a tenth of a CPU as the limit. Anyways, the point is that requests are close to the observed usage and limits are higher so that applications have some space to breathe in case of a temporary spike in resource usage.

All that's left is to apply the new definition:

```
kubectl apply \
    -f res/go-demo-2.yml \
    --record

kubectl rollout status \
    deployment go-demo-2-api
```

The `deployment "go-demo-2-api"` was successfully rolled out, and we can move onto the next subject.

Exploring quality of service (QoS) contracts

When we send a request to Kubernetes API to create a Pod (directly or through one of the Controllers), it initiates the scheduling process. What happens next or, to be more precise, where it will decide to run a Pod, depends hugely on the resources we defined for the containers that form the Pod. In a nutshell, Kubernetes will decide to deploy a Pod, whenever it is possible, inside one of the nodes that has enough available memory.

When memory requests are defined, Pods will get the memory they requested. If memory usage of one of the containers exceeds the requested amount, or if some other Pod needs that memory, the Pod hosting it might be killed. Please note that I wrote that a Pod *might* be killed. Whether that will happen depends on the requests from other Pods and the available memory in the cluster. On the other hand, containers that exceed their memory limits are always killed (unless it was a temporary situation).

CPU requests and limits work a bit differently. Containers that exceed specified CPU resources are not killed. Instead, they are throttled.

Now that we shed a bit of light around Kubernetes' killing activities, we should note that (almost) nothing happens randomly. When there aren't enough resources to serve the needs of all the Pods, Kubernetes will destroy one or more containers. The decision which one it will be is anything but random. Who will be the unlucky one depends on the assigned **Quality of Service (QoS)**. Those with the lowest priority are killed first.

Since this might be the first time you heard about QoS, we'll spend some time explaining what they are and how they work.

Pods are the smallest units in Kubernetes. Since almost everything ends up as a Pod (one way or another), it is no wonder that Kubernetes promises specific guarantees to all the Pods running inside the cluster. Whenever we send a request to the API to create or update a Pod, it gets assigned one of the QoS classes. They are used to make decisions such as where to schedule a Pod or whether to evict it.

We do not specify QoS directly. Instead, they are assigned based on the decisions we make with resource requests and limits.

At the moment, three QoS classes are available. Each Pod can have the *Guaranteed*, the *Burstable*, or the *BestEffort* QoS.

Guaranteed QoS is assigned only to Pods which have set both CPU requests and limits, and memory requests and limits for all of their containers. The Pods we created with the last definition match that criteria. However, there's one more necessary condition that must be met. The requests and limits values must be the same per container. Still, there is a catch. When a container specifies only limits, requests are automatically set to the same values. In other words, containers without requests will have Guaranteed QoS if their limits are defined.

We can summarize criteria for Guaranteed QoS as follows:

- Both memory and CPU limits must be set
- Memory and CPU requests must be set to the same values as the limits, or they can be left empty, in which case they default to the limits (we'll explore them soon)

Pods with Guaranteed QoS assigned are the top priority and will never be killed unless they exceed their limits or are unhealthy. They are the last to go when things go wrong. As long as their resource usage is within limits, Kubernetes will always choose to kill Pods with other QoS assignments when resource usage is over the capacity.

Let's move to the next QoS.

Burstable QoS is assigned to Pods that do not meet the criteria for Guaranteed QoS but have at least one container with memory or CPU requests defined.

Pods with the Burstable QoS are guaranteed minimal (requested) memory usage. They might be able to use more resources if they are available. If the system is under pressure and needs more available memory, containers belonging to the Pods with the Burstable QoS are more likely to be killed than those with Guaranteed QoS when there are no Pods with the BestEffort QoS. You can consider the Pods with this QoS as medium priority.

Finally, we reached the last QoS.

BestEffort QoS is given to the Pods that do not qualify as Guaranteed or Burstable. They are Pods that consist of containers that have none of the resources defined. Containers in Pods qualified as BestEffort can use any available memory they need.

When in need of more resources, Kubernetes will start killing containers residing in the Pods with BestEffort QoS. They are the lowest priority, and they are the first to disappear when more memory is needed.

Let's take a look which QoS our `go-demo-2-db` Pod got assigned.

```
kubectl describe pod go-demo-2-db
```

The output, limited to the relevant parts, is as follows:

```
...
Containers:
  db:
    ...
    Limits:
      cpu:     100m
      memory:  100Mi
    Requests:
      cpu:     10m
      memory:  50Mi
...
QoS Class:        Burstable
...
```

The Pod was assigned Burstable QoS. Its limits are different from requests, so it did not qualify for Guaranteed QoS. Since its resources are set, and it is not eligible for Guaranteed QoS, Kubernetes assigned it the second best QoS.

Now, let's take a look at a slightly modified definition:

```
cat res/go-demo-2-qos.yml
```

The output, limited to the relevant parts, is as follows:

```
apiVersion: apps/v1beta2
kind: Deployment
metadata:
  name: go-demo-2-db
spec:
  ...
  template:
    ...
    spec:
      containers:
      - name: db
        image: mongo:3.3
        resources:
          limits:
            memory: "50Mi"
            cpu: 0.1
          requests:
            memory: "50Mi"
            cpu: 0.1
...
apiVersion: apps/v1beta2
kind: Deployment
metadata:
  name: go-demo-2-api
spec:
  ...
  template:
    ...
    spec:
      containers:
      - name: api
        image: vfarcic/go-demo-2
...
```

This time, we specified that both `cpu` and `memory` should have the same values for both the `requests` and the `limits` for the containers that will be created with the `go-demo-2-db` Deployment. As a result, it should be assigned Guaranteed QoS.

The containers of the `go-demo-2-api` Deployment are void of any `resources` definitions and, therefore, will be assigned BestEffort QoS.

Let's confirm that both assumptions (not to say guesses) are indeed correct.

```
kubectl apply \
    -f res/go-demo-2-qos.yml \
    --record
```

```
kubectl rollout status \
    deployment go-demo-2-db
```

We applied the new definition and output the rollout status of the `go-demo-2-db` Deployment.

Now we can describe the Pod created thought the `go-demo-2-db` Deployment and check its QoS.

kubectl describe pod go-demo-2-db

The output, limited to the relevant parts, is as follows:

```
Containers:
  db:
    ...
    Limits:
      cpu:     100m
      memory: 50Mi
    Requests:
      cpu:     100m
      memory: 50Mi
  ...
QoS Class: Guaranteed
...
```

Memory and CPU limits and requests are the same and, as a result, the QoS is `Guaranteed`.

Let's check the QoS of the Pods created through the `go-demo-2-api` Deployment.

kubectl describe pod go-demo-2-api

The output, limited to the relevant parts, is as follows:

```
...
QoS Class:        BestEffort
...
QoS Class:        BestEffort
...
QoS Class:        BestEffort
...
```

The three Pods created through the `go-demo-2-api` Deployment are without any resources definitions and, therefore, their QoS is set to `BestEffort`.

We won't be needing the objects we created so far so we'll remove them before moving onto the next subject.

```
kubectl delete \
    -f res/go-demo-2-qos.yml
```

Defining resource defaults and limitations within a namespace

We already learned how to leverage Kubernetes namespaces to create clusters within a cluster. When combined with RBAC, we can create namespaces and give users permissions to use them without exposing the whole cluster. Still, one thing is missing.

We can, let's say, create a `test` namespace and allow users to create objects without permitting them to access other namespaces. Even though that is better than allowing everyone full access to the cluster, such a strategy would not prevent people from bringing the whole cluster down or affecting the performance of applications running in other namespaces. The piece of the puzzle we're missing is resource control on the namespace level.

We already discussed that every container should have resource `limits` and `requests` defined. That information helps Kubernetes schedule Pods more efficiently. It also provides it with the information it can use to decide whether a Pod should be evicted or restarted. Still, the fact that we can specify `resources` does not mean that we are forced to define them. We should have the ability to set default `resources` that will be applied when we forget to specify them explicitly.

Even if we define default `resources`, we also need a way to set limits. Otherwise, everyone with permissions to deploy a Pod can potentially run an application that requests more resources than we're willing to give.

All in all, our next task is to define default requests and limits as well as to specify minimum and maximum values someone can define for a Pod.

We'll start by creating a `test` Namespace.

```
kubectl create namespace test
```

With a playground namespace created, we can take a look at a new definition.

```
cat res/limit-range.yml
```

The output is as follows:

```
apiVersion: v1
kind: LimitRange
metadata:
  name: limit-range
spec:
  limits:
  - default:
      memory: 50Mi
      cpu: 0.2
    defaultRequest:
      memory: 30Mi
      cpu: 0.05
    max:
      memory: 80Mi
      cpu: 0.5
    min:
      memory: 10Mi
      cpu: 0.01
    type: Container
```

We specified that the resource should be of `LimitRange` kind. It's `spec` has four `limits`.

The `default` limit and `defaultRequest` entries will be applied to the containers that do not specify resources. If a container does not have memory or CPU limits, it'll be assigned the values set in the `LimitRange`. The `default` entries are used as limits, and the `defaultRequest` entries are used as requests.

When a container does have the resources defined, they will be evaluated against `LimitRange` thresholds specified as `max` and `min`. If a container does not meet the criteria, the Pod that hosts the containers will not be created.

We'll see a practical implementation of the four `limits` soon. For now, the next step is to create the `limit-range` resource:

```
kubectl --namespace test create \
    -f res/limit-range.yml \
    --save-config --record
```

We created the `LimitRange` resource.

Let's describe the `test` namespace where the resource was created.

kubectl describe namespace test

The output, limited to the relevant parts, is as follows.

```
...
Resource Limits
  Type         Resource Min  Max  Default Request Default Limit  Max
Limit/Request Ratio
  ----         -------- ---  ---  --------------- -------------  ----- --------
----------
  Container cpu         10m  500m 50m             200m           -
  Container memory      10Mi 80Mi 30Mi            50Mi           -
```

We can see that the `test` namespace has the resource limits we specified. We set four out of five possible values. The `maxLimitRequestRatio` is missing and we'll describe it only briefly. When `MaxLimitRequestRatio` is set, container request and limit resources must both be non-zero, and the limit divided by the request must be less than or equal to the enumerated value.

Let's take a look at yet another variation of the `go-demo` definition:

`cat res/go-demo-2-no-res.yml`

The only thing to note is that none of the containers have any resources defined.

Next, we'll create the objects defined in the `go-demo-2-no-res.yml` file.

```
kubectl --namespace test create \
    -f res/go-demo-2-no-res.yml \
    --save-config --record

kubectl --namespace test \
    rollout status \
    deployment go-demo-2-api
```

We created the objects inside the `test` namespace and waited until the `deployment "go-demo-2-api"` was successfully rolled out.

Let's describe one of the Pods we created:

```
kubectl --namespace test describe \
    pod go-demo-2-db
```

The output, limited to the relevant parts, is as follows:

```
...
Containers:
  db:
    ...
```

```
Limits:
    cpu:        200m
    memory:     50Mi
Requests:
    cpu:            50m
    memory:         30Mi
...
```

Even though we did not specify the resources of the db container inside the go-demo-2-db Pod, the resources are set. The db container was assigned the default limits of the test Namespace as the container limit. Similarly, the defaultRequest limits were used as container requests.

As we can see, any attempt to create Pods hosting containers without resources will result in the namespace limits applied.

 We should still define container resources instead of relying on namespace default limits. They are, after all, only a fallback in case someone forgot to define resources.

Let's see what happens when resources are defined, but they do not match the namespace min and max limits.

We'll use the same go-demo-2.yml we used before.

cat res/go-demo-2.yml

The output, limited to the relevant parts, is as follows:

```
...
apiVersion: apps/v1beta2
kind: Deployment
metadata:
  name: go-demo-2-db
spec:
  ...
  template:
    ...
    spec:
      containers:
      - name: db
        image: mongo:3.3
        resources:
          limits:
            memory: "100Mi"
            cpu: 0.1
```

```
            requests:
              memory: "50Mi"
              cpu: 0.01
...
apiVersion: apps/v1beta2
kind: Deployment
metadata:
  name: go-demo-2-api
spec:
  ...
  template:
    ...
    spec:
      containers:
      - name: api
        ...
        resources:
          limits:
            memory: "10Mi"
            cpu: 0.1
          requests:
            memory: "5Mi"
            cpu: 0.01
...
```

What matters is that the `resources` for both Deployments are defined.

Let's create the objects and retrieve the events. They will help us understand better what is happening.

```
kubectl --namespace test apply \
    -f res/go-demo-2.yml \
    --record
kubectl --namespace test get events -w
```

The output of the latter command, limited to the relevant parts, is as follows:

```
... Error creating: pods "go-demo-2-db-868dbbc488-s92nm" is forbi
dden: maximum memory usage per Container is 80Mi, but limit is 100Mi.
    ...
... Error creating: pods "go-demo-2-api-6bd767ffb6-96mbl" is
forbidden: minimum memory usage per Container is 10Mi, but request is
5Mi.
    ...
```

We can see that we are forbidden from creating either of the two Pods. The difference between those events is in what caused Kubernetes to reject our request.

The `go-demo-2-db-*` Pod could not be created because its `maximum memory usage per Container is 80Mi, but limit is 100Mi`. On the other hand, we are forbidden from creating the `go-demo-2-api-*` Pods because the `minimum memory usage per Container is 10Mi, but request is 5Mi`.

All the containers within the `test` namespace will have to comply with the `min` and `max` limits. Otherwise, we are forbidden from creating them. Container limits cannot be higher than the namespace `max` limits. On the other hand, container resource requests cannot be smaller than namespace `min` limits.

If we think about namespace limits as lower and upper thresholds, we can say that container requests cannot be below them, and that container limits can't be above.

Press the *Ctrl + C* keys to stop watching the events.

It might be easier to observe the effects of the `max` and `min` limits if we create Pods directly, instead of through Deployments.

```
kubectl --namespace test run test \
    --image alpine \
    --requests memory=100Mi \
    --restart Never \
    sleep 10000
```

We tried to create a Pod with the memory request set to `100Mi`. Since the namespace limit is `80Mi`, the API returned the error message stating that the `Pod "test" is invalid`. Even though the `max` limit refers to container `limit`, memory request was used in its absence.

We'll run a similar exercise but, this time, with only `1Mi` set as memory request.

```
kubectl --namespace test run test \
    --image alpine \
    --requests memory=1Mi \
    --restart Never \
    sleep 10000
```

This time, the error is slightly different. We can see that `pods "test" is forbidden: minimum memory usage per Container is 10Mi, but request is 1Mi`. What we requested is below the `min` limit of the `test` namespace and, therefore, we are forbidden from creating the Pod.

We'll delete the `test` namespace before we move into the next subject.

```
kubectl delete namespace test
```

Defining resource quotas for a namespace

Resource defaults and limitations are a good first step towards preventing malicious or accidental deployment of Pods that can potentially produce adverse effects on the cluster. Still, any user with the permissions to create Pods in a namespace can overload the system. Even if `max` values are set to some reasonably small amount of memory and CPU, a user could deploy thousands, or even millions of Pods, and "eat" all the available cluster resources. Such an effect might not be even produced out of malice but accidentally. A Pod might be attached to a system that scales it automatically without defining upper bounds and, before we know it, it might scale to too many replicas. There are also many other ways things might get out of control.

What we need is to define namespace boundaries through quotas.

With quotas, we can guarantee that each namespace gets its fair share of resources. Unlike `LimitRange` rules that are applied to each container, `ResourceQuota` defines namespace limits based on aggregate resource consumption.

We can use `ResourceQuota` objects to define the total amount of compute resources (memory and CPU) that can be spent in a namespace. We can also use it to limit storage utilization or the number of objects of a certain type that can be created in a namespace.

Let's take a look at the cluster resources we have in our Minikube cluster. It is small, and it's not even a real cluster. However, it's the only one we have (for now), so please use your imagination and pretend that it's "real".

Our cluster has 2 CPUs and 2 GB of memory. Now, let's say that this cluster serves only development and production purposes. We can use the `default` namespace for production and create a `dev` namespace for development. We can assume that the production should consume all the resources of the cluster minus those given to the `dev` namespace which, on the other hand, should not exceed a specific limit.

The truth is that with 2 CPUs and 2 GB of memory, there isn't much we can give to developers. Still, we'll try to be generous. We'll give them 500 MB and 0.8 CPUs for requests. We'll allow occasional bursts in resource usage by defining limits of 1 CPU and 1 GB of memory. Furthermore, we might want to limit the number of Pods to ten. Finally, as a way to reduce risks, we will deny developers the right to expose node ports.

Isn't that a decent plan? I'll imagine that, at this moment, you are nodding as a sign of approval so we'll move on and create the quotas we discussed.

Let's take a look at the `dev.yaml` definition:

```
cat res/dev.yml
```

The output is as follows:

```
apiVersion: v1
kind: Namespace
metadata:
  name: dev
---
apiVersion: v1
kind: ResourceQuota
metadata:
  name: dev
  namespace: dev
spec:
  hard:
    requests.cpu: 0.8
    requests.memory: 500Mi
    limits.cpu: 1
    limits.memory: 1Gi
    pods: 10
    services.nodeports: "0"
```

Besides creating the `dev` namespace, we're also creating a `ResourceQuota`. It specifies a set of `hard` limits. Remember, they are based on aggregated data, and not on per-container basis like LimitRanges.

We set requests quotas to 0.8 CPUs and $500Mi$ of RAM. Similarly, limit quotas as set to 1 CPU and $1Gi$ of memory. Finally, we specified that the `dev` namespace can have only 10 Pods and that there can be no NodePorts. That's the plan we formulated and defined. Now let's create the objects and explore the effects.

```
kubectl create \
    -f res/dev.yml \
    --record --save-config
```

We can see from the output that the `namespace "dev"` was created as well as the `resourcequota "dev"`. To be on the safe side, we'll describe the newly created `devquota`.

```
kubectl --namespace dev describe \
    quota dev
```

The output is as follows:

```
Name:              dev
Namespace:         dev
Resource           Used  Hard
--------           ----  ----
limits.cpu         0     1
limits.memory      0     1Gi
pods               0     10
requests.cpu       0     800m
requests.memory    0     500Mi
services.nodeports 0     0
```

We can see that the hard limits are set and that there's currently no usage. That was to be expected since we're not running any objects in the dev namespace. Let's spice it up a bit by creating the already too familiar go-demo-2 objects.

```
kubectl --namespace dev create \
    -f res/go-demo-2.yml \
    --save-config --record
kubectl --namespace dev \
    rollout status \
    deployment go-demo-2-api
```

We created the objects from the go-demo-2.yml file and waited until the go-demo-2-api Deployment rolled out. Now we can revisit the values of the dev quota:

```
kubectl --namespace dev describe \
    quota dev
```

The output is as follows:

```
Name:              dev
Namespace:         dev
Resource           Used  Hard
--------           ----  ----
limits.cpu         400m  1
limits.memory      130Mi 1Gi
pods               4     10
requests.cpu       40m   800m
requests.memory    65Mi  500Mi
services.nodeports 0     0
```

Judging from the `Used` column, we can see that we are, for example, currently running 4 Pods and that we are still below the limit of 10. One of those Pods was created through the `go-demo-2-db` Deployment, and the other three with the `go-demo-2-api`. If you summarize resources we specified for the containers that form those Pods, you'll see that the values match the used `limits` and `requests`.

So far, we did not reach any of the quotas. Let's try to break at least one of them.

```
cat res/go-demo-2-scaled.yml
```

The output, limited to the relevant parts, is as follows:

```
...
apiVersion: apps/v1beta2
kind: Deployment
metadata:
  name: go-demo-2-api
spec:
  replicas: 15
...
```

The definition of the `go-demo-2-scaled.yml` is almost the same as the one in `go-demo-2.yml`. The only difference is that the number of replicas of the `go-demo-2-api` Deployment is increased to fifteen. As you already know, that should result in fifteen Pods created through that Deployment.

I'm sure you can guess what will happen if we apply the new definition. We'll do it anyway.

```
kubectl --namespace dev apply \
    -f res/go-demo-2-scaled.yml \
    --record
```

We applied the new definition. We'll give Kubernetes a few moments to do the work before we take a look at the events it'll generate. So, take a deep breath and count from one to the number of processors in your Laptop. In my case, it's one Mississippi, two Mississippi, three Mississippi, all the way until sixteen Mississippi.

```
kubectl --namespace dev get events
```

The output of a few of the events generated inside the `dev` namespace is as follows:

```
...
... Error creating: pods "go-demo-2-api-..." is forbidden: exceeded quota:
dev, requested: limits.cpu=100m,pods=1, used: limits.cpu=1,pods=10,
limited: limits.cpu=1,pods=10
```

```
    13s            13s            1              go-demo-2-api-6bd767ffb6.150f5
1f4b3a7ed3f            ReplicaSet                          Warning .
  .. Error creating: pods "go-demo-2-api-..." is forbidden: exceeded quota:
dev, requested: limits.cpu=100m,pods=1, used: limits.cpu=1,pods=10,
limited: limits.cpu=1,pods=10
...
```

We can see that we reached two of the limits imposed by the namespace quota. We reached the maximum amount of CPU (1) and Pods (10). As a result, ReplicaSet controller was forbidden from creating new Pods.

We should be able to confirm which hard limits were reached by describing the dev namespace.

kubectl describe namespace dev

The output, limited to the Resource Quotas section, is as follows:

```
...
Resource Quotas
  Name:               dev
  Resource            Used    Hard
  --------            ---     ---
  limits.cpu          1       1
  limits.memory       190Mi   1Gi
  pods                10      10
  requests.cpu        100m    800m
  requests.memory     95Mi    500Mi
  services.nodeports  0       0
...
```

As the events showed us, the values of limits.cpu and pods resources are the same in both User and Hard columns. As a result, we won't be able to create any more Pods, nor will we be allowed to increase CPU limits for those that are already running.

Finally, let's take a look at the Pods inside the dev namespace.

kubectl get pods --namespace dev

Following is the output of the preceding command:

NAME	READY	STATUS	RESTARTS	AGE
go-demo-2-api-...	1/1	Running	0	3m
go-demo-2-api-...	1/1	Running	0	3m
go-demo-2-api-...	1/1	Running	0	5m
go-demo-2-api-...	1/1	Running	0	3m
go-demo-2-api-...	1/1	Running	0	5m

```
go-demo-2-api-... 1/1    Running 0        3m
go-demo-2-api-... 1/1    Running 0        3m
go-demo-2-api-... 1/1    Running 0        3m
go-demo-2-api-... 1/1    Running 0        5m
go-demo-2-db-...  1/1    Running 0        5m
```

The `go-demo-2-api` Deployment managed to create nine Pods. Together with the Pod created through the `go-demo-2-db`, we reached the limit of ten.

We confirmed that the limit and the Pod quotas work. We'll revert to the previous definition (the one that does not reach any of the quotas) before we move onto the next verification.

```
kubectl --namespace dev apply \
    -f res/go-demo-2.yml \
    --record
kubectl --namespace dev \
    rollout status \
    deployment go-demo-2-api
```

The output of the latter command should indicate that the `deployment "go-demo-2-api" was successfully rolled out`.

Let's take a look at yet another slightly modified definition of the `go-demo-2` objects:

```
cat res/go-demo-2-mem.yml
```

The output, limited to the relevant parts, is as follows:

```
...
apiVersion: apps/v1beta2
kind: Deployment
metadata:
  name: go-demo-2-db
spec:
  ...
  template:
    ...
    spec:
      containers:
      - name: db
        image: mongo:3.3
        resources:
          limits:
            memory: "100Mi"
            cpu: 0.1
          requests:
            memory: "50Mi"
```

```
            cpu: 0.01
...
apiVersion: apps/v1beta2
kind: Deployment
metadata:
  name: go-demo-2-api
spec:
  replicas: 3
  ...
  template:
    ...
    spec:
      containers:
      - name: api
        ...
        resources:
          limits:
            memory: "200Mi"
            cpu: 0.1
          requests:
            memory: "200Mi"
            cpu: 0.01
...
```

Both memory request and limit of the `api` container of the `go-demo-2-api` Deployment is set to `200Mi` while the database remains with the memory request of `50Mi`. Knowing that the `requests.memory` quota of the `dev` namespace is `500Mi`, it's enough to do simple math and come to the conclusion that we won't be able to run all three replicas of the `go-demo-2-api` Deployment.

```
kubectl --namespace dev apply \
    -f res/go-demo-2-mem.yml \
    --record
```

Just as before, we should wait for a while before taking a look at the events of the `dev` namespace.

```
kubectl --namespace dev get events \
    | grep mem
```

The output, limited to one of the entries, is as follows:

```
... Error creating: pods "go-demo-2-api-..." is forbidden: exceeded quota:
dev, requested: requests.memory=200Mi, used: requests.memory=455Mi,
limited: requests.memory=500Mi
```

We reached the quota of the `requests.memory`. As a result, creation of at least one of the Pods is forbidden. We can see that we requested creation of a Pod that requests `200Mi` of memory. Since the current summary of the memory requests is `455Mi`, creating that Pod would exceed the allocated `500Mi`.

Let's take a closer look at the namespace.

```
kubectl describe namespace dev
```

The output, limited to the `Resource Quotas` section, is as follows:

```
. . .
Resource Quotas
  Name:                  dev
  Resource             Used    Hard
  --------             ----    ----
  limits.cpu           400m    1
  limits.memory        510Mi   1Gi
  pods                 4       10
  requests.cpu         40m     800m
  requests.memory      455Mi   500Mi
  services.nodeports   0       0
. . .
```

Indeed, the amount of used memory requests is `455Mi`, meaning that we could create additional Pods with up to `45Mi`, not `200Mi`.

We'll revert to the `go-demo-2.yml` one more time before we explore the last quota we defined.

```
kubectl --namespace dev apply \
    -f res/go-demo-2.yml \
    --record
kubectl --namespace dev \
    rollout status \
    deployment go-demo-2-api
```

The only quota we did not yet verify is `services.nodeports`. We set it to `0` and, as a result, we should not be allowed to expose any node ports. Let's confirm that is indeed true.

```
kubectl expose deployment go-demo-2-api \
    --namespace dev \
    --name go-demo-2-api \
    --port 8080 \
    --type NodePort
```

The output is as follows:

```
Error from server (Forbidden): services "go-demo-2-api" is forbidden:
exceeded quota: dev, requested: services.nodeports=1, used:
services.nodeports=0, limited: services.nodeports=0
```

All our quotas work as expected. But, there are others. We won't have time to explore examples of all the quotas we can use. Instead, we'll list them all for future reference.

We can divide quotas into several groups:

Compute resource quotas limit the total sum of the compute resources. They are as follows:

Resource name	Description
cpu	Across all pods in a non-terminal state, the sum of CPU requests cannot exceed this value.
limits.cpu	Across all pods in a non-terminal state, the sum of CPU limits cannot exceed this value.
limits.memory	Across all pods in a non-terminal state, the sum of memory limits cannot exceed this value.
memory	Across all pods in a non-terminal state, the sum of memory requests cannot exceed this value.
requests.cpu	Across all pods in a non-terminal state, the sum of CPU requests cannot exceed this value.
requests.memory	Across all pods in a non-terminal state, the sum of memory requests cannot exceed this value.

Storage resource quotas limit the total sum of the storage resources. We did not yet explore storage (beyond a few local examples) so you might want to keep the list that follows for future reference:

Resource name	Description
requests.storage	Across all persistent volume claims, the sum of storage requests cannot exceed this value.
persistentvolumeclaims	The total number of persistent volume claims that can exist in the namespace.
[PREFIX]/requests.storage	Across all persistent volume claims associated with the storage-class-name, the sum of storage requests cannot exceed this value.
[PREFIX]/persistentvolumeclaims	Across all persistent volume claims associated with the storage-class-name, the total number of persistent volume claims that can exist in the namespace.

`requests.ephemeral-storage`	Across all pods in the namespace, the sum of local ephemeral storage requests cannot exceed this value.
`limits.ephemeral-storage`	Across all pods in the namespace, the sum of local ephemeral storage limits cannot exceed this value.

Please note that `[PREFIX]` should be replaced with `<storage-class-name>.storageclass.storage.k8s.io`.

Object count quotas limit the number of objects of a given type. They are as follows:

Resource name	Description
`configmaps`	The total number of config maps that can exist in the namespace.
`persistentvolumeclaims`	The total number of persistent volume claims that can exist in the namespace.
`pods`	The total number of pods in a non-terminal state that can exist in the namespace. A pod is in a terminal state if status.phase in (Failed, Succeeded) is true.
`replicationcontrollers`	The total number of replication controllers that can exist in the namespace.
`resourcequotas`	The total number of resource quotas that can exist in the namespace.
`services`	The total number of services that can exist in the namespace.
`services.loadbalancers`	The total number of services of type load balancer that can exist in the namespace.
`services.nodeports`	The total number of services of type node port that can exist in the namespace.
`secrets`	The total number of secrets that can exist in the namespace.

What now?

Wasn't that a ride?

Kubernetes relies heavily on available resources spread throughout the cluster. Still, it cannot do magic. We need to help it out by defining resources we expect our containers will consume.

Even though Heapster is not the best solution for collecting metrics, it is already available in our Minikube cluster, and we used it to learn how much resources our applications use and, through that information, we refined our resource definitions. Without metrics, our definitions are pure guesses. When we guess, Kubernetes needs to guess as well. A stable system is a predictable system based on facts, not someone's imagination. Heapster helped us transform our assumptions into measurable facts which we fed into Kubernetes which, in turn, used them in its scheduling algorithms.

Exploration of resource definitions led us to **Quality Of Service (QoS)**. Even though Kubernetes decides which QoS will be used, knowing the rules used in the decision process is essential if we are to prioritize applications and their availability.

All that leads us to the culmination of the strategies that make our clusters secure, stable, and robust. Dividing a cluster into Namespaces and employing RBAC is not enough. RBAC prevents unauthorized users from accessing the cluster and provides permissions to those we trust. However, RBAC does not prevent users from accidentally (or intentionally) putting the cluster in danger through too many deployments, too big applications, or inaccurate sizing. Only by combining RBAC with resource defaults, limitations, and quotas can we hope for a fault tolerant and robust cluster capable of reliably hosting our applications.

We learned almost all the essential Kubernetes objects and principles. The time has come to move to a "real" cluster. We are about to delete the Minikube cluster for the last time (at least in this book).

```
minikube delete
```

Kubernetes resource management compared to docker swarm equivalent

Resource management can be divided into a few categories. We need to define how much memory and CPU we except a container will use and what are the limits. This information is crucial for a scheduler to make "intelligent" decisions when calculating where to place containers. In this aspect, there is no essential difference between Kubernetes and Docker Swarm. Both are using requested resources to decide where to deploy containers and limits when to evict them. Both of them are, more or less, the same in this aspect.

How can we know how much memory and CPU to dedicate to each of our containers? That's one of the questions I heard way too many times. The answer is simple. Collect metrics, evaluate them, adjust resources, take a break, repeat. Where do we collect metrics? Wherever you want. Prometheus is a good choice. Where will it get metrics? Well, it depends which scheduler you use. If it's Docker Swarm, you'll need to run a bunch of exporters. Or, you might be brave enough and try the experimental feature that exposes Docker's internal metrics in Prometheus format. You might even be enthusiastic enough to think that they will be enough for all your monitoring and alerting needs. Maybe, by the time you read this, the feature is not experimental anymore. On the other hand, Kubernetes has it all, and so much more. You can use Heapster, or you might discover that it is too limiting and configure Prometheus to scrape metrics directly from Kubernetes API. Kubernetes exposes a vast amount of data. More than you'll probably ever need. You will be able to fetch memory, CPU, IO, network, and a myriad of other metrics and make intelligent decisions not only about the resources your containers require but about so much more.

To make things clear, you can get the same metrics no matter whether you're running Kubernetes or Docker Swarm. The major difference is that Kubernetes exposes them through its API, while with Swarm you'll have to struggle between the decisions whether to use its limited metrics or go into the trouble of setting up the exporters like cAdvisor and Node Exporter. Most likely, you'll discover that you'll need both the metrics from Swarm's API and those from the exporters. Kubernetes has a more robust solution, even though you might still need an exporter or two. Still, having most, if not all, of the metrics you'll need from its API is a handy thing to have.

Frankly, the differences in the way we retrieve metrics from the two schedulers are not of great importance. If this would be where the story about resources ends, I'd conclude that both solutions are, more or less, equally good. But, the narrative continues. This is where similarities stop. Or, to be more precise, this is where Docker Swarm ends, and Kubernetes only just began.

Kubernetes allows us to define resource defaults and limitations that are applied to containers that do not specify resources. It allows us to specify resource quotas that prevent accidental or malicious over-usage of resources. The two combined with Namespaces provide very powerful safeguards. They give us some of the means with which we can design the system that is truly fault tolerant by preventing rogue containers, uncontrolled scaling, and human errors from bringing our clusters to a grinding halt. Don't think, even for a second, that quotas are the only thing required for building a robust system. It isn't the only piece of the puzzle, but it is a significant one never the less.

Namespaces combined with quotas are important. I'd even say that they are crucial. Without them, we would be forced to create a cluster for every group, team, or a department in our organizations. Or, we might have to resort to further tightening of the processes that prevent our teams from exploiting the benefits behind container orchestrators. If the goal is to provide freedom to our teams without sacrificing cluster stability, Kubernetes has a clear edge over Docker Swarm.

This battle is won by Kubernetes, but the war still rages.

OK. I exaggerated a bit with the words *battle* and *war*. It's not a conflict, and both communities are increasing collaboration and sharing ideas and solutions. Both platforms are merging. Still, for now, Kubernetes has a clear edge over Docker Swarm on the subject of resource management.

14
Creating a Production-Ready Kubernetes Cluster

Creating a Kubernetes cluster is not trivial. We have to make many choices, and we can easily get lost in the myriad of options. The number of permutations is getting close to infinite and, yet, our clusters need to be configured consistently. Experience from the first attempt to set up a cluster can easily convert into a nightmare that will haunt you for the rest of your life.

Unlike Docker Swarm that packs almost everything into a single binary, Kubernetes clusters require quite a few separate components running across the nodes. Setting them up can be very easy, or it can become a challenge. It all depends on the choices we make initially. One of the first things we need to do is choose a tool that we'll use to create a Kubernetes cluster.

If we'd decide to install a Docker Swarm cluster, all we'd need to do is to install Docker engine on all the servers, and execute `docker swarm init` or `docker swarm join` command on each of the nodes. That's it. Docker packs everything into a single binary. Docker Swarm setup process is as simple as it can get. The same cannot be said for Kubernetes. Unlike Swarm that is highly opinionated, Kubernetes provides much higher freedom of choice. It is designed around extensibility. We need to choose among many different components. Some of them are maintained by the core Kubernetes project, while others are provided by third-parties. Extensibility is probably one of the main reasons behind Kubernetes' rapid growth. Almost every software vendor today is either building components for Kubernetes or providing a service that sits on top of it.

Besides the intelligent design and the fact that it solves problems related to distributed, scalable, fault-tolerant, and highly available systems, Kubernetes' power comes from adoption and support from a myriad of individuals and companies. You can use that power, as long as you understand that it comes with responsibilities. It's up to you, dear reader, to choose how will your Kubernetes cluster look like, and which components it'll host. You can decide to build it from scratch, or you can use one of the hosted solutions like **Google Cloud Platform (GCE)** Kubernetes Engine. There is a third option though. We can choose to use one of the installation tools. Most of them are highly opinionated with a limited amount of arguments we can use to tweak the outcome.

You might be thinking that creating a cluster from scratch using `kubeadm` cannot be that hard. You'd be right if running Kubernetes is all we need. But, it isn't. We need to make it fault tolerant and highly available. It needs to stand the test of time. Constructing a robust solution would require a combination of Kubernetes core and third-party components, AWS know-how, and quite a lot of custom scripts that would tie the two together. We won't go down that road. At least, not now.

We'll use **Kubernetes Operations (kops)** to create a cluster. It is somewhere in the middle between do-it-yourself-from-scratch and hosted solutions (for example, GCE). It's an excellent fit for both newbies and veterans. You'll learn which components are required for running a Kubernetes cluster. You'll be able to make some choices. And, yet, we won't go down the rabbit hole of setting up the cluster from scratch. Believe me, that hole is very deep, and it might take us a very long time to get out of it.

Typically, this would be a great place to explain the most significant components of a Kubernetes cluster. Heck, you were probably wondering why we didn't do that early on when we began the journey. Still, we'll postpone the discussion for a while longer. I believe it'll be better to create a cluster first and discuss the components through live examples. I feel that it's easier to understand something we can see and touch, instead of keeping it purely on the theoretical level.

All in all, we'll create a cluster first, and discuss its components later.

Since I already mentioned that we'll use **kops** to create a cluster, we'll start with a very brief introduction to the project behind it.

What is kubernetes operations (kops) project?

If you visit **Kubernetes Operations (kops)** (`https://github.com/kubernetes/kops`) project, the first sentence you'll read is that it is "the easiest way to get a production-grade Kubernetes cluster up and running." In my humble opinion, that sentence is accurate only if we exclude **Google Kubernetes Engine (GKE)**. Today (February 2018), other hosting vendors did not yet release their Kubernetes-as-a-service solutions. Amazon's **Elastic Container Service for Kubernetes (EKS)** (`https://aws.amazon.com/eks/`) is still not open to the public. **Azure Container Service (AKS)** (`https://azure.microsoft.com/en-us/services/kubernetes-service/`) is also a new addition that still has a few pain points. By the time you read this, all major hosting providers might have their solutions. Still, I prefer kops since it provides almost the same level of simplicity without taking away the control of the process. It allows us to tweak the cluster more than we would be permitted with hosted solutions. It is entirely open source, it can be stored in version control, and it is not designed to lock you into a vendor.

If your hosting vendor is AWS, kops is, in my opinion, the best way to create a Kubernetes cluster. Whether that's true for GCE, is open for debate since GKE works great. We can expect kops to be extended in the future to other vendors. For example, at the time of this writing, VMWare is in alpha and should be stable soon. Azure and Digital Ocean support are being added as I write this.

We'll use kops to create a Kubernetes cluster in AWS. This is the part of the story that might get you disappointed. You might have chosen to run Kubernetes somewhere else. Don't be depressed. Almost all Kubernetes clusters follow the same principles even though the method of setting them up might differ. The principles are what truly matters, and I'm confident that, once you set it up successfully on AWS, you'll be able to transfer that knowledge anywhere else.

The reason for choosing AWS lies in its adoption. It is the hosting vendor with, by far, the biggest user-base. If I'd have to place a blind bet on your choice, it would be AWS solely because that is statistically the most likely choice. I could not explore all the options in a single chapter. If I am to go through all hosting vendors and different projects that might help with the installation, we'd need to dedicate a whole book to that. Instead, I invite you to explore the subject further once you're finished with installing Kubernetes in AWS with kops. As an alternative, ping me on `slack.devops20toolkit.com` or send me an email to `viktor@farcic.com` and I'll give you a hand. If I receive enough messages, I might even dedicate a whole book to Kubernetes installations.

I went astray from kops...

Kops lets us create a production-grade Kubernetes cluster. That means that we can use it not only to create a cluster, but also to upgrade it (without downtime), update it, or destroy it if we don't need it anymore. A cluster cannot be called "production grade" unless it is highly available and fault tolerant. We should be able to execute it entirely from the command line if we'd like it to be automated. Those and quite a few other things are what kops provides, and what makes it great.

Kops follows the same philosophy as Kubernetes. We create a set of JSON or YAML objects which are sent to controllers that create a cluster.

We'll discuss what kops can and cannot do in more detail soon. For now, we'll jump into the hands-on part of this chapter and ensure that all the prerequisites for the installation are set.

Preparing for the cluster setup

We'll continue using the specifications from the `vfarcic/k8s-specs` repository, so the first thing we'll do is to go inside the directory where we cloned it, and pull the latest version.

All the commands from this chapter are available in the `14-aws.sh` (`https://gist.github.com/vfarcic/04af9efcd1c972e8199fc014b030b13 4`) Gist.

```
cd k8s-specs
git pull
```

I will assume that you already have an AWS account. If that's not the case, please head over to Amazon Web Services (`https://aws.amazon.com/`) and sign-up.

If you are already proficient with AWS, you might want to skim through the text that follows and only execute the commands.

The first thing we should do is get the AWS credentials.

Please open Amazon EC2 Console (`https://console.aws.amazon.com/ec2/v2/home`), click on your name from the top-right menu and select **My Security Credentials**. You will see the screen with different types of credentials. Expand the **Access Keys (Access Key ID and Secret Access Key)** section and click the **Create New Access Key** button. Expand the **Show Access Key** section to see the keys.

You will not be able to view the keys later on, so this is the only chance you'll have to *Download Key File*.

We'll put the keys as environment variables that will be used by the **AWS Command Line Interface** (**AWS CLI**) (`https://aws.amazon.com/cli/`).

Please replace `[...]` with your keys before executing the commands that follow:

```
export AWS_ACCESS_KEY_ID=[...]

export AWS_SECRET_ACCESS_KEY=[...]
```

We'll need to install AWS **Command Line Interface** (**CLI**) (`https://aws.amazon.com/cli/`) and gather info about your account.

If you haven't already, please open the Installing the AWS Command Line Interface (`https://docs.aws.amazon.com/cli/latest/userguide/installing.html`) page, and follow the installation method best suited for your OS.

 A note to Windows users: I found the most convenient way to get AWS CLI installed on Windows is to use Chocolatey (`https://chocolatey.org/`). Download and install Chocolatey, then run `choco install awscli` from an Administrator Command Prompt. Later on in the chapter, Chocolatey will be used to install jq.

Once you're done, we'll confirm that the installation was successful by outputting the version.

 A note to Windows users: You might need to reopen your *GitBash* terminal for the changes to the environment variable PATH to take effect.

```
aws --version
```

The output (from my laptop) is as follows:

```
aws-cli/1.11.15 Python/2.7.10 Darwin/16.0.0 botocore/1.4.72
```

Amazon EC2 is hosted in multiple locations worldwide. These locations are composed of regions and availability zones. Each region is a separate geographic area composed of multiple isolated locations known as availability zones. Amazon EC2 provides you the ability to place resources, such as instances, and data in multiple locations.

Next, we'll define the environment variable `AWS_DEFAULT_REGION` that will tell AWS CLI which region we'd like to use by default.

```
export AWS_DEFAULT_REGION=us-east-2
```

For now, please note that you can change the value of the variable to any other region, as long as it has at least three availability zones. We'll discuss the reasons for using `us-east-2` region and the need for multiple availability zones soon.

Next, we'll create a few **Identity and Access Management (IAM)** resources. Even though we could create a cluster with the user you used to register to AWS, it is a good practice to create a separate account that contains only the privileges we'll need for the exercises that follow:

First, we'll create an IAM group called `kops`:

```
aws iam create-group \
    --group-name kops
```

The output is as follows:

```
{
    "Group": {
        "Path": "/",
        "CreateDate": "2018-02-21T12:58:47.853Z",
        "GroupId": "AGPAIF2Y6HJF7YFYQBQK2",
        "Arn": "arn:aws:iam::036548781187:group/kops",
        "GroupName": "kops"
    }
}
```

We don't care much for any of the information from the output except that it does not contain an error message thus confirming that the group was created successfully.

Next, we'll assign a few policies to the group thus providing the future users of the group with sufficient permissions to create the objects we'll need.

Since our cluster will consist of EC2 (https://aws.amazon.com/ec2/) instances, the group will need to have the permissions to create and manage them. We'll need a place to store the state of the cluster so we'll need access to S3 (https://aws.amazon.com/s3/). Furthermore, we need to add VPCs (https://aws.amazon.com/vpc/) to the mix so that our cluster is isolated from prying eyes. Finally, we'll need to be able to create additional IAMs.

In AWS, user permissions are granted by creating policies. We'll need *AmazonEC2FullAccess, AmazonS3FullAccess, AmazonVPCFullAccess*, and *IAMFullAccess*.

The commands that attach the required policies to the `kops` group are as follows:

```
aws iam attach-group-policy \
    --policy-arn arn:aws:iam::aws:policy/AmazonEC2FullAccess \
    --group-name kops
aws iam attach-group-policy \
    --policy-arn arn:aws:iam::aws:policy/AmazonS3FullAccess \
    --group-name kops
aws iam attach-group-policy \
    --policy-arn arn:aws:iam::aws:policy/AmazonVPCFullAccess \
    --group-name kops
aws iam attach-group-policy \
    --policy-arn arn:aws:iam::aws:policy/IAMFullAccess \
    --group-name kops
```

Now that we have a group with the sufficient permissions, we should create a user as well.

```
aws iam create-user \
    --user-name kops
```

The output is as follows:

```
{
    "User": {
        "UserName": "kops",
        "Path": "/",
        "CreateDate": "2018-02-21T12:59:28.836Z",
        "UserId": "AIDAJ22UOS7JVYQIAVMWA",
        "Arn": "arn:aws:iam::036548781187:user/kops"
    }
}
```

Just as when we created the group, the contents of the output are not important, except as a confirmation that the command was executed successfully.

The user we created does not yet belong to the `kops` group. We'll fix that next:

```
aws iam add-user-to-group \
    --user-name kops \
    --group-name kops
```

Finally, we'll need access keys for the newly created user. Without them, we would not be able to act on its behalf.

```
aws iam create-access-key \
    --user-name kops >kops-creds
```

We created access keys and stored the output in the `kops-creds` file. Let's take a quick look at its content.

```
cat kops-creds
```

The output is as follows:

```
{
    "AccessKey": {
        "UserName": "kops",
        "Status": "Active",
        "CreateDate": "2018-02-21T13:00:24.733Z",
        "SecretAccessKey": "...",
        "AccessKeyId": "..."
    }
}
```

Please note that I removed the values of the keys. I do not yet trust you enough with the keys of my AWS account.

We need the `SecretAccessKey` and `AccessKeyId` entries. So, the next step is to parse the content of the `kops-creds` file and store those two values as the environment variables `AWS_ACCESS_KEY_ID` and `AWS_SECRET_ACCESS_KEY`.

In the spirit of full automation, we'll use `jq` (`https://stedolan.github.io/jq/`) to parse the contents of the `kops-creds` file. Please download and install the distribution suited for your OS.

A note to Windows users: Using Chocolatey, install `jq` from an Administrator Command Prompt via `choco install jq`.

```
export AWS_ACCESS_KEY_ID=$(\
    cat kops-creds | jq -r \
    '.AccessKey.AccessKeyId')
export AWS_SECRET_ACCESS_KEY=$(
    cat kops-creds | jq -r \
    '.AccessKey.SecretAccessKey')
```

We used `cat` to output contents of the file and combined it with `jq` to filter the input so that only the field we need is retrieved.

From now on, all the AWS CLI commands will not be executed by the administrative user you used to register to AWS, but as `kops`.

 It is imperative that the `kops-creds` file is secured and not accessible to anyone but people you trust. The best method to secure it depends from one organization to another. No matter what you do, do not write it on a post-it and stick it to your monitor. Storing it in one of your GitHub repositories is even worse.

Next, we should decide which availability zones we'll use. So, let's take a look at what's available in the `us-east-2` region.

```
aws ec2 describe-availability-zones \
    --region $AWS_DEFAULT_REGION
```

The output is as follows:

```
{
    "AvailabilityZones": [
        {
            "State": "available",
            "RegionName": "us-east-2",
            "Messages": [],
            "ZoneName": "us-east-2a"
        },
        {
            "State": "available",
            "RegionName": "us-east-2",
            "Messages": [],
            "ZoneName": "us-east-2b"
        },
        {
            "State": "available",
            "RegionName": "us-east-2",
            "Messages": [],
            "ZoneName": "us-east-2c"
        }
```

```
    ]
}
```

As we can see, the region has three availability zones. We'll store them in an environment variable.

 A note to Windows users: Please use `tr '\r\n' ','` instead of `tr '\n' ','` in the command that follows.

```
export ZONES=$(aws ec2 \
    describe-availability-zones \
    --region $AWS_DEFAULT_REGION \
    | jq -r \
    '.AvailabilityZones[].ZoneName' \
    | tr '\n' ',' | tr -d ' ')
ZONES=${ZONES%?}
echo $ZONES
```

Just as with the access keys, we used `jq` to limit the results only to the zone names, and we combined that with `tr` that replaced new lines with commas. The second command removes the trailing comma.

The output of the last command that echoed the values of the environment variable is as follows:

```
us-east-2a,us-east-2b,us-east-2c
```

We'll discuss the reasons behind the usage of three availability zones later on. For now, just remember that they are stored in the environment variable `ZONES`.

The last preparation step is to create SSH keys required for the setup. Since we might create some other artifacts during the process, we'll create a directory dedicated to the creation of the cluster.

```
mkdir -p cluster
cd cluster
```

SSH keys can be created through the `aws ec2` command `create-key-pair`:

```
aws ec2 create-key-pair \
    --key-name devops23 \
    | jq -r '.KeyMaterial' \
    >devops23.pem
```

We created a new key pair, filtered the output so that only the `KeyMaterial` is returned, and stored it in the `devops23.pem` file.

For security reasons, we should change the permissions of the `devops23.pem` file so that only the current user can read it.

```
chmod 400 devops23.pem \
```

Finally, we'll need only the public segment of the newly generated SSH key, so we'll use `ssh-keygen` to extract it.

```
ssh-keygen -y -f devops23.pem
    >devops23.pub
```

All those steps might look a bit daunting if this is your first contact with AWS. Nevertheless, they are pretty standard. No matter what you do in AWS, you'd need to perform, more or less, the same actions. Not all of them are mandatory, but they are good practice. Having a dedicated (non-admin) user and a group with only required policies is always a good idea. Access keys are necessary for any `aws` command. Without SSH keys, no one can enter into a server.

The good news is that we're finished with the prerequisites, and we can turn our attention towards creating a Kubernetes cluster.

Creating a kubernetes cluster in AWS

We'll start by deciding the name of our soon to be created cluster. We'll choose to call it `devops23.k8s.local`. The latter part of the name (`.k8s.local`) is mandatory if we do not have a DNS at hand. It's a naming convention kops uses to decide whether to create a gossip-based cluster or to rely on a publicly available domain. If this would be a "real" production cluster, you would probably have a DNS for it. However, since I cannot be sure whether you do have one for the exercises in this book, we'll play it safe, and proceed with the gossip mode.

We'll store the name into an environment variable so that it is easily accessible.

```
export NAME=devops23.k8s.local
```

When we create the cluster, kops will store its state in a location we're about to configure. If you used Terraform, you'll notice that kops uses a very similar approach. It uses the state it generates when creating the cluster for all subsequent operations. If we want to change any aspect of a cluster, we'll have to change the desired state first, and then apply those changes to the cluster.

At the moment, when creating a cluster in AWS, the only option for storing the state are Amazon S3 (https://aws.amazon.com/s3/) buckets. We can expect availability of additional stores soon. For now, S3 is our only option.

The command that creates an S3 bucket in our region is as follows:

```
export BUCKET_NAME=devops23-$(date +%s)
aws s3api create-bucket \
    --bucket $BUCKET_NAME \
    --create-bucket-configuration \
    LocationConstraint=$AWS_DEFAULT_REGION
```

We created a bucket with a unique name and the output is as follows:

```
{
    "Location": http://devops23-1519993212.s3.amazonaws.com/
}
```

For simplicity, we'll define the environment variable `KOPS_STATE_STORE`. Kops will use it to know where we store the state. Otherwise, we'd need to use `--store` argument with every `kops` command.

```
export KOPS_STATE_STORE=s3://$BUCKET_NAME
```

There's only one thing missing before we create the cluster. We need to install kops.

If you are a **MacOS user**, the easiest way to install `kops` is through `Homebrew` (https://brew.sh/).

```
brew update && brew install kops
```

As an alternative, we can download a release from GitHub.

```
curl -Lo kops https://github.com/kubernetes/kops/releases/download/$(curl -
s
https://api.github.com/repos/kubernetes/kops/releases/latest | grep
tag_name | cut -d '"' -f 4)/kops-darwin-amd64
chmod +x ./kops
sudo mv ./kops /usr/local/bin/
```

If, on the other hand, you're a **Linux user**, the commands that will install kops are as follows:

```
wget -O kops https://github.com/kubernetes/kops/releases/download/$(curl -s
https://api.github.com/repos/kubernetes/kops/releases/latest | grep
tag_name |
cut -d '"' -f 4)/kops-linux-amd64
chmod +x ./kops
sudo mv ./kops /usr/local/bin/
```

Finally, if you are a **Windows user**, you cannot install *kops*. At the time of this writing, its releases do not include Windows binaries. Don't worry. I am not giving up on you, dear *Windows user*. We'll manage to overcome the problem soon by exploiting Docker's ability to run any Linux application. The only requirement is that you have Docker for Windows (https://www.docker.com/docker-windows) installed.

I already created a Docker image that contains kops and its dependencies. So, we'll create an alias kops that will create a container instead running a binary. The result will be the same.

The command that creates the kops alias is as follows. Execute it only if you are a **Windows user**:

```
mkdir config
alias kops="docker run -it --rm \
    -v $PWD/devops23.pub:/devops23.pub \
    -v $PWD/config:/config \
    -e KUBECONFIG=/config/kubecfg.yaml \
    -e NAME=$NAME -e ZONES=$ZONES \
    -e AWS_ACCESS_KEY_ID=$AWS_ACCESS_KEY_ID \
    -e AWS_SECRET_ACCESS_KEY=$AWS_SECRET_ACCESS_KEY \
    -e KOPS_STATE_STORE=$KOPS_STATE_STORE \
    vfarcic/kops"
```

We won't go into details of all the arguments the docker run command uses. Their usage will become clear when we start using kops. Just remember that we are passing all the environment variables we might use as well as mounting the SSH key and the directory where kops will store kubectl configuration.

We are, finally, ready to create a cluster. But, before we do that, we'll spend a bit of time discussing the requirements we might have. After all, not all clusters are created equal, and the choices we are about to make might severely impact our ability to accomplish the goals we might have.

The first question we might ask ourselves is whether we want to have high-availability. It would be strange if anyone would answer no. Who doesn't want to have a cluster that is (almost) always available? Instead, we'll ask ourselves what the things that might bring our cluster down are.

When a node is destroyed, Kubernetes will reschedule all the applications that were running inside it into the healthy nodes. All we have to do is to make sure that, later on, a new server is created and joined the cluster, so that its capacity is back to the desired values. We'll discuss later how are new nodes created as a reaction to failures of a server. For now, we'll assume that will happen somehow.

Still, there is a catch. Given that new nodes need to join the cluster, if the failed server was the only master, there is no cluster to join. All is lost. The part is where master servers are. They host the critical components without which Kubernetes cannot operate.

So, we need more than one master node. How about two? If one fails, we still have the other one. Still, that would not work.

Every piece of information that enters one of the master nodes is propagated to the others, and only after the majority agrees, that information is committed. If we lose majority (50%+1), masters cannot establish a quorum and cease to operate. If one out of two masters is down, we can get only half of the votes, and we would lose the ability to establish the quorum. Therefore, we need three masters or more. Odd numbers greater than one are "magic" numbers. Given that we won't create a big cluster, three should do.

With three masters, we are safe from a failure of any single one of them. Given that failed servers will be replaced with new ones, as long as only one master fails at the time, we should be fault tolerant and have high availability.

 Always set an odd number greater than one for master nodes.

The whole idea of having multiple masters does not mean much if an entire data center goes down.

Attempts to prevent a data center from failing are commendable. Still, no matter how well a data center is designed, there is always a scenario that might cause its disruption. So, we need more than one data center. Following the logic behind master nodes, we need at least three. But, as with almost anything else, we cannot have any three (or more) data centers. If they are too far apart, the latency between them might be too high. Since every piece of information is propagated to all the masters in a cluster, slow communication between data centers would severely impact the cluster as a whole.

All in all, we need three data centers that are close enough to provide low latency, and yet physically separated, so that failure of one does not impact the others. Since we are about to create the cluster in AWS, we'll use **availability zones (AZs)** which are physically separated data centers with low latency.

> Always spread your cluster between at least three data centers which are close enough to warrant low latency.

There's more to high-availability to running multiple masters and spreading a cluster across multiple availability zones. We'll get back to this subject later. For now, we'll continue exploring the other decisions we have to make.

Which networking shall we use? We can choose between *kubenet, CNI, classic,* and *external* networking.

The classic Kubernetes native networking is deprecated in favor of kubenet, so we can discard it right away.

The external networking is used in some custom implementations and for particular use cases, so we'll discard that one as well.

That leaves us with kubenet and CNI.

Container Network Interface (CNI) allows us to plug in a third-party networking driver. Kops supports Calico (`https://docs.projectcalico.org/v2.0/getting-started/kubernetes/installation/hosted/`), flannel (`https://github.com/coreos/flannel`), Canal (Flannel + Calico) (`https://github.com/projectcalico/canal`), kopeio-vxlan (`https://github.com/kopeio/networking`), kube-router (`https://github.com/kubernetes/kops/blob/master/docs/networking.md#kube-router-example-for-cni-ipvs-based-service-proxy-and-network-policy-enforcer`), romana (`https://github.com/romana/romana`), weave (`https://github.com/weaveworks-experiments/weave-kube`), and amazon-vpc-routed-

`eni`
(`https://github.com/kubernetes/kops/blob/master/docs/networking.md#amazon-vpc-b ackend`) networks. Each of those networks comes with pros and cons and differs in its implementation and primary objectives. Choosing between them would require a detailed analysis of each. We'll leave a comparison of all those for some other time and place. Instead, we'll focus on `kubenet`.

Kubenet is kops' default networking solution. It is Kubernetes native networking, and it is considered battle tested and very reliable. However, it comes with a limitation. On AWS, routes for each node are configured in AWS VPC routing tables. Since those tables cannot have more than fifty entries, kubenet can be used in clusters with up to fifty nodes. If you're planning to have a cluster bigger than that, you'll have to switch to one of the previously mentioned CNIs.

Use kubenet networking if your cluster is smaller than fifty nodes.

The good news is that using any of the networking solutions is easy. All we have to do is specify the `--networking` argument followed with the name of the network.

Given that we won't have the time and space to evaluate all the CNIs, we'll use kubenet as the networking solution for the cluster we're about to create. I encourage you to explore the other options on your own (or wait until I write a post or a new book).

Finally, we are left with only one more choice we need to make. What will be the size of our nodes? Since we won't run many applications, `t2.small` should be more than enough and will keep AWS costs to a minimum. `t2.micro` is too small, so we elected the second smallest among those AWS offers.

You might have noticed that we did not mention persistent volumes. We'll explore them in the next chapter.

The command that creates a cluster using the specifications we discussed is as follows:

```
kops create cluster \
    --name $NAME \
    --master-count 3 \
    --node-count 1 \
    --node-size t2.small \
    --master-size t2.small \
```

```
--zones $ZONES \
--master-zones $ZONES \
--ssh-public-key devops23.pub \
--networking kubenet \
--kubernetes-version v1.8.4 \
--yes
```

We specified that the cluster should have three masters and one worker node. Remember, we can always increase the number of workers, so there's no need to start with more than what we need at the moment.

The sizes of both worker nodes and masters are set to t2.small. Both types of nodes will be spread across the three availability zones we specified through the environment variable ZONES. Further on, we defined the public key and the type of networking.

We used --kubernetes-version to specify that we prefer to run version v1.8.4. Otherwise, we'd get a cluster with the latest version considered stable by kops. Even though running latest stable version is probably a good idea, we'll need to be a few versions behind to demonstrate some of the features kops has to offer.

By default, kops sets authorization to AlwaysAllow. Since this is a simulation of a production-ready cluster, we changed it to RBAC, which we already explored in one of the previous chapters.

The --yes argument specifies that the cluster should be created right away. Without it, kops would only update the state in the S3 bucket, and we'd need to execute kops apply to create the cluster. Such two-step approach is preferable, but I got impatient and would like to see the cluster in all its glory as soon as possible.

The output of the command is as follows:

```
. . .
kops has set your kubectl context to devops23.k8s.local
Cluster is starting.  It should be ready in a few minutes.
Suggestions:
 * validate cluster: kops validate cluster
 * list nodes: kubectl get nodes --show-labels
 * ssh to the master: ssh -i ~/.ssh/id_rsa admin@api.devops23.k8s.local
The admin user is specific to Debian. If not using Debian please use the
appropriate user based on your OS.
 * read about installing addons:
https://github.com/kubernetes/kops/blob/master/docs/addons.md
```

We can see that the kubectl context was changed to point to the new cluster which is starting, and will be ready soon. Further down are a few suggestions of the next actions. We'll skip them, for now.

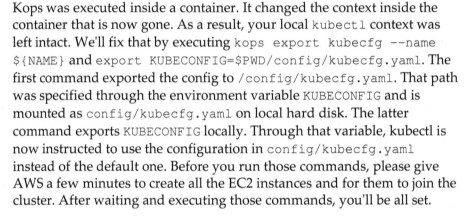

A note to Windows users
Kops was executed inside a container. It changed the context inside the container that is now gone. As a result, your local kubectl context was left intact. We'll fix that by executing kops export kubecfg --name ${NAME} and export KUBECONFIG=$PWD/config/kubecfg.yaml. The first command exported the config to /config/kubecfg.yaml. That path was specified through the environment variable KUBECONFIG and is mounted as config/kubecfg.yaml on local hard disk. The latter command exports KUBECONFIG locally. Through that variable, kubectl is now instructed to use the configuration in config/kubecfg.yaml instead of the default one. Before you run those commands, please give AWS a few minutes to create all the EC2 instances and for them to join the cluster. After waiting and executing those commands, you'll be all set.

We'll use kops to retrieve the information about the newly created cluster.

```
kops get cluster
```

The output is as follows:

```
NAME              CLOUD ZONES
devops23.k8s.local aws    us-east-2a,us-east-2b,us-east-2c
```

This information does not tell us anything new. We already knew the name of the cluster and the zones it runs in.

How about kubectl cluster-info?

```
kubectl cluster-info
```

The output is as follows:

```
Kubernetes master is running at
https://api-devops23-k8s-local-ivnbim-6094461
90.us-east-2.elb.amazonaws.com
KubeDNS is running at
https://api-devops23-k8s-local-ivnbim-609446190.us-east
-2.elb.amazonaws.com/api/v1/namespaces/kube-system/services/kube-
dns:dns/proxy
To further debug and diagnose cluster problems, use 'kubectl cluster-info
dump'.
```

We can see that the master is running as well as KubeDNS. The cluster is probably ready. If in your case KubeDNS did not appear in the output, you might need to wait for a few more minutes.

We can get more reliable information about the readiness of our new cluster through the `kops validate` command.

```
kops validate cluster
```

The output is as follows:

```
Using cluster from kubectl context: devops23.k8s.local
Validating cluster devops23.k8s.local
INSTANCE GROUPS
NAME                ROLE    MACHINETYPE MIN MAX SUBNETS
master-us-east-2a Master t2.small     1   1   us-east-2a
master-us-east-2b Master t2.small     1   1   us-east-2b
master-us-east-2c Master t2.small     1   1   us-east-2c
nodes               Node    t2.small    1   1   us-east-2a,us-east-2b,us-
east-2c
NODE STATUS
NAME                    ROLE    READY
ip-172-20-120-133...  master  True
ip-172-20-34-249...   master  True
ip-172-20-65-28...    master  True
ip-172-20-95-101...   node    True
Your cluster devops23.k8s.local is ready
```

That is useful. We can see that the cluster uses four instance groups or, to use AWS terms, four **auto-scaling groups** (**ASGs**). There's one for each master, and there's one for all the (worker) nodes.

The reason each master has a separate ASG lies in need to ensure that each is running in its own **availability zone** (**AZ**). That way we can guarantee that failure of the whole AZ will affect only one master. Nodes (workers), on the other hand, are not restricted to any specific AZ. AWS is free to schedule nodes in any AZ that is available.

We'll discuss ASGs in more detail later on.

Further down the output, we can see that there are four servers, three with masters, and one with worker node. All are ready.

Finally, we got the confirmation that our `cluster devops23.k8s.local is ready`.

Using the information we got so far, we can describe the cluster through the *figure 14-1*.

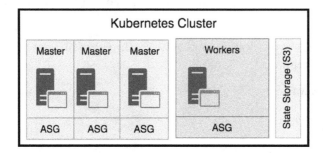

Figure 14-1: The servers that form the Kubernetes cluster

There's apparently much more to the cluster than what is depicted in the *figure 14-1*. So, let's try to discover the goodies kops created for us.

Exploring the components that constitute the cluster

When kops created the VMs (EC2 instances), the first thing it did was to execute *nodeup*. It, in turn, installed a few packages. It made sure that Docker, Kubelet, and Protokube are up and running.

Docker runs containers. It would be hard for me to imagine that you don't know what Docker does, so we'll skip to the next in line.

Kubelet is Kubernetes' node agent. It runs on every node of a cluster, and its primary purpose is to run Pods. Or, to be more precise, it ensures that the containers described in PodSpecs are running as long as they are healthy. It primarily gets the information about the Pods it should run through Kubernetes' API server. As an alternative, it can get the info through files, HTTP endpoints, and HTTP servers.

Unlike Docker and Kubelet, **Protokube** is specific to kops. Its primary responsibilities are to discover master disks, to mount them, and to create manifests. Some of those manifests are used by Kubelet to create system-level Pods and to make sure that they are always running.

Besides starting the containers defined through Pods in the manifests (created by Protokube), Kubelet also tries to contact the API server which, eventually, is also started by it. Once the connection is established, Kubelet registers the node where it is running.

All three packages are running on all the nodes, no matter whether they are masters or workers:

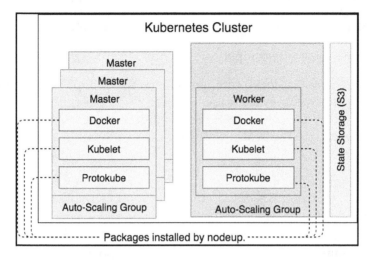

Figure 14-2: The servers that form the Kubernetes cluster

Let's take a look at the system-level Pods currently running in our cluster:

```
kubectl --namespace kube-system get pods
```

The output is as follows:

NAME	READY	STATUS	RESTARTS	AGE
dns-controller-...	1/1	Running	0	5m
etcd-server-events-ip-172-20-120-133...	1/1	Running	0	5m
etcd-server-events-ip-172-20-34-249...	1/1	Running	1	4m
etcd-server-events-ip-172-20-65-28...	1/1	Running	0	4m
etcd-server-ip-172-20-120-133...	1/1	Running	0	4m
etcd-server-ip-172-20-34-249...	1/1	Running	1	3m
etcd-server-ip-172-20-65-28...	1/1	Running	0	4m
kube-apiserver-ip-172-20-120-133...	1/1	Running	0	4m
kube-apiserver-ip-172-20-34-249...	1/1	Running	3	3m
kube-apiserver-ip-172-20-65-28...	1/1	Running	1	4m
kube-controller-manager-ip-172-20-120-133...	1/1	Running	0	4m
kube-controller-manager-ip-172-20-34-249...	1/1	Running	0	4m
kube-controller-manager-ip-172-20-65-28...	1/1	Running	0	4m
kube-dns-7f56f9f8c7-...	3/3	Running	0	5m
kube-dns-7f56f9f8c7-...	3/3	Running	0	2m
kube-dns-autoscaler-f4c47db64-...	1/1	Running	0	5m
kube-proxy-ip-172-20-120-133...	1/1	Running	0	4m
kube-proxy-ip-172-20-34-249...	1/1	Running	0	4m

```
kube-proxy-ip-172-20-65-28...            1/1    Running 0        4m
kube-proxy-ip-172-20-95-101...           1/1    Running 0        3m
kube-scheduler-ip-172-20-120-133...      1/1    Running 0        4m
kube-scheduler-ip-172-20-34-249...       1/1    Running 0        4m
kube-scheduler-ip-172-20-65-28...        1/1    Running 0        4m
```

As you can see, quite a few core components are running.

We can divide core (or system-level) components into two groups. Master components run only on masters. In our case, they are `kube-apiserver`, `kube-controller-manager`, `kube-scheduler`, `etcd`, and `dns-controller`. Node components run on all the nodes, both masters and workers. We already discussed a few of those. In addition to Protokube, Docker, and Kubelet, we got `kube-proxy`, as one more node component. Since this might be the first time you heard about those core components, we'll briefly explain each of their functions.

Kubernetes API Server (`kube-apiserver`) accepts requests to create, update, or remove Kubernetes resources. It listens on ports `8080` and `443`. The former is insecure and is only reachable from the same server. Through it, the other components can register themselves without requiring a token. The former port (`443`) is used for all external communications with the API Server. That communication can be user-facing like, for example, when we send a `kubectl` command. Kubelet also uses `443` port to reach the API server and register itself as a node.

No matter who initiates communication with the API Server, its purpose is to validate and configure API object. Among others, those can be Pods, Services, ReplicaSets, and others. Its usage is not limited to user-facing interactions. All the components in the cluster interact with the API Server for the operations that require a cluster-wide shared state.

The shared state of the cluster is stored in `etcd` (`https://github.com/coreos/etcd`). It is a key/value store where all cluster data is kept, and it is highly available through consistent data replication. It is split into two Pods, where `etcd-server` holds the state of the cluster and `etcd-server-events` stores the events.

Kops creates an **EBS volume** for each `etcd` instance. It serves as its storage.

Kubernetes Controller Manager (`kube-controller-manager`) is in charge of running controllers. You already saw a few controllers in action like `ReplicaSets` and `Deployments`. Apart from object controllers like those, `kube-controller-manager` is also in charge of Node Controllers responsible for monitoring servers and responding when one becomes unavailable.

Kubernetes Scheduler (kube-scheduler) watches the API Server for new Pods and assigns them to a node. From there on, those Pods are run by Kubelet on the allocated node.

DNS Controller (dns-controller) allows nodes and users to discover the API Server.

Kubernetes Proxy (kube-proxy) reflects Services defined through the API Server. It is in charge of TCP and UDP forwarding. It runs on all nodes of the cluster (both masters and workers).

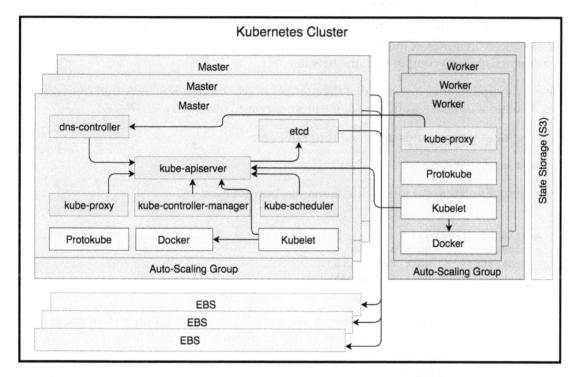

Figure 14-3: The core components of the cluster

There's much more going on in our new cluster. For now, we explored only the major components.

Next, we'll try to update our cluster.

Updating the cluster

No matter how much we plan, we will never manage to have a cluster with capacity that should serve us equally well today as tomorrow. Things change, and we'll need to be able to adapt to those changes. Ideally, our cluster should increase and decrease its capacity automatically by evaluating metrics and firing alerts that would interact with kops or directly with AWS. However, that is an advanced topic that we won't be able to cover. For now, we'll limit the scope to manual cluster updates.

With kops, we cannot update the cluster directly. Instead, we edit the desired state of the cluster stored, in our case, in the S3 bucket. Once the state is changed, kops will make the necessary changes to comply with the new desire.

We'll try to update the cluster so that the number of worker nodes is increased from one to two. In other words, we want to add one more server to the cluster.

Let's see the sub-commands provided through `kops edit`.

```
kops edit --help
```

The output, limited to the available commands, is as follows:

```
. . .
Available Commands:
  cluster         Edit cluster.
  federation      Edit federation.
  instancegroup Edit instancegroup.
. . .
```

We have three types of edits we can make. We did not set up federation, so that one is out of the game. You might think that `cluster` would provide the possibility to create a new worker node. However, that is not the case. If you execute `kops edit cluster --name $NAME`, you'll see that nothing in the configuration indicates how many nodes we should have. That is normal considering that we should not create servers in AWS directly. Just as Kubernetes, AWS also prefers declarative approach over imperative. At least, when dealing with EC2 instances.

Instead of sending an imperative instruction to create a new node, we'll change the value of the **Auto-Scaling Group** (**ASG**) related to worker nodes. Once we change ASG values, AWS will make sure that it complies with the new desire. It'll not only create a new server to comply with the new ASG sizes, but it will also monitor EC2 instances and maintain the desired number in case one of them fails.

So, we'll choose the third `kops edit` option.

```
kops edit ig --name $NAME nodes
```

We executed `kops edit ig` command, where `ig` is one of the aliases of `instancegroup`. We specified the name of the cluster with the `--name` argument. Finally, we set the type of the servers to `nodes`. As a result, we are presented with the `InstanceGroup` config for the Auto-Scaling Group associated with worker nodes.

The output is as follows.

```
apiVersion: kops/v1alpha2
kind: InstanceGroup
metadata:
  creationTimestamp: 2018-02-23T00:04:50Z
  labels:
    kops.k8s.io/cluster: devops23.k8s.local
  name: nodes
spec:
  image: kope.io/k8s-1.8-debian-jessie-amd64-hvm-ebs-2018-01-14
  machineType: t2.small
  maxSize: 1
  minSize: 1
  nodeLabels:
    kops.k8s.io/instancegroup: nodes
  role: Node
  subnets:
  - us-east-2a
  - us-east-2b
  - us-east-2c
```

Bear in mind that what you're seeing on the screen is not the standard output (`stdout`). Instead, the configuration is opened in your default editor. In my case, that is `vi`.

We can see some useful information from this config. For example, the `image` used to create EC2 instances is based on Debian. It is custom made for kops. The `machineType` represents EC2 size which is set to `t2.small`. Further down, you can see that we're running the VMs in three subnets or, since we're in AWS, three availability zones.

The parts of the config we care about are the `spec` entries `maxSize` and `minSize`. Both are set to `1` since that is the number of worker nodes we specified when we created the cluster. Please change the values of those two entries to `2`, save, and exit.

TIP

If you're using vi as your default editor, you'll need to press *I* to enter into the insert mode. From there on, you can change the values. Once you're finished editing, please press the *ESC* key, followed by :wq. Colon (:) allows us to enter commands, w is translated to save, and q to quit. Don't forget to press the enter key. If, on the other hand, you are not using vi, you're on your own. I'm sure that you'll know how to operate your default editor. If not, Google is your friend.

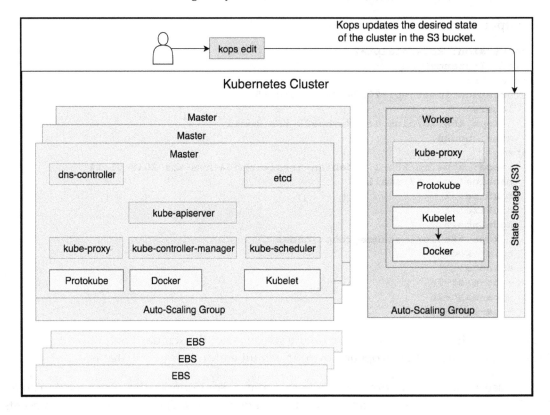

Figure 14-4: The process behind the kops edit command

Now that we changed the configuration, we need to tell kops that we want it to update the cluster to comply with the new desired state.

```
kops update cluster --name $NAME --yes
```

The output, limited to the last few lines, is as follows:

```
. . .
kops has set your kubectl context to devops23.k8s.local
Cluster changes have been applied to the cloud.
Changes may require instances to restart: kops rolling-update cluster
```

We can see that kops set our `kubectl` context to the cluster we updated. There was no need for that since that was already our context, but it did that anyway. Further on, we got the confirmation that the changes `have been applied to the cloud`.

The last sentence is interesting. It informed us that we can use `kops rolling-update`. The `kops update` command applies all the changes to the cluster at once. That can result in downtime. For example, if we wanted to change the image to a newer version, running `kops update` would recreate all the worker nodes at once. As a result, we'd have downtime from the moment instances are shut down until the new ones are created, and Kubernetes schedules the Pods in them. Kops knows that such an action should not be allowed so, if the update requires that servers are replaced, it does nothing expecting that you'll execute `kops rolling-update` afterward. That is not our case. Adding new nodes does not require restarts or replacement of the existing servers.

The `kops rolling-update` command intends to apply the changes without downtime. It would apply them to one server at the time so that most of the servers are always running. In parallel, Kubernetes would be rescheduling the Pods that were running on the servers that were brought down.

As long as our applications are scaled, `kops rolling-update` should not produce downtime.

Let's see what happened when we executed the `kops update` command.

1. Kops retrieved the desired state from the S3 bucket.
2. Kops sent requests to AWS API to change the values of the workers ASG.
3. AWS modified the values of the workers ASG by increasing them by 1.
4. ASG created a new EC2 instance to comply with the new sizing.
5. Protokube installed Kubelet and Docker and created the manifest file with the list of Pods.
6. Kubelet read the manifest file and run the container that forms the `kube-proxy` Pod (the only Pod on the worker nodes).

7. Kubelet sent a request to the `kube-apiserver` (through the `dns-controller`) to register the new node and join it to the cluster. The information about the new node is stored in `etcd`.

This process is almost identical to the one used to create the nodes of the cluster.

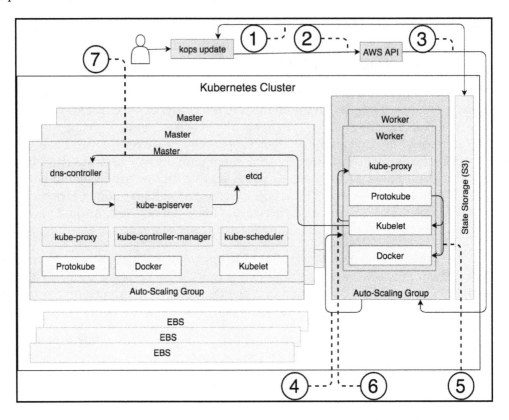

Figure 14-5: The process behind the kops update command

Unless you are a very slow reader, ASG created a new EC2 instance, and Kubelet joined it to the cluster. We can confirm that through the `kops validate` command.

```
kops validate cluster
```

The output is as follows:

```
Validating cluster devops23.k8s.local
INSTANCE GROUPS
NAME                ROLE    MACHINETYPE MIN MAX SUBNETS
master-us-east-2a Master t2.small     1   1   us-east-2a
master-us-east-2b Master t2.small     1   1   us-east-2b
master-us-east-2c Master t2.small     1   1   us-east-2c
nodes             Node    t2.small     2   2   us-east-2a,us-east-2b,us-
east-2c
NODE STATUS
NAME                ROLE    READY
ip-172-20-120-133... master True
ip-172-20-33-237...  node    True
ip-172-20-34-249...  master True
ip-172-20-65-28...   master True
ip-172-20-95-101...  node    True
Your cluster devops23.k8s.local is ready
```

We can see that now we have two nodes (there was one before) and that they are located somewhere inside the three us-east-2 availability zones.

Similarly, we can use kubectl to confirm that Kubernetes indeed added the new worker node to the cluster.

```
kubectl get nodes
```

The output is as follows:

```
NAME                STATUS ROLES  AGE VERSION
ip-172-20-120-133... Ready  master 13m v1.8.4
ip-172-20-33-237...  Ready  node    1m  v1.8.4
ip-172-20-34-249...  Ready  master 13m v1.8.4
ip-172-20-65-28...   Ready  master 13m v1.8.4
ip-172-20-95-101...  Ready  node   12m v1.8.4
```

That was easy, wasn't it? From now on, we can effortlessly add or remove nodes.

How about upgrading?

Upgrading the cluster manually

The process to upgrade the cluster depends on what we want to do.

If we'd like to upgrade it to a specific Kubernetes version, we can execute a similar process like the one we used to add a new worker node.

```
kops edit cluster $NAME
```

Just as before, we are about to edit the cluster definition. The only difference is that this time we're not editing a specific instance group, but the cluster as a whole.

If you explore the YAML file in front of you, you'll see that it contains the information we specified when we created the cluster, combined with the kops default values that we omitted to set.

For now, we're interested in `kubernetesVersion`. Please find it and change the version from `v1.8.4` to `v1.8.5`. Save and exit.

Now that we modified the desired state of the cluster, we can proceed with `kops update`.

```
kops update cluster $NAME
```

The last line of the output indicates that we *must specify --yes to apply changes*. Unlike the previous time we executed `kops update`, now we did not specify the argument `--yes`. As a result, we got a preview, or a dry-run, of what would happen if we apply the change. Previously, we added a new worker node, and that operation did not affect the existing servers. We were brave enough to update the cluster without previewing which resources will be created, updated, or destroyed. However, this time we are upgrading the servers in the cluster. Existing nodes will be replaced with new ones, and that is potentially dangerous operation. Later on, we might trust kops to do what's right and skip the preview altogether. But, for now, we should evaluate what will happen if we proceed.

Please go through the output. You'll see a git-like diff of the changes that will be applied to some of the resources that form the cluster. Take your time.

Now that you are confident with the changes, we can apply them.

```
kops update cluster $NAME --yes
```

The last line of the output states that `changes may require instances to restart:`
`kops rolling-update cluster`. We already saw that message before but, this time, the
update was not performed. The reason is simple, even though not necessarily very
intuitive. We can update auto-scaling groups since that results in creation or destruction of
nodes. But, when we need to replace them, as in this case, it would be disastrous to execute
a simple update. Updating everything at once would, at best, produce a downtime. In our
case, it's even worse. Destroying all the masters at once would likely result in a loss of
quorum. A new cluster might not be able to recuperate.

All in all, kops requires an extra step when "big bang" updating of the cluster might result
in undesirable results. So, we need to execute the `kops rolling-update` command. Since
we're still insecure, we'll run a preview first.

```
kops rolling-update cluster $NAME
```

The output is as follows:

```
NAME                STATUS      NEEDUPDATE READY MIN MAX NODES
master-us-east-2a NeedsUpdate 1          0     1   1   1
master-us-east-2b NeedsUpdate 1          0     1   1   1
master-us-east-2c NeedsUpdate 1          0     1   1   1
nodes             NeedsUpdate 2          0     2   2   2
Must specify --yes to rolling-update.
```

We can see that all the nodes require an update. Since we already evaluated the changes
through the output of the `kops update` command, we'll proceed and apply rolling
updates.

```
kops rolling-update cluster $NAME --yes
```

The rolling update process started, and it will take approximately 30 minutes to complete.

We'll explore the output as it comes:

```
NAME                STATUS      NEEDUPDATE READY MIN MAX NODES
master-us-east-2a NeedsUpdate 1          0     1   1   1
master-us-east-2b NeedsUpdate 1          0     1   1   1
master-us-east-2c NeedsUpdate 1          0     1   1   1
nodes             NeedsUpdate 2          0     2   2   2
```

The output starts with the same information we got when we asked for a preview, so there's not much to comment:

```
I0225 23:03:03.993068         1 instancegroups.go:130] Draining the node:
"ip-1
72-20-40-167...".
node "ip-172-20-40-167..." cordoned
node "ip-172-20-40-167..." cordoned
WARNING: Deleting pods not managed by ReplicationController,
 ReplicaSet, Job, DaemonSet or StatefulSet: etcd-server-events-
 ip-172-20-40-167..., etcd-server-ip-172-20-40-167..., kube-apiserver-
 ip-172-20-40-167..., kube-controller-manager-ip-172-20-40-167...,
 kube-proxy-ip-172-20-40-167..., kube-scheduler-ip-172-20-40-167...
node "ip-172-20-40-167..." drained
```

Instead of destroying the first node, kops picked one masters and drained it. That way, the applications running on it can shut down gracefully. We can see that it drained etcd-server-events, etcd-server-ip, kube-apiserver, kube-controller-manager, kube-proxy, kube-scheduler Pods running on the server ip-172-20-40-167. As a result, Kubernetes rescheduled them to one of the healthy nodes. That might not be true for all the Pods but only for those that can be rescheduled.

```
I0225 23:04:37.479407 1 instancegroups.go:237] Stopping instance "i-
06d40d6ff583fe10b", node "ip-172-20-40-167...", in group "master-us-east-
2a.masters.devops23.k8s.local".
```

We can see that after draining finished, the master node was stopped. Since each master is associated with an auto-scaling group, AWS will detect that the node is no more, and start a new one. Once the new server is initialized, nodeup will execute and install Docker, Kubelet, and Protokube. The latter will create the manifest that will be used by Kubelet to run the Pods required for a master node. Kubelet will also register the new node with one of the healthy masters.

That part of the process is the same as the one executed when creating a new cluster or when adding new servers. It is the part that takes longest to complete (around five minutes).

```
I0225 23:09:38.218945 1 instancegroups.go:161] Validating the cluster.
I0225 23:09:39.437456 1 instancegroups.go:212] Cluster validated.
```

We can see that, after waiting for everything to settle, kops validated the cluster, thus confirming that upgrade of the first master node finished successfully.

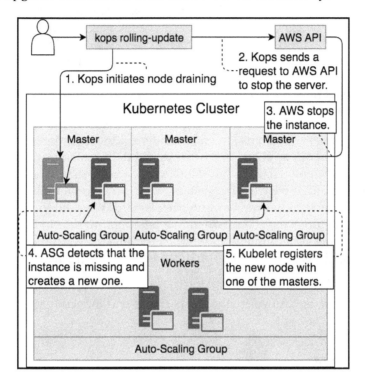

Figure 14-6: Rolling upgrade of one of the master nodes

As soon as it validated the upgrade of the first master, kops proceeded with the next node. During next ten to fifteen minutes, the same process will be repeated with the other two masters. Once all three are upgraded, kops will execute the same process with the worker nodes, and we'll have to wait for another ten to fifteen minutes.

```
I0225 23:34:01.148318 1 rollingupdate.go:191] Rolling update
    completed for cluster "devops23.k8s.local"!
```

Finally, once all the servers were upgraded, we can see that rolling update was completed.

The experience was positive but long. Auto-scaling groups need a bit of time to detect that a server is down. It takes a minute or two for a new VM to be created and initialized. Docker, Kubelet, and Protokube need to be installed. Containers that form core Pods need to be pulled. All in all, quite a few things need to happen.

The upgrade process would be faster if kops would use immutable approach and bake everything into images (AMIs). However, the choice was made to decouple OS with packages and core Pods, so the installation needs to be done at runtime. Also, the default distribution is Debian, which is not as light as, let's say, CoreOS. Due to those, and a few other design choices, the process is somehow lengthy. When combined with inevitable time AWS needs to do its part of the process, we're looking at over five minutes of upgrade duration for each node in a cluster. Even with only five nodes, the whole process is around thirty minutes. If we'd have a bigger cluster, it could take hours, or even days to upgrade.

Even though it takes considerable time to upgrade, the process is hands-free. If we are brave enough, we can let kops do its job and spend our time working on something more exciting. Assuming that our applications are designed to be scalable and fault-tolerant, we won't experience downtime. That is what matters much more than whether we'll be able to watch the process unfold. If we trust the system, we can just as well run it in the background and ignore it. However, earning trust is hard. We need to successfully run the process a few times before we put our fate in it. Even then, we should build a robust monitoring and alerting system that will notify us if things go wrong. Unfortunately, we won't cover those subjects in this book. You'll have to wait for the next one or explore it yourself.

Let's go back to our cluster and verify that Kubernetes was indeed upgraded.

```
kubectl get nodes
```

The output is as follows:

```
NAME                   STATUS ROLES   AGE VERSION
ip-172-20-107-172...   Ready  node    4m  v1.8.5
ip-172-20-124-177...   Ready  master  16m v1.8.5
ip-172-20-44-126...    Ready  master  28m v1.8.5
ip-172-20-56-244...    Ready  node    10m v1.8.5
ip-172-20-67-40...     Ready  master  22m v1.8.5
```

Judging by versions of each of the nodes, all were upgraded to v1.8.5. The process worked.

> Try to upgrade often. As a rule of thumb, you should upgrade one minor release at a time.

Even if you are a couple of minor releases behind the stable kops-recommended release, it's better if you execute multiple rolling upgrades (one for each minor release) than to jump to the latest at once. By upgrading to the next minor release, you'll minimize potential problems and simplify rollback if required.

Even though kops is fairly reliable, you should not trust it blindly. It's relatively easy to create a small testing cluster running the same release as production, execute the upgrade process, and validate that everything works as expected. Once finished, you can destroy the test cluster and avoid unnecessary expenses.

 Don't trust anyone. Test upgrades in a separate cluster.

Upgrading the cluster automatically

We edited cluster's desired state before we started the rolling update process. While that worked well, we're likely to always upgrade to the latest stable version. In those cases, we can execute the `kops upgrade` command.

```
kops upgrade cluster $NAME --yes
```

Please note that this time we skipped the preview by setting the `--yes` argument. The output is as follows:

```
ITEM     PROPERTY           OLD      NEW
Cluster  KubernetesVersion  v1.8.5   1.8.6
Updates applied to configuration.
You can now apply these changes, using 'kops update cluster
devops23.k8s.local'
```

We can see that the current Kubernetes version is `v1.8.5` and, in case we choose to proceed, it will be upgraded to the latest which, at the time of this writing, is `v1.8.6`.

```
kops update cluster $NAME --yes
```

Just as before, we can see from the last entry that `changes may require instances to restart: kops rolling-update cluster`.

Let's proceed:

```
kops rolling-update cluster $NAME --yes
```

I'll skip commenting on the output since it is the same as the previous time we upgraded the cluster. The only significant difference, from the process perspective, is that we did not edit cluster's desired state by specifying the version we want, but initiated the process through the `kops upgrade` command. Everything else was the same in both cases.

If we are to create a test cluster and write a set of tests that verify the upgrade process, we could execute the upgrade process periodically. We could, for example, create a job in Jenkins that would upgrade every month. If there isn't new Kubernetes release, it would do nothing. If there is, it would create a new cluster with the same release as production, upgrade it, validate that everything works as expected, destroy the testing cluster, upgrade the production cluster, and run another round of test. However, it takes time and experience to get to that point. Until then, manually executed upgrades are the way to go.

We are missing one more thing before we can deploy applications to our simulation of a production cluster.

Accessing the cluster

We need a way to access the cluster. So far, we saw that we can, at least, interact with the Kubernetes API. Every time we executed `kubectl`, it communicated with the cluster through the API server. That communication is established through AWS Elastic Load Balancer (ELB). Let's take a quick look at it.

```
aws elb describe-load-balancers
```

The output, limited to the relevant parts, is as follows:

```
{
    "LoadBalancerDescriptions": [
        {
            ...
            "ListenerDescriptions": [
                {
                    "Listener": {
                        "InstancePort": 443,
                        "LoadBalancerPort": 443,
                        "Protocol": "TCP",
                        "InstanceProtocol": "TCP"
                    },
                    ...
            "Instances": [
                {
                    "InstanceId": "i-01f5c2ca47168b248"
                },
```

```
    {
      "InstanceId": "i-0305e3b2d3da6e1ce"
    },
    {
      "InstanceId": "i-04291ef2432b462f2"
    }
  ],
  "DNSName": "api-devops23-k8s-local-ivnbim-1190013982.us-
east-2.elb.amazonaws.com",
  . . .
  "LoadBalancerName": "api-devops23-k8s-local-ivnbim",
  . . .
```

Judging from the `Listener` section, we can see that only port `443` is opened, thus allowing only SSL requests. The three instances belong to managers. We can safely assume that this load balancer is used only for the access to Kubernetes API. In other words, we are still missing access to worker nodes through which we'll be able to communicate with our applications. We'll come back to this issue in a moment.

The entry that matters, from user's perspective, is `DNSName`. That is the address we need to use if we want to communicate with Kubernetes' API Server. Load Balancer is there to ensure that we have a fixed address and that requests will be forwarded to one of the healthy masters.

Finally, the name of the load balancer is `api-devops23-k8s-local-ivnbim`. It is important that you remember that it starts with `api-devops23`. You'll see soon why the name matters.

We can confirm that the `DNSName` is indeed the door to the API by examining `kubectl` configuration:

```
kubectl config view
```

The output, limited to the relevant parts, is as follows:

```
apiVersion: v1
clusters:
- cluster:
    certificate-authority-data: REDACTED
    server:
https://api-devops23-k8s-local-ivnbim-1190013982.us-east-2.elb.am
 azonaws.com
  name: devops23.k8s.local
. . .
current-context: devops23.k8s.local
. . .
```

We can see that the `devops23.k8s.local` is set to use `amazonaws.com` subdomain as the server address and that it is the current context. That is the DNS of the ELB.

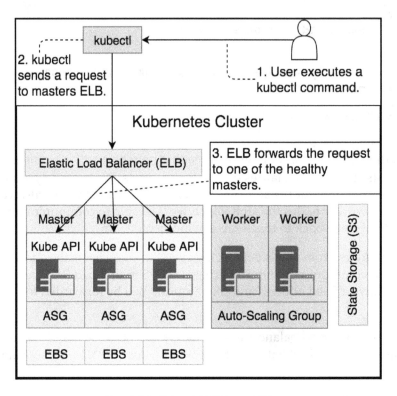

Figure 14-7: Load balancer behind Kubernetes API Server

The fact that we can access the API does not get us much closer to having a way to access applications we are soon to deploy. We already learned that we can use Ingress to channel requests to a set of ports (usually `80` and `443`). However, even if we deploy Ingress, we still need an entry point to the worker nodes. We need another load balancer sitting above the nodes.

Fortunately, kops has a solution.

We can use kops' add-ons to deploy additional core services. You can get the list of those currently available by exploring directories in
`https://github.com/kubernetes/kops/tree/master/addons`. Even though most of them are useful, we'll focus only on the task at hand.

Add-ons are, in most cases, Kubernetes resources defined in a YAML file. All we have to do is pick the addon we want, choose the version we prefer, and execute `kubectl create`. We'll create the resources defined in `ingress-nginx` version `v1.6.0`.

We won't go into details behind the definition YAML file we are about to use to create the resources kops assembled for us. I'll leave that up to you. Instead, we'll proceed with `kubectl create`.

```
kubectl create \
    -f
https://raw.githubusercontent.com/kubernetes/kops/master/addons/ingress-ngi
nx/v1.6.0.yaml
```

The output is as follows:

```
namespace "kube-ingress" created
serviceaccount "nginx-ingress-controller" created
clusterrole "nginx-ingress-controller" created
role "nginx-ingress-controller" created
clusterrolebinding "nginx-ingress-controller" created
rolebinding "nginx-ingress-controller" created
service "nginx-default-backend" created
deployment "nginx-default-backend" created
configmap "ingress-nginx" created
service "ingress-nginx" created
deployment "ingress-nginx" created
```

We can see that quite a few resources were created in the Namespace `kube-ingress`. Let's take a look what's inside.

```
kubectl --namespace kube-ingress \
    get all
```

The output is as follows:

```
NAME                                DESIRED CURRENT UP-TO-DATE AVAILABLE AGE
deploy/ingress-nginx                3       3       3          3         1m
deploy/nginx-default-backend 1      1       1       1          1m
NAME                                DESIRED CURRENT READY AGE
rs/ingress-nginx-768fc7997b         3       3       3     1m
rs/nginx-default-backend-74f9cd546d 1       1       1     1m
NAME                                READY  STATUS  RESTARTS AGE
```

```
po/ingress-nginx-768fc7997b-4xfq8      1/1   Running 0       1m
po/ingress-nginx-768fc7997b-c7zvx      1/1   Running 0       1m
po/ingress-nginx-768fc7997b-clr5m      1/1   Running 0       1m
po/nginx-default-backend-74f9cd546d-mtct8 1/1  Running 0     1m
NAME                    TYPE         CLUSTER-IP      EXTERNAL-IP
PORT(S)                 AGE
svc/ingress-nginx            LoadBalancer 100.66.190.165 abb5117871831...
80:301
    07/TCP,443:30430/TCP 1m
svc/nginx-default-backend ClusterIP     100.70.227.240 <none>
80/TCP
                   1m
```

We can see that it created two deployments, which created two ReplicaSets, which
created Pods. In addition, we got two Services as well. As a result, Ingress is running inside
our cluster and are a step closer to being able to test it. Still, we need to figure out how to
access the cluster.

One of the two Services (ingress-nginx) is LoadBalancer. We did not explore that type
when we discussed Services.

LoadBalancer Service type exposes the service externally using a cloud provider's load
balancer. NodePort and ClusterIP services, to which the external load balancer will
route, are automatically created. Ingress is "intelligent" enough to know how to create and
configure an AWS ELB. All it needed is an annotation
service.beta.kubernetes.io/aws-load-balancer-proxy-protocol (defined in the
YAML file).

You'll notice that the ingress-nginx Service published port 30107 and mapped it to 80.
30430 was mapped to 443. This means that, from inside the cluster, we should be able to
send HTTP requests to 30107 and HTTPS to 30430. However, that is only part of the story.
Since the Service is the LoadBalancer type, we should expect some changes to AWS
Elastic Load Balancers (**ELBs**) as well.

Let's check the state of the load balancers in our cluster.

```
aws elb describe-load-balancers
```

The output, limited to the relevant parts, is as follows:

```
{
    "LoadBalancerDescriptions": [
    {
        ...
        "LoadBalancerName": "api-devops23-k8s-local-ivnbim",
        ...
    },
    {
        ...
        "ListenerDescriptions": [
        {
            "Listener": {
                "InstancePort": 30107,
                "LoadBalancerPort": 80,
                "Protocol": "TCP",
                "InstanceProtocol": "TCP"
            },
            "PolicyNames": []
        },
        {
            "Listener": {
                "InstancePort": 30430,
                "LoadBalancerPort": 443,
                "Protocol": "TCP",
                "InstanceProtocol": "TCP"
            },
            "PolicyNames": []
        }
        ],
        ...
        "Instances": [
        {
            "InstanceId": "i-063fabc7ad5935db5"
        },
        {
            "InstanceId": "i-04d32c91cfc084369"
        }
        ],
        "DNSName": "a1c431cef1bfa11e88b600650be36f73-2136831960.us-
east-2.elb.amazonaws.com",
        ...
        "LoadBalancerName": "a1c431cef1bfa11e88b600650be36f73",
        ...
```

We can observe from the output that a new load balancer was added.

The new load balancer publishes port `80` (HTTP) and maps it to `30107`. This port is the same as the `ingress-nginx` Service published. Similarly, the LB published port `443` (HTTPS) and mapped it to `30430`. From the `Instances` section, we can see that it currently maps to the two worker nodes.

Further down, we can see the `DNSName`. We should retrieve it but, unfortunately, `LoadBalancerName` does not follow any format. However, we do know that now there are two load balancers and that the one dedicated to masters has a name that starts with `api-devops23`. So, we can retrieve the other LB by specifying that it should not contain that prefix. We'll use `jq` instruction `not` for that.

The command that retrieves DNS from the new load balancer is as follows:

```
CLUSTER_DNS=$(aws elb \
    describe-load-balancers | jq -r \
    ".LoadBalancerDescriptions[] \
    | select(.DNSName \
    | contains (\"api-devops23\") \
    | not).DNSName")
```

We'll come back to the newly created Ingress and the load balancer soon. For now, we'll move on and deploy the `go-demo-2` application.

Deploying applications

Deploying resources to a Kubernetes cluster running in AWS is no different from deployments anywhere else, including Minikube. That's one of the big advantages of Kubernetes, or of any other container scheduler. We have a layer of abstraction between hosting providers and our applications. As a result, we can deploy (almost) any YAML definition to any Kubernetes cluster, no matter where it is. That's huge. It gives up a very high level of freedom and allows us to avoid vendor locking. Sure, we cannot effortlessly switch from one scheduler to another, meaning that we are "locked" into the scheduler we chose. Still, it's better to depend on an open source project than on a commercial hosting vendor like AWS, GCE, or Azure.

We need to spend time setting up a Kubernetes cluster, and the steps will differ from one hosting provider to another. However, once a cluster is up-and-running, we can create any Kubernetes resource (almost) entirely ignoring what's underneath it. The result is the same no matter whether our cluster is AWS, GCE, Azure, on-prem, or anywhere else.

Let's get back to the task at hand and create `go-demo-2` resources:

```
cd ..
kubectl create \
    -f aws/go-demo-2.yml \
    --record --save-config
```

We moved back to the repository's root directory, and created the resources defined in `aws/go-demo-2.yml`. The output is as follows:

```
ingress "go-demo-2" created
deployment "go-demo-2-db" created
service "go-demo-2-db" created
deployment "go-demo-2-api" created
service "go-demo-2-api" created
```

Next, we should wait until `go-demo-2-api` Deployment is rolled out.

```
kubectl rollout status \
    deployment go-demo-2-api
```

The output is as follows:

```
deployment "go-demo-2-api" successfully rolled out
```

Finally, we can validate that the application is running and is accessible through the DNS provided by the AWS **Elastic Load Balancer (ELB)**:

```
curl -i "http://$CLUSTER_DNS/demo/hello"
```

We got response code `200` and the message `hello, world!`. The Kubernetes cluster we set up in AWS works!

When we sent the request to the ELB dedicated to workers, it performed round-robin and forwarded it to one of the healthy nodes. Once inside the worker, the request was picked by the `nginx` Service, forwarded to Ingress, and, from there, to one of the containers that form the replicas of the `go-demo-2-api` ReplicaSet.

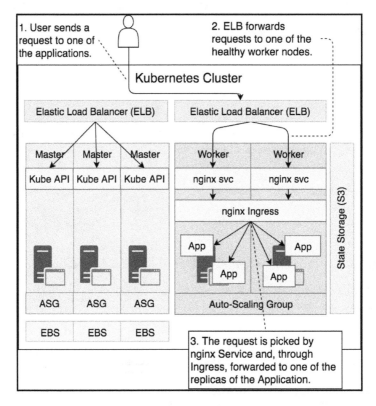

Figure 14-8: Load balancer behind Kubernetes worker nodes

It might be worth pointing out that containers that form our applications are always running in worker nodes. Master servers, on the other hand, are entirely dedicated to running Kubernetes system. That does not mean that we couldn't create a cluster in the way that masters and workers are combined into the same servers, just as we did with Minikube. However, that is risky, and we're better off separating the two types of nodes. Masters are more reliable when they are running on dedicated servers. Kops knows that, and it does not even allow us to mix the two.

Exploring high-availability and fault-tolerance

The cluster would not be reliable if it wouldn't be fault tolerant. Kops intents to make it so, but we're going to validate that anyways.

Let's retrieve the list of worker node instances:

```
aws ec2 \
    describe-instances | jq -r \
    ".Reservations[].Instances[] \
    | select(.SecurityGroups[]\
    .GroupName==\"nodes.$NAME\")\
    .InstanceId"
```

We used `aws ec2 describe-instances` to retrieve all the instances (five in total). The output was sent to `jq`, which filtered them by the security group dedicated to worker nodes.

The output is as follows:

```
i-063fabc7ad5935db5
i-04d32c91cfc084369
```

We'll terminate one of the worker nodes. To do that, we'll pick a random one, and retrieve its ID.

```
INSTANCE_ID=$(aws ec2 \
    describe-instances | jq -r \
    ".Reservations[].Instances[] \
    | select(.SecurityGroups[]\
    .GroupName==\"nodes.$NAME\")\
    .InstanceId" | tail -n 1)
```

We used the same command as before and added `tail -n 1`, so that the output is limited to a single line (entry). We stored the result in the `INSTANCE_ID` variable. Now we know which instance to terminate.

```
aws ec2 terminate-instances \
    --instance-ids $INSTANCE_ID
```

The output is as follows:

```
{
  "TerminatingInstances": [
    {
```

```
    "InstanceId": "i-063fabc7ad5935db5",
    "CurrentState": {
      "Code": 32,
      "Name": "shutting-down"
    },
    "PreviousState": {
      "Code": 16,
      "Name": "running"
    }
   }
  ]
 }
```

We can see from the output that the instance is shutting down. We can confirm that by listing all the instances from the security group `nodes.devops23.k8s.local`.

```
aws ec2 describe-instances | jq -r \
    ".Reservations[].Instances[] \
    | select(\
    .SecurityGroups[].GroupName \
    ==\"nodes.$NAME\").InstanceId"
```

The output is as follows:

```
i-04d32c91cfc084369
```

As expected, we are now running only one instance. All that's left is to wait for a minute, and repeat the same command.

```
aws ec2 \
    describe-instances | jq -r \
    ".Reservations[].Instances[] \
    | select(.SecurityGroups[]\
    .GroupName==\"nodes.$NAME\")\
    .InstanceId"
```

The output is as follows:

```
i-003b4b1934d85641a
i-04d32c91cfc084369
```

This time, we can see that there are again two instances. The only difference is that this time one of the instance IDs is different.

AWS auto-scaling group discovered that the instances do not match the desired number, and it created a new one.

The fact that AWS created a node to replace the one we terminated does not mean that the new server joined the Kubernetes cluster. Let's verify that:

```
kubectl get nodes
```

The output is as follows:

```
NAME                                         STATUS ROLES   AGE VERSION
ip-172-20-55-183.us-east-2.compute.internal Ready  master 30m v1.
  8.6
ip-172-20-61-82.us-east-2.compute.internal  Ready  node   13m v1.
  8.6
ip-172-20-71-53.us-east-2.compute.internal  Ready  master 30m v1.
  8.6
ip-172-20-97-39.us-east-2.compute.internal  Ready  master 30m v1.
  8.6
```

If you were fast enough, your output should also show that there is only one (worker) node. Once AWS created a new server, it takes a bit of time until Docker, Kubelet, and Protokube are installed, containers are pulled and run, and the node is registered through one of the masters.

Let's try it again.

```
kubectl get nodes
```

The output is as follows:

```
NAME                                         STATUS ROLES   AGE VERSION
ip-172-20-55-183.us-east-2.compute.internal Ready  master 32m v1.
  8.6
ip-172-20-61-82.us-east-2.compute.internal  Ready  node   15m v1.
  8.6
ip-172-20-71-53.us-east-2.compute.internal  Ready  master 32m v1.
  8.6
ip-172-20-79-161.us-east-2.compute.internal Ready  node   2m  v1.
  8.6
ip-172-20-97-39.us-east-2.compute.internal  Ready  master 32m v1.
  8.6
```

This time, the number of (worker) nodes is back to two. Our cluster is back in the desired state.

What we just experienced is, basically, the same as when we executed the rolling upgrade. The only difference is that we terminated an instance as a way to simulate a failure. During the upgrade process, kops does the same. It shuts down one instance at a time and waits until the cluster goes back to the desired state.

Feel free to do a similar test with master nodes. The only difference is that you'll have to use `masters` instead of `nodes` as the prefix of the security group name. Since everything else is the same, I trust you won't need instructions and explanations.

Giving others access to the cluster

Unless you're planning to be the only person in your organization with the access to the cluster, you'll need to create a `kubectl` configuration that you can distribute to your coworkers. Let's see the steps:

```
cd cluster
mkdir -p config
export KUBECONFIG=$PWD/config/kubecfg.yaml
```

We went back to the `cluster` directory, created the sub-directory `config`, and exported `KUBECONFIG` variable with the path to the file where we'd like to store the configuration. Now we can execute `kops export`:

```
kops export kubecfg --name ${NAME}
cat $KUBECONFIG
```

The output of the latter command is as follows:

```
apiVersion: v1
clusters:
- cluster:
    certificate-authority-data: ...
    server:
https://api-devops23-k8s-local-ivnbim-609446190.us-east-2.elb.amazonaws.com
  name: devops23.k8s.local
contexts:
- context:
    cluster: devops23.k8s.local
    user: devops23.k8s.local
  name: devops23.k8s.local
current-context: devops23.k8s.local
kind: Config
preferences: {}
users:
```

```
  - name: devops23.k8s.local
    user:
      as-user-extra: {}
      client-certificate-data: ...
      client-key-data: ...
      password: oeezRbhG4yz3oBUO5kf7DSWcOwvjKZ61
      username: admin
  - name: devops23.k8s.local-basic-auth
    user:
      as-user-extra: {}
      password: oeezRbhG4yz3oBUO5kf7DSWcOwvjKZ61
      username: admin
```

Now you can pass that configuration to one of your coworkers, and he'll have the same access as you.

Truth be told, you should create a new user and a password or, even better, an SSH key and let each user in your organization access the cluster with their own authentication. You should also create RBAC permissions for each user or a group of users. We won't go into the steps how to do that since they are already explained in the `Chapter 12`, *Securing Kubernetes Clusters*.

Destroying the cluster

The chapter is almost finished, and we do not need the cluster anymore. We want to destroy it as soon as possible. There's no good reason to keep it running when we're not using it. But, before we proceed with the destructive actions, we'll create a file that will hold all the environment variables we used in this chapter. That will help us the next time we want to recreate the cluster.

```
echo "export AWS_ACCESS_KEY_ID=$AWS_ACCESS_KEY_ID
export AWS_SECRET_ACCESS_KEY=$AWS_SECRET_ACCESS_KEY
export AWS_DEFAULT_REGION=$AWS_DEFAULT_REGION
export ZONES=$ZONES
export NAME=$NAME
export KOPS_STATE_STORE=$KOPS_STATE_STORE" \
    >kops
```

We echoed the variables with the values into the `kops` file, and now we can delete the cluster:

```
kops delete cluster \
    --name $NAME \
    --yes
```

The output is as follows:

```
...
Deleted kubectl config for devops23.k8s.local
Deleted cluster: "devops23.k8s.local"
```

Kops removed references of the cluster from our `kubectl` configuration and proceeded to delete all the AWS resources it created. Our cluster is no more. We can proceed and delete the S3 bucket as well.

```
aws s3api delete-bucket \
    --bucket $BUCKET_NAME
```

We will not remove the IAM resources (group, user, access key, and policies). It does not cost to keep them in AWS, and we'll save ourselves from re-running the commands that create them. However, I will list the commands as a reference.

Do NOT execute following commands. They are only a reference. We'll need those resources in the next chapter.

```
# Replace `[...]` with the administrative access key ID.
export AWS_ACCESS_KEY_ID=[...]
# Replace `[...]` with the administrative secret access key.
export AWS_SECRET_ACCESS_KEY=[...]
aws iam remove-user-from-group \
    --user-name kops \
    --group-name kops
aws iam delete-access-key \
    --user-name kops \
    --access-key-id $(\
    cat kops-creds | jq -r\
    '.AccessKey.AccessKeyId')
aws iam delete-user \
    --user-name kops
aws iam detach-group-policy \
    --policy-arn arn:aws:iam::aws:policy/AmazonEC2FullAccess \
    --group-name kops
aws iam detach-group-policy \
```

```
    --policy-arn arn:aws:iam::aws:policy/AmazonS3FullAccess \
    --group-name kops

aws iam detach-group-policy \
    --policy-arn arn:aws:iam::aws:policy/AmazonVPCFullAccess \
    --group-name kops
aws iam detach-group-policy \
    --policy-arn arn:aws:iam::aws:policy/IAMFullAccess \
    --group-name kops
aws iam delete-group \
    --group-name kops
```

What now?

We have a production-ready Kubernetes cluster running in AWS. Isn't that something worthwhile a celebration?

Kops proved to be relatively easy to use. We executed more `aws` than `kops` commands. If we exclude them, the whole cluster can be created with a single `kops` command. We can easily add or remove worker nodes. Upgrades are simple and reliable, if a bit long. The important part is that through rolling upgrades we can avoid downtime.

There are a few `kops` command we did not explore. I feel that now you know the important parts and that you will be able to figure out the rest through the documentation.

You might be inclined to think that you are ready to apply everything you learned so far. Do not open that champagne bottle you've been saving for special occasions. There's still one significant topic we need to explore. We postponed the discussion about stateful services since we did not have the ability to use external drives. We did use volumes, but they were all local, and do not qualify as persistent. Failure of a single server would prove that. Now that we are running a cluster in AWS, we can explore how to deploy stateful applications.

Kubernetes operations (kops) compared to Docker for AWS

Docker for AWS (D4AWS) quickly became the preferable way to create a Docker Swarm cluster in AWS (and Azure). Similarly, kops is the most commonly used tool to create Kubernetes clusters in AWS. At least, at the time of this writing.

The result, with both tools, is more or less the same. Both create Security Groups, VPCs, Auto-Scaling Groups, Elastic Load Balancers, and everything else a cluster needs. In both cases, Auto-Scaling Groups are in charge of creating EC2 instances. Both rely on external storage to keep the state of the cluster (kops in S3 and D4AWS in DynamoDB). In both cases, EC2 instances brought to life by Auto-Scaling Groups know how to run system-level services and join the cluster. If we exclude the fact that one solution runs Docker Swarm and that the other uses Kubernetes, there is no significant functional difference if we observe only the result (the cluster). So, we'll focus on user experience instead.

Both tools can be executed from the command line and that's where we can spot the first difference.

Docker for AWS relies on CloudFormation templates, so we need to execute `aws cloudformation` command. Docker provides a template and we should use parameters to customize it. In my humble opinion, the way CloudFormation expects us to pass parameters is just silly.

Let's take a look at an example:

```
aws cloudformation create-stack \
    --template-url
https://editions-us-east-1.s3.amazonaws.com/aws/stable/Docker.tmpl \
    --capabilities CAPABILITY_IAM \
    --stack-name devops22 \
    --parameters \
    ParameterKey=ManagerSize,ParameterValue=3 \
    ParameterKey=ClusterSize,ParameterValue=2 \
    ParameterKey=KeyName,ParameterValue=workshop \
    ParameterKey=EnableSystemPrune,ParameterValue=yes \
    ParameterKey=EnableCloudWatchLogs,ParameterValue=no \
    ParameterKey=EnableCloudStorEfs,ParameterValue=yes \
    ParameterKey=ManagerInstanceType,ParameterValue=t2.small \
    ParameterKey=InstanceType,ParameterValue=t2.small
```

Having to write something like `ParameterKey=ManagerSize,ParameterValue=3` instead of `ManagerSize=3` is annoying at best.

A sample command that creates Kubernetes cluster using `kops` is as follows:

```
kops create cluster \
    --name $NAME \
    --master-count 3 \
    --node-count 1 \
    --node-size t2.small \
    --master-size t2.small \
    --zones $ZONES \
    --master-zones $ZONES \
    --ssh-public-key devops23.pub \
    --networking kubenet \
    --kubernetes-version v1.8.4 \
    --yes
```

Isn't that easier and more intuitive?

Moreover, kops is a binary with everything we would expect. We can, for example, execute `kops --help` and see the available options and a few examples. If we'd like to know which parameters are available with Docker For AWS, we'd need to go through the template. That's definitely less intuitive and more difficult than running `kops create cluster --help`. Even if we don't mind browsing through the Docker For AWS template, we still don't have examples at hand (from the command line, not browser). From user experience perspective, kops wins over Docker For AWS if we restrict the comparison only to command line interface. Simply put, executing a well-defined binary dedicated to managing a cluster is better than executing `aws cloudformation` commands with remote templates.

Did Docker make a mistake for choosing CloudFormation? I don't think so. Even if command line experience is suboptimal, it is apparent that they wanted to provide an experience native to hosting vendor. In our case that's AWS, but the same can be said for Azure. If you will always operate cluster from the command line (as I think you should), this is where the story ends and kops is a winner with a very narrow margin.

The fact that we can create Docker For AWS cluster using CloudFormation means that we can take advantage of it from AWS Console. That translates into UI experience. We can use AWS Console UI to create, update, or delete a cluster. We can see the events as they progress, explore the resources that were created, roll back to the previous version, and so on. By choosing CloudFormation template, Docker decided to provide not only command line but also a visual experience.

Personally, I think that UIs are evil and that we should do everything from the command line. That being said, I'm fully aware that not everybody feels the same. Even if you do choose never to use UI for "real" work, it is very helpful, at least at the beginning, as a learning experience of what can and what cannot be done, and how all the steps tie together.

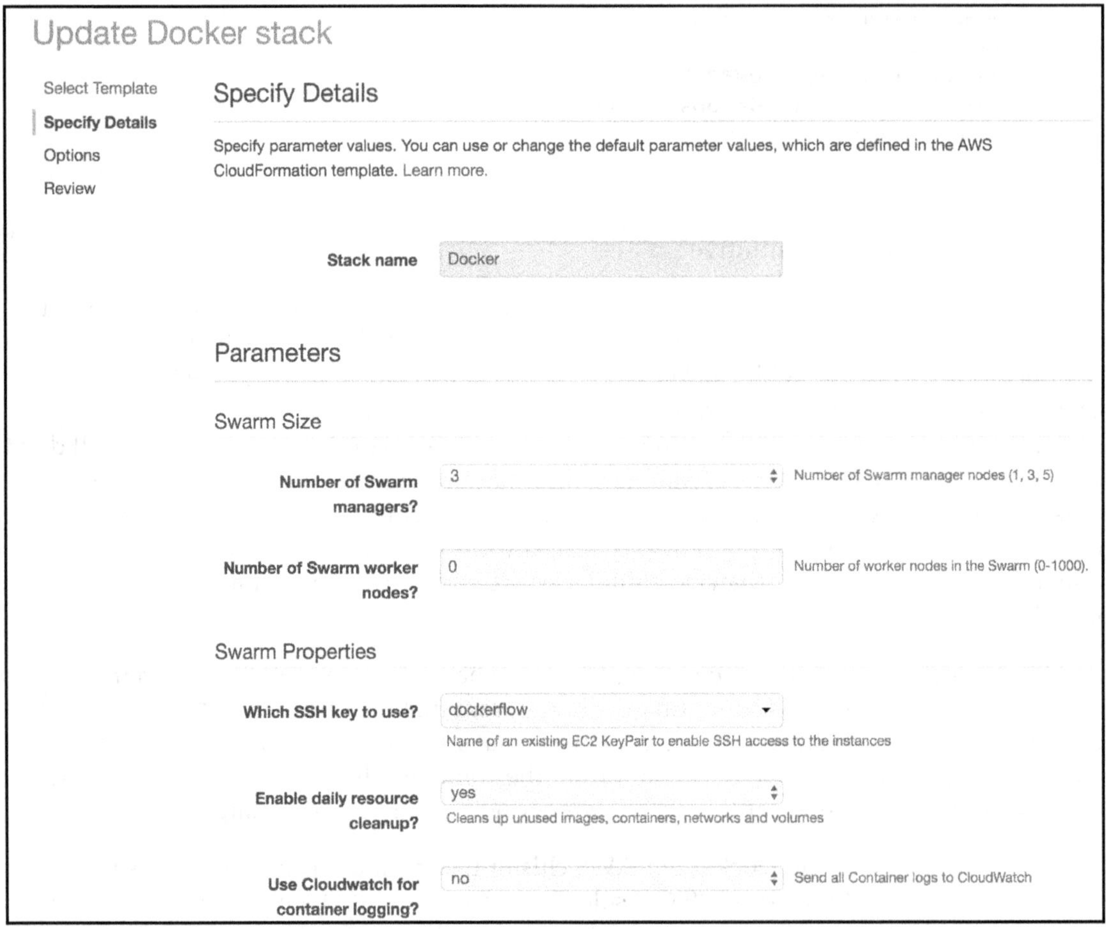

Update Docker stack

Select Template

Specify Details

Options

Review

Specify Details

Specify parameter values. You can use or change the default parameter values, which are defined in the AWS CloudFormation template. Learn more.

Stack name Docker

Parameters

Swarm Size

Number of Swarm managers?	3 — Number of Swarm manager nodes (1, 3, 5)
Number of Swarm worker nodes?	0 — Number of worker nodes in the Swarm (0-1000).

Swarm Properties

Which SSH key to use?	dockerflow ▼ — Name of an existing EC2 KeyPair to enable SSH access to the instances
Enable daily resource cleanup?	yes — Cleans up unused images, containers, networks and volumes
Use Cloudwatch for container logging?	no — Send all Container logs to CloudWatch

Figure 14-9: Docker For AWS UI

It's a tough call. What matters is that both tools are creating reliable clusters. Kops is more user-friendly from the command line, but it has no UI. Docker For AWS, on the other hand, works as native AWS solution through CloudFormation. That gives it the UI, but at the cost of suboptimal command line experience.

You won't have to choose one over the other since the choice will not depend on which one you like more, but whether you want to use Docker Swarm or Kubernetes.

15
Persisting State

> Having fault-tolerance and high-availability is of no use if we lose
> application state during rescheduling. Having state is unavoidable, and
> we need to preserve it no matter what happens to our applications,
> servers, or even a whole datacenter.

The way to preserve the state of our applications depends on their architecture. Some are
storing data in-memory and rely on periodic backups. Others are capable of synchronizing
data between multiple replicas, so that loss instance of one does not result in loss of data.
Most, however, are relying on disk to store their state. We'll focus on that group of stateful
applications.

If we are to build fault-tolerant systems, we need to make sure that failure of any part of the
system is recoverable. Since speed is of the essence, we cannot rely on manual operations to
recuperate from failures. Even if we could, no one wants to be the person sitting in front of
a screen, waiting for something to fail, only to bring it back to its previous state.

We already saw that Kubernetes would, in most cases, recuperate from a failure of an
application, of a server, or even of a whole datacenter. It'll reschedule Pods to healthy
nodes. We also experienced how AWS and kops accomplish more or less the same effect on
the infrastructure level. Auto-scaling groups will recreate failed nodes and, since they are
provisioned with kops startup processes, new instances will have everything they need,
and they will join the cluster.

The only thing that prevents us from saying that our system is (mostly) highly available
and fault tolerant is the fact that we did not solve the problem of persisting state across
failures. That's the subject we'll explore next.

We'll try to preserve our data no matter what happens to our stateful applications or the
servers where they run.

Creating a Kubernetes cluster

We'll start by recreating a similar cluster as the one we used in the previous chapter:

 All the commands from this chapter are available in the 15-pv.sh (https://gist.github.com/vfarcic/41c86eb385dfc5c881d910c5e98596f 2) Gist.

```
cd k8s-specs
git pull
cd cluster
```

We entered the local copy of the k8s-specs repository, pulled the latest code, and went into the cluster directory.

In the previous chapter, we stored the environment variables we used in the kops file. Let's take a quick look at them.

```
cat kops
```

The output, without the keys, is as follows:

```
export AWS_ACCESS_KEY_ID=...
export AWS_SECRET_ACCESS_KEY=...
export AWS_DEFAULT_REGION=us-east-2
export ZONES=us-east-2a,us-east-2b,us-east-2c
export NAME=devops23.k8s.local
export KOPS_STATE_STORE=s3://devops23-1520933480
```

By storing the environment variables in a file, we can fast-track the process by loading them using the source command.

 In the older editions of the book, there was an error in the command we used to store the environment variables in the kops file. The export commands were missing. Please ensure that your copy of the file has all the lines starting with export. If that's not the case, please update it accordingly.

```
source kops
```

Now that the environment variables are set, we can proceed to create an S3 bucket:

```
export BUCKET_NAME=devops23-$(date +%s)
aws s3api create-bucket \
    --bucket $BUCKET_NAME \
```

```
    --create-bucket-configuration \
    LocationConstraint=$AWS_DEFAULT_REGION
export KOPS_STATE_STORE=s3://$BUCKET_NAME
```

The command that creates the `kops` alias is as follows. Execute it only if you are a **Windows user**:

```
alias kops="docker run -it --rm \
    -v $PWD/devops23.pub:/devops23.pub \
    -v $PWD/config:/config \
    -e KUBECONFIG=/config/kubecfg.yaml \
    -e NAME=$NAME -e ZONES=$ZONES \
    -e AWS_ACCESS_KEY_ID=$AWS_ACCESS_KEY_ID \
    -e AWS_SECRET_ACCESS_KEY=$AWS_SECRET_ACCESS_KEY \
    -e KOPS_STATE_STORE=$KOPS_STATE_STORE \
    vfarcic/kops"
```

Now we can, finally, create a new Kubernetes cluster in AWS.

```
kops create cluster \
    --name $NAME \
    --master-count 3 \
    --master-size t2.small \
    --node-count 2 \
    --node-size t2.medium \
  --zones $ZONES \
    --master-zones $ZONES \
    --ssh-public-key devops23.pub \
    --networking kubenet \
    --yes
```

If we compare that command with the one we executed in the previous chapter, we'll notice only a few minor changes. We increased `node-count` to 2 and `node-size` to `t2.medium`. That will give us more than enough capacity for the exercises we'll run in this chapter.

Let's validate the cluster:

```
kops validate cluster
```

Assuming that enough time passed since we executed `kops create cluster`, the output should indicate that the `cluster devops23.k8s.local is ready`.

A note to Windows users

Kops was executed inside a container. It changed the context inside the container that is now gone. As a result, your local `kubectl` context was left intact. We'll fix that by executing `kops export kubecfg --name ${NAME}` and `export KUBECONFIG=$PWD/config/kubecfg.yaml`. The first command exported the config to `/config/kubecfg.yaml`. That path was specified through the environment variable `KUBECONFIG` and is mounted as `config/kubecfg.yaml` on local hard disk. The latter command exports `KUBECONFIG` locally. Through that variable, `kubectl` is now instructed to use the configuration in `config/kubecfg.yaml` instead of the default one. Before you run those commands, please give AWS a few minutes to create all the EC2 instances and for them to join the cluster. After waiting and executing those commands, you'll be all set.

We'll need Ingress if we'd like to access the applications we'll deploy.

```
kubectl create \
    -f
https://raw.githubusercontent.com/kubernetes/kops/master/addons/ingress-ngi
nx/v1.6.0.yaml
```

Ingress will not help us much without the ELB DNS, so we'll get that as well:

```
CLUSTER_DNS=$(aws elb \
    describe-load-balancers | jq -r \
    ".LoadBalancerDescriptions[] \
    | select(.DNSName \
    | contains (\"api-devops23\") \
    | not).DNSName")
echo $CLUSTER_DNS
```

The output of the latter command should end with `us-east-2.elb.amazonaws.com`.

Finally, now that we are finished with the cluster setup, we can go back to the repository root directory.

```
cd ..
```

Deploying stateful applications without persisting state

We'll start the exploration by deploying a stateful application without any mechanism to persist its state. That will give us a better insight into benefits behind of some of the Kubernetes concepts and resources we'll use in this chapter.

We already deployed Jenkins a few times. Since it is a stateful application, it is an excellent candidate to serve as a playground.

Let's take a look at a definition stored in the `pv/jenkins-no-pv.yml` file.

```
cat pv/jenkins-no-pv.yml
```

The YAML defines the `jenkins` namespace, an Ingress controller, and a service. We're already familiar with those types of resources so we'll skip explaining them and jump straight to the Deployment definition.

The output of the `cat` command, limited to the `jenkins` Deployment, is as follows:

```
. . .
apiVersion: apps/v1beta2
kind: Deployment
metadata:
  name: Jenkins
    namespace: Jenkins
  spec:
    selector:
      matchLabels:
        app: Jenkins
    strategy:
      type: Recreate
    template:
      metadata:
        labels:
          app: Jenkins
      spec:
        containers:
        - name: Jenkins
          image: vfarcic/Jenkins
          env:
          - name: JENKINS_OPTS
            value: --prefix=/Jenkins
          volumeMounts:
          - name: jenkins-creds
            mountPath: /etc/secrets
```

```
            resources:
              limits:
                memory: 2Gi
                cpu: 1
              requests:
                memory: 1Gi
                cpu: 0.5
          volumes:
          - name: jenkins-creds
            secret:
              secretName: jenkins-creds
```

There's nothing special about this Deployment. We already used a very similar one. Besides, by now, you're an expert at Deployment controllers.

The only thing worth mentioning is that there is only one volume mount and it references a secret we're using to provide Jenkins with the initial administrative user. Jenkins is persisting its state in `/var/jenkins_home`, and we are not mounting that directory.

Let's create the resources defined in `pv/jenkins-no-pv.yml`:

```
kubectl create \
    -f pv/jenkins-no-pv.yml \
    --record --save-config
```

The output is as follows:

```
namespace "jenkins" created
ingress "jenkins" created
service "jenkins" created
deployment "jenkins" created
```

We'll take a quick look at the events as a way to check that everything was deployed successfully:

```
kubectl --namespace jenkins \
    get events
```

The output, limited to relevant parts, is as follows:

```
...
2018-03-14 22:36:26 +0100 CET   2018-03-14 22:35:54 +0100 CET   7
jenkins-8768d486-lmv6b.151be70fd682e40d   Pod                     Warning
FailedMount  kubelet, ip-172-20-99-208.us-east-2.compute.internal
MountVolume.SetUp
```

```
failed for volume "jenkins-creds" : secrets "jenkins-creds" not found
    ...
```

We can see that the setup of the only volume failed since it could not find the secret referenced as `jenkins-creds`. Let's create it:

```
kubectl --namespace jenkins \
    create secret \
    generic jenkins-creds \
    --from-literal=jenkins-user=jdoe \
    --from-literal=jenkins-pass=incognito
```

Now, with the secret `jenkins-creds` created in the `jenkins` namespace, we can confirm that the rollout of the Deployment was successful.

```
kubectl --namespace jenkins \
    rollout status \
    deployment jenkins
```

We can see, from the output, that the `deployment "jenkins" was successfully rolled out`.

Now that everything is up and running, we can open Jenkins UI in a browser:

```
open "http://$CLUSTER_DNS/jenkins"
```

A note to Windows users
Git Bash might not be able to use the `open` command. If that's the case, please replace the `open` command with `echo`. As a result, you'll get the full address that should be opened directly in your browser of choice.

Please click the **Log in** link, type `jdoe` as the **User,** and `incognito` as the **Password**. When finished, click the **log in** button.

Now that we are authenticated as **jdoe** administrator, we can proceed and create a job. That will generate a state that we can use to explore what happens when a stateful application fails.

Please click the **create new jobs** link, type `my-job` as the item name, select **Pipeline** as the job type, and press the **OK** button.

You'll be presented with the job configuration screen. There's no need to do anything here since we are not, at the moment, interested in any specific Pipeline definition. It's enough to click the **Save** button.

Next, we'll simulate a failure by killing `java` process running inside the Pod created by the `jenkins` Deployment. To do that, we need to find out the name of the Pod.

```
kubectl --namespace jenkins \
    get pods \
    --selector=app=jenkins \
    -o json
```

We retrieved the Pods from the `jenkins` namespace, filtered them with the selector `api=jenkins`, and formatted the output as `json`.

The output, limited to the relevant parts, as is follows:

```
{
  "apiVersion": "v1",
    "items": [
    {
      ...
      "metadata": {
        ...
        "name": "jenkins-8768d486-1mv6b",
        ...
```

We can see that the name is inside `metadata` entry of one of the `items`. We can use that to formulate `jsonpath` that will retrieve only the name of the Pod:

```
POD_NAME=$(kubectl \
    --namespace jenkins \
    get pods \
    --selector=app=jenkins \
    -o jsonpath="{.items[*].metadata.name}")
echo $POD_NAME
```

The name of the Pod is now stored in the environment variable `POD_NAME`.

The output of the latter command is as follows:

```
jenkins-8768d486-1mv6b
```

Now that we know the name of the Pod hosting Jenkins, we can proceed and kill the `java` process:

```
kubectl --namespace jenkins \
    exec -it $POD_NAME pkill java
```

The container failed once we killed Jenkins process. We already know from experience that a failed container inside a Pod will be recreated. As a result, we had a short downtime, but Jenkins is running once again.

Let's see what happened to the job we created earlier. I'm sure you know the answer, but we'll check it anyway:

```
open "http://$CLUSTER_DNS/jenkins"
```

As expected, `my-job` is nowhere to be found. The container that was hosting `/var/jenkins_home` directory failed, and it was replaced with a new one. The state we created is lost.

Truth be told, we already saw in the `Chapter 8`, *Using Volumes to Access Host's File System* that we can mount a volume in an attempt to preserve state across failures. However, in the past, we used `emptyDir` which mounts a local volume. Even though that's better than nothing, such a volume exists only as long as the server it is stored in is up and running. If the server would fail, the state stored in `emptyDir` would be gone. Such a solution would be only slightly better than not using any volume. By using local disk we would only postpone inevitable, and, sooner or later, we'd get to the same situation. We'd be left wondering why we lost everything we created in Jenkins. We can do better than that.

Creating AWS volumes

If we want to persist state that will survive even server failures, we have two options we can choose. We could, for example, store data locally and replicate it to multiple servers. That way, a container could use local storage knowing that the files are available on all the servers. Such a setup would be too complicated if we'd like to implement the process ourselves. Truth be told, we could use one of the volume drivers for that. However, we'll opt for a more commonly used method to persist the state across failures. We'll use external storage.

Since we are running our cluster in AWS, we can choose between S3 (`https://aws.amazon.com/s3/`), **Elastic File System** (**EFS**) (`https://aws.amazon.com/efs/`), and **Elastic Block Store** (**EBS**) (`https://aws.amazon.com/ebs/`).

S3 is meant to be accessed through its API and is not suitable as a local disk replacement. That leaves us with EFS and EBS.

EFS, has a distinct advantage that it can be mounted to multiple EC2 instances spread across multiple availability zones. It is closest we can get to fault-tolerant storage. Even if a whole zone (datacenter) fails, we'll still be able to use EFS in the rest of the zones used by our cluster. However, that comes at a cost. EFS introduces a performance penalty. It is, after all, a **network file system (NFS)**, and that entails higher latency.

Elastic Block Store (EBS) is the fastest storage we can use in AWS. Its data access latency is very low thus making it the best choice when performance is the primary concern. The downside is availability. It doesn't work in multiple availability zones. Failure of one will mean downtime, at least until the zone is restored to its operational state.

We'll choose EBS for our storage needs. Jenkins depends heavily on IO, and we need data access to be as fast as possible. However, there is another reason for such a choice. EBS is fully supported by Kubernetes. EFS will come but, at the time of this writing, it is still in the experimental stage. As a bonus advantage, EBS is much cheaper than EFS.

Given the requirements and what Kubernetes offers, the choice is obvious. We'll use EBS, even though we might run into trouble if the availability zone where our Jenkins will run goes down. In such a case, we'd need to migrate EBS volume to a healthy zone. There's no such thing as a perfect solution.

We are jumping ahead of ourselves. We'll leave Kubernetes aside for a while and concentrate on creating an EBS volume.

Each EBS volume is tied to an availability zone. Unlike EFS, EBS cannot span multiple zones. So, the first thing we need to do is to find out which are the zones worker nodes are running in. We can get that information by describing the EC2 instances belonging to the security group `nodes.devops23.k8s.local`.

```
aws ec2 describe-instances
```

The output, limited to the relevant parts, is as follows:

```
{
  "Reservations": [
    {
      "Instances": [
        {
          ...
          "SecurityGroups": [
            {
              "GroupName": "nodes.devops23.k8s.local",
              "GroupId": "sg-33fd8c58"
            }
          ],
```

```
. . .
"Placement": {
  "Tenancy": "default",
  "GroupName": "",
  "AvailabilityZone": "us-east-2a"
},
. . .
```

We can see that the information is inside the `Reservations.Instances` array. To get the zone, we need to filter the output by the `SecurityGroups.GroupName` field. Zone name is located in the `Placement.AvailabilityZone` field.

The command that does the filtering and retrieves the availability zones of the worker nodes is as follows:

```
aws ec2 describe-instances \
    | jq -r \
    ".Reservations[].Instances[] \
    | select(.SecurityGroups[]\
    .GroupName==\"nodes.$NAME\")\
    .Placement.AvailabilityZone"
```

The output is as follows:

```
us-east-2a
us-east-2c
```

We can see that the two worker nodes are located in the zones `us-east-2a` and `us-east-2c`.

The commands that retrieve the zones of the two worker nodes and store them in environment variables is as follows:

```
aws ec2 describe-instances \
    | jq -r \
    ".Reservations[].Instances[] \
    | select(.SecurityGroups[]\
    .GroupName=="\nodes.$NAME\")\
    .Placement.AvailabilityZone" \
    | tee zones
AZ_1=$(cat zones | head -n 1)
AZ_2=$(cat zones | tail -n 1)
```

We retrieved the zones and stored the output into the `zones` file. Further on, we retrieved the first row with the `head` command and stored it in the environment variable `AZ_1`. Similarly, we stored the last (the second) row in the variable `AZ_2`.

Now we have all the information we need to create a few volumes.

 The command that follows requires a relatively newer version of `aws`. If it fails, please update your AWS CLI binary to the latest version.

```
VOLUME_ID_1=$(aws ec2 create-volume \
    --availability-zone $AZ_1 \
    --size 10 \
    --volume-type gp2 \
    --tag-specifications
"ResourceType=volume,Tags=[{Key=KubernetesCluster,Value=$NAME}]" \
    | jq -r '.VolumeId')
VOLUME_ID_2=$(aws ec2 create-volume \
    --availability-zone $AZ_1 \
    --size 10 \
    --volume-type gp2 \
    --tag-specifications
"ResourceType=volume,Tags=[{Key=KubernetesCluster,Value=$NAME}]" \
    | jq -r '.VolumeId')
VOLUME_ID_3=$(aws ec2 create-volume \
    --availability-zone $AZ_2 \
    --size 10 \
    --volume-type gp2 \
    --tag-specifications
"ResourceType=volume,Tags=[{Key=KubernetesCluster,Value=$NAME}]" \
    | jq -r '.VolumeId')
```

We executed `aws ec2 create-volume` command three times. As a result, we created three EBS volumes. Two of them are in one zone, while the third is in another. They all have 10 GB of space. We chose gp2 as the type of the volumes. The other types either require bigger sizes or are more expensive. When in doubt, gp2 is usually the best choice for EBS volumes.

We also defined a tag that will help us distinguish the volumes dedicated to this cluster from those we might have in our AWS account for other purposes.

Finally, jq filtered the output so that only the volume ID is retrieved. The results are stored in the environment variables VOLUME_ID_1, VOLUME_ID_2, and VOLUME_ID_3.

Let's take a quick look at one of the IDs we stored as an environment variable:

```
echo $VOLUME_ID_1
```

The output is as follows:

```
vol-092b8980b1964574a
```

Finally, to be on the safe side, we'll list the volume that matches the ID and thus confirm, without doubt, that the EBS was indeed created.

```
aws ec2 describe-volumes \
    --volume-ids $VOLUME_ID_1
```

The output is as follows:

```
{
    "Volumes": [
        {
            "AvailabilityZone": "us-east-2c",
            "Attachments": [],
            "Tags": [
                {
                    "Value": "devops23.k8s.local",
                    "Key": "KubernetesCluster"
                }
            ],
            "Encrypted": false,
            "VolumeType": "gp2",
            "VolumeId": "vol-092b8980b1964574a",
            "State": "available",
            "Iops": 100,
            "SnapshotId": "",
            "CreateTime": "2018-03-14T21:47:13.242Z",
            "Size": 10
        }
    ]
}
```

Now that the EBS volumes are indeed `available` and in the same zones as the worker nodes, we can proceed and create Kubernetes persistent volumes.

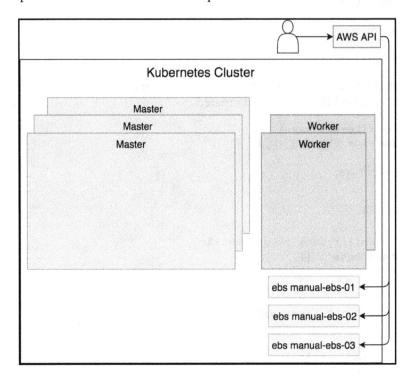

Figure 15-1: EBS volumes created in the same zones as the worker nodes

Creating Kubernetes persistent volumes

The fact that we have a few EBS volumes available does not mean that Kubernetes knows about their existence. We need to add PersistentVolumes that will act as a bridge between our Kubernetes cluster and AWS EBS volumes.

PersistentVolumes allow us to abstract details of how storage is provided (for example, EBS) from how it is consumed. Just like Volumes, PersistentVolumes are resources in a Kubernetes cluster. The main difference is that their lifecycle is independent of individual Pods that are using them.

Let's take a look at a definition that will create a few PersistentVolumes:

```
cat pv/pv.yml
```

The output, limited to the first of the three volumes, is as follows:

```
kind: PersistentVolume
apiVersion: v1
metadata:
  name: manual-ebs-01
  labels:
    type: ebs
spec:
  storageClassName: manual-ebs
  capacity:
    storage: 5Gi
  accessModes:
    - ReadWriteOnce
  awsElasticBlockStore:
    volumeID: REPLACE_ME_1
    fsType: ext4
...
```

The `spec` section features a few interesting details. We set `manual-ebs` as the storage class name. We'll see later what is its function. For now, just remember the name.

We defined that the storage capacity is `5Gi`. It does not need to be the same as the capacity of the EBS we created earlier, as long as it is not bigger. Kubernetes will try to match `PersistentVolume` with, in this case, EBS that has a similar, if not the same capacity. Since we have only one EBS volume with 10 GB, it is the closest (and the only) match to the `PersistentVolume` request of `5Gi`. Ideally, persistent volumes capacity should match EBS size, but I wanted to demonstrate that any value equal to or less then the actual size should do.

We specified that the access mode should be `ReadWriteOnce`. That means that we'll be able to mount the volume as read-write only once. Only one Pod will be able to use it at any given moment. Such a strategy fits us well since EBS cannot be mounted to multiple instances. Our choice of the access mode is not truly a choice, but more an acknowledgment of the way how EBS works. The alternative modes are `ReadOnlyMany` and `ReadWriteMany`. Both modes would result in volumes that could be mounted to multiple Pods, either as read-only or read-write. Those modes would be more suitable for NFS like, for example, EFS, which can be mounted by multiple instances.

The `spec` fields we explored so far are common to all persistent volume types. Besides those, there are entries specific to the actual volume we are associating with a Kubernetes `PersistentVolume`. Since we're going to use EBS, we specified `awsElasticBlockStore` with the volume ID and file system type. Since I could not know in advance what will be the ID of your EBS volume, the definition has the value set to `REPLACE_ME`. Later on, we'll replace it with the ID of the EBS we created earlier.

There are many other types we could have specified instead. If this cluster would run on Azure, we could use `azureDisk` or `azureFile`. In **Google Compute Engine** (**GCE**) it would be `GCEPersistentDisk`. We could have setup `Glusterfs`. Or, if we would have this cluster running in an on-prem data center, it would probably be `nfs`. There are quite a few others we could use but, since we're running the cluster in AWS, many would not work, while others could be too difficult to set up. Since EBS is already available, we'll just roll with it. All in all, this cluster is in AWS, and `awsElasticBlockStore` is the easiest, if not the best choice.

Now that we have an understanding of the YAML definition, we can proceed and create the `PersistentVolume`:

```
cat pv/pv.yml \
    | sed -e \
    "s@REPLACE_ME_1@$VOLUME_ID_1@g" \
    | sed -e \
    "s@REPLACE_ME_2@$VOLUME_ID_2@g" \
    | sed -e \
    "s@REPLACE_ME_3@$VOLUME_ID_3@g" \
    | kubectl create -f - \
    --save-config --record
```

We used `cat` to output the contents of the `pv/pv.yml` file and pipe it into `sed` commands which, in turn, replaced the `REPLACE_ME_*` strings with the IDs of the EBS volumes we created earlier. The result was sent to the `kubectl create` command that created persistent volumes. As a result, we can see from the output that all three PersistentVolumes were created.

Let's take a look at the persistent volumes currently available in our cluster.

```
kubectl get pv
```

The output is as follows:

```
NAME           CAPACITY ACCESS MODES RECLAIM POLICY STATUS    CLAIM
STORAGECLASS REASON AGE
manual-ebs-01 5Gi       RWO          Retain         Available manual-
ebs           11s
```

manual-ebs-02 5Gi	RWO	Retain	Available	manual-	
ebs 11s					
manual-ebs-03 5Gi	RWO	Retain	Available	manual-	
ebs 11s					

It should come as no surprise that we have three volumes:

The interesting part of the information we're seeing are the statuses. The persistent volumes are `available`. We created them, but no one is using them. They just sit there waiting for someone to claim them.

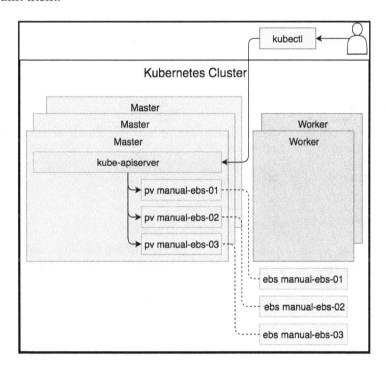

Figure 15-2: Kubernetes persistent volumes tied to EBS volumes

Claiming persistent volumes

Kubernetes persistent volumes are useless if no one uses them. They exist only as objects with relation to, in our case, specific EBS volumes. They are waiting for someone to claim them through the `PersistentVolumeClaim` resource.

Just like Pods which can request specific resources like memory and CPU, PersistentVolumeClaims can request particular sizes and access modes. Both are, in a way, consuming resources, even though of different types. Just as Pods should not specify on which node they should run, PersistentVolumeClaims cannot define which volume they should mount. Instead, Kubernetes scheduler will assign them a volume depending on the claimed resources.

We'll use pv/pvc.yml to explore how we could claim a persistent volume:

```
cat pv/pvc.yml
```

The output is as follows:

```
kind: PersistentVolumeClaim
apiVersion: v1
metadata:
  name: jenkins
  namespace: jenkins
spec:
  storageClassName: manual-ebs
  accessModes:
    - ReadWriteOnce
  resources:
    requests:
      storage: 1Gi
```

The YAML file defines a PersistentVolumeClaim with the storage class name manual-ebs. That is the same class as the persistent volumes manual-ebs-* we created earlier. The access mode and the storage request are also matching what we defined for the persistent volume.

Please note that we are not specifying which volume we'd like to use. Instead, this claim specifies a set of attributes (`storageClassName`, `accessModes`, and `storage`). Any of the volumes in the system that match those specifications might be claimed by the `PersistentVolumeClaim` named `jenkins`. Bear in mind that `resources` do not have to be the exact match. Any volume that has the same or bigger amount of storage is considered a match. A claim for `1Gi` can be translated to *at least 1Gi*. In our case, a claim for `1Gi` matches all three persistent volumes since they are set to `5Gi`.

Now that we explored the definition of the claim, we can proceed, and create it:

```
kubectl create -f pv/pvc.yml \
    --save-config --record
```

The output indicates that the `persistentvolumeclaim "jenkins" was created`.

Let's list the claims and see what we got:

```
kubectl --namespace jenkins \
    get pvc
```

The output is as follows:

```
NAME     STATUS VOLUME         CAPACITY ACCESS MODES STORAGECLASS AGE
jenkins  Bound  manual-ebs-02  5Gi      RWO          manual-ebs   17s
```

We see from the output that the status of the claim is `Bound`. That means that the claim found a matching persistent volume and bounded it. We can confirm that by listing the volumes:

```
kubectl get pv
```

The output is as follows:

```
NAME             CAPACITY ACCESS MODES RECLAIM POLICY STATUS     CLAIM
STORAGECLASS REASON AGE
manual-ebs-01 5Gi         RWO          Retain         Available
manual-ebs              7m
manual-ebs-02 5Gi         RWO          Retain         Bound
jenkins/jenkins manual-ebs           7m
manual-ebs-03 5Gi         RWO          Retain         Available
manual-ebs              7m
```

We can see that one of the volumes (`manual-ebs-02`) changed the status from `Available` to `Bound`. That is the volume bound to the claim we created a moment ago. We can see that the claim comes from `jenkins` namespace and `jenkinsPersistentVolumeClaim`.

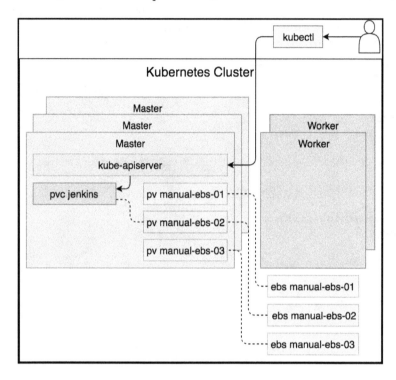

Figure 15-3: Creation of a Persistent Volume Claim

Please note that if a PersistentVolumeClaim cannot find a matching volume, it will remain unbound indefinitely, unless we add a new PersistentVolume with the matching specifications.

We still haven't accomplished our goal. The fact that we claimed a volume does not mean that anyone uses it. On the other hand, our Jenkins needs to persist its state. We'll join our `PersistentVolumeClaim` with a Jenkins container.

Attaching claimed volumes to Pods

```
cat pv/jenkins-pv.yml
```

The relevant parts of the output is as follows:

```
...
apiVersion: apps/v1beta2
kind: Deployment
metadata:
  name: jenkins
  namespace: jenkins
spec:
  ...
  template:
    ...
    spec:
      containers:
      - name: jenkins
        ...
        volumeMounts:
        - name: jenkins-home
          mountPath: /var/jenkins_home
        ...
      volumes:
      - name: jenkins-home
        persistentVolumeClaim:
          claimName: jenkins
      ...
```

You'll notice that, this time, we added a new volume jenkins-home, which references the PersistentVolumeClaim called jenkins. From the container's perspective, the claim is a volume.

Let's deploy Jenkins resources and confirm that everything works as expected.

```
kubectl apply \
    -f pv/jenkins-pv.yml \
    --record
```

The output is as follows:

```
namespace "jenkins" configured
ingress "jenkins" configured
service "jenkins" configured
deployment "jenkins" configured
```

We'll wait until the Deployment rolls out before proceeding with a test that will confirm whether Jenkins state is now persisted.

```
kubectl --namespace jenkins \
    rollout status \
    deployment jenkins
```

Once the rollout is finished, we'll see a message stating that the `deployment "jenkins"` `was successfully rolled out`.

We sent a request to the Kubernetes API to create a Deployment. As a result, we got a `ReplicaSet` that, in turn, created the `jenkins` Pod. It mounted the `PersistentVolumeClaim`, which is bound to the `PersistenceVolume`, that is tied to the EBS volume. As a result, the EBS volume was mounted to the `jenkins` container running in a Pod.

A simplified version of the sequence of events is depicted in the *Figure 15-4*.

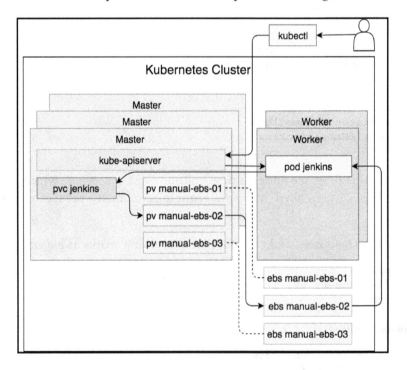

Figure 15-4: The sequence of events initiated with a request to create a Jenkins Pod with the PersistentVolumeClaim

1. We executed `kubectl` command
2. `kubectl` sent a request to `kube-apiserver` to create the resources defined in `pv/jenkins-pv.yml`
3. Among others, the `jenkins` Pod was created in one of the worker nodes
4. Since `jenkins` container in the Pod has a `PersistentVolumeClaim`, it mounted it as a logical volume
5. The `PersistentVolumeClaim` was already bound to one of the PersistentVolumes
6. The PersistentVolume is associated with one of the EBS volumes
7. The EBS volume was mounted as a physical volume to the `jenkins` Pod

Now that Jenkins is up-and-running, we'll execute a similar set of steps as before, and validate that the state is persisted across failures.

```
open "http://$CLUSTER_DNS/jenkins"
```

We opened Jenkins home screen. If you are not authenticated, please click the **Log in** link and type `jdoe` as the **User** and `**incognito*` as the **Password**. Click the **log in** button.

You'll see the **create new jobs** link. Click it. Type `my-job` as the item name, select `Pipeline` as the job type, and click the **OK** button. Once inside the job configuration screen, all we have to do is click the **Save** button. An empty job will be enough to test persistence.

Now we need to find out the name of the Pod created through the `jenkins` Deployment.

```
POD_NAME=$(kubectl \
    --namespace jenkins \
    get pod \
    --selector=app=jenkins \
    -o jsonpath="{.items[*].metadata.name}")
```

With the name of the Pod stored in the environment variable POD_NAME, we can proceed and kill `java` process that's running Jenkins.

```
kubectl --namespace jenkins \
    exec -it $POD_NAME pkill java
```

We killed the Jenkins process and thus simulated failure of the container. As a result, Kubernetes detected the failure and recreated the container.

A minute later, we can open Jenkins home screen again, and check whether the state (the job we created) was preserved.

```
open "http://$CLUSTER_DNS/jenkins"
```

As you can see, the job is still available thus proving that we successfully mounted the EBS volume as the directory where Jenkins preserves its state.

If instead of destroying the container, we terminated the server where the Pod is running, the result, from the functional perspective, would be the same. The Pod would be rescheduled to a healthy node. Jenkins would start again and restore its state from the EBS volume. Or, at least, that's what we'd hope. However, such behavior is not guaranteed to happen in our cluster.

We have only two worker nodes, distributed in two (out of three) availability zones. If the node that hosted Jenkins failed, we'd be left with only one node. To be more precise, we'd have only one worker node running in the cluster until the auto-scaling group detects that an EC2 instance is missing and recreates it. During those few minutes, the single node we're left with is not in the same zone. As we already mentioned, each EBS instance is tied to a zone, and the one we mounted to the Jenkins Pod would not be associated with the zone where the other EC2 instance is running. As a result, the PersistentVolume could not re-bound the EBS volume and, therefore, the failed container could not be recreated, until the failed EC2 instance is recreated.

The chances are that the new EC2 instance would not be in the same zone as the one where the failed server was running. Since we're using three availability zones, and one of them already has an EC2 instance, AWS would recreate the failed server in one of the other two zones. We'd have fifty percent chances that the new EC2 would be in the same zone as the one where the failed server was running. Those are not good odds.

In the real-world scenario, we'd probably have more than two worker nodes. Even a slight increase to three nodes would give us a very good chance that the failed server would be recreated in the same zone. Auto-scaling groups are trying to distribute EC2 instances more or less equally across all the zones. However, that is not guaranteed to happen. A good minimum number of worker nodes would be six.

The more servers we have, the higher are the chances that the cluster is fault tolerant. That is especially true if we are hosting stateful applications. As it goes, we almost certainly have those. There's hardly any system that does not have a state in some form or another.

If it's better to have more servers than less, we might be in a complicated position if our system is small and needs, let's say, less than six servers. In such cases, I'd recommend running smaller VMs. If, for example, you planned to use three `t2.xlarge` EC2 instances for worker nodes, you might reconsider that and switch to six `t2.large` servers. Sure, more nodes mean more resource overhead spent on operating systems, Kubernetes system Pods, and few other things. However, I believe that is compensated with bigger stability of your cluster.

There is still one more situation we might encounter. A whole availability zone (data center) might fail. Kubernetes will continue operating correctly. It'll have two instead of three master nodes, and the failed worker nodes will be recreated in healthy zones. However, we'd run into trouble with our stateful services. Kubernetes would not be able to reschedule those that were mounted to EBS volumes from the failed zone. We'd need to wait for the availability zone to come back online, or we'd need to move the EBS volume to a healthy zone manually. The chances are that, in such a case, the EBS would not be available and, therefore, could not be moved.

We could create a process that would be replicating data in (near) real-time between EBS volumes spread across multiple availability zones, but that also comes with a downside. Such an operation would be expensive and would likely slow down state retrieval while everything is fully operational. Should we choose lower performance over high-availability? Is the increased operational overhead worth the trouble? The answer to those questions will differ from one use-case to another.

There is yet another option. We could use EFS (https://aws.amazon.com/efs/) instead of EBS. But, that would also impact performance since EFS tends to be slower than EBS. On top of that, there is no production-ready EFS support in Kubernetes. At the time of this writing, the EFS provisioner (https://github.com/kubernetes-incubator/external-storage/tree/master/aws/efs) is still in beta phase. By the time you read this, things might have changed. Or maybe they didn't. Even when the *efs provisioner* becomes stable, it will still be slower and more expensive solution than EBS.

Maybe you'll decide to ditch EBS (and EFS) in favor of some other type of persistent storage. There are many different options you can choose. We won't explore them since an in-depth comparison of all the popular solutions would require much more space than what we have left. Consider them an advanced topic that will be covered in the next book. Or maybe it won't. I do not yet know the scope of *The DevOps 2.4 Toolkit* book.

All in all, every solution has pros and cons and none would fit all use-cases. For good or bad, we'll stick with EBS for the remainder of this book.

Going back to PersistentVolumes tied to EBS...

Now that we explored how to manage static persistent volumes, we'll try to accomplish the same results using dynamic approach. But, before we do that, we'll see what happens when some of the resources we created are removed.

Let's delete the `jenkins` Deployment.

```
kubectl --namespace jenkins delete \
    deploy jenkins
```

The output shows us that the `deployment "jenkins" was deleted`.

Did anything happen with the PersistentVolumeClaim and the PersistentVolume?

```
kubectl --namespace jenkins get pvc
kubectl get pv
```

The combined output of both commands is as follows:

```
NAME      STATUS VOLUME         CAPACITY ACCESS MODES STORAGECLASS    AGE
jenkins Bound  manual-ebs-02 5Gi        RWO          manual-ebs      57s
NAME             CAPACITY ACCESS MODES RECLAIM POLICY STATUS     CLAIM
STORAGECLASS REASON AGE
manual-ebs-01 5Gi        RWO                Retain        Available
jenkins/jenkins manual-ebs         10m
manual-ebs-02 5Gi        RWO                Retain        Bound
jenkins/jenkins manual-ebs         10m
manual-ebs-03 5Gi        RWO                Retain        Available
jenkins/jenkins manual-ebs         10m
```

Even though we removed Jenkins Deployment and, with it, the Pod that used the claim, both the PersistentVolumeClaim and PersistentVolumes are intact. The `manual-ebs-01` volume is still bound to the `jenkins` claim.

What would happen if we remove the PersistentVolumeClaim `jenkins`?

```
kubectl --namespace jenkins \
    delete pvc jenkins
```

The output shows that the `persistentvolumeclaim "jenkins" was deleted`.

Now, let's see what happened with the PersistentVolumes:

```
kubectl get pv
```

The output is as follows:

```
NAME              CAPACITY ACCESS MODES RECLAIM POLICY STATUS    CLAIM
STORAGECLASS REASON AGE
manual-ebs-01 5Gi        RWO           Retain         Available
jenkins/jenkins manual-ebs            10m
manual-ebs-02 5Gi        RWO           Retain         Released
jenkins/jenkins manual-ebs            10m
manual-ebs-03 5Gi        RWO           Retain         Available
jenkins/jenkins manual-ebs            10m
```

This time, the `manual-ebs-2` volume is `Released`.

This might be a good moment to explain the `Retain` policy applied to the PersistentVolumes we created.

`ReclaimPolicy` defines what should be done with a volume after it's released from its claim. The policy was applied the moment we deleted the PersistentVolumeClaim that was bound to `manual-ebs-02`. When we created the PersistentVolumes, we did not specify `ReclaimPolicy`, so the volumes were assigned the default policy which is `Retain`.

The `Retain` reclaim policy enforces manual reclamation of the resource. When the PersistentVolumeClaim is deleted, the PersistentVolume still exists, and the volume is considered `released`. But it is not yet available for other claims because the previous claimant's data remains on the volume. In our case, that data is Jenkins state. If we'd like this PersistentVolume to become available, we'd need to delete all the data on the EBS volume.

Since we are running the cluster in AWS, it is easier to delete than to recycle resources, so we'll remove the released PersistentVolume instead of trying to clean everything we generated inside the EBS. Actually, we'll remove all the volumes since we are about to explore how we can accomplish the same effects dynamically.

The other two reclaim policies are `Recycle` and `Delete`. `Recycle` is considered deprecated so we won't waste time explaining it. The `Delete` policy requires dynamic provisioning, but we'll postpone the explanation until we explore that topic.

Let's delete some stuff:

```
kubectl delete -f pv/pv.yml
```

The output is as follows:

```
persistentvolume "manual-ebs-01" deleted
persistentvolume "manual-ebs-02" deleted
persistentvolume "manual-ebs-03" deleted
```

We can see that all three PersistentVolumes were deleted. However, only Kubernetes resources were removed. We still need to manually delete the EBS volumes.

If you go to your AWS console, you'll see that all three EBS volumes are now in the `available` state and waiting to be mounted. We'll delete them all:

```
aws ec2 delete-volume \
    --volume-id $VOLUME_ID_1
aws ec2 delete-volume \
    --volume-id $VOLUME_ID_2
aws ec2 delete-volume \
    --volume-id $VOLUME_ID_3
```

We are finished with our tour around manual creation of persistent volumes. If we'd use this approach to volume management, cluster administrator would need to ensure that there is always an extra number of available volumes that can be used by new claims. It is tedious work that often results in having more volumes than we need. On the other hand, if we don't have a sufficient number of available (unused) volumes, we're risking that someone will create a claim that will not find a suitable volume to mount.

Manual volume management is sometimes unavoidable, especially if chose to use on-prem infrastructure combined with NFS. However, this is not our case. AWS is all about dynamic resource provisioning, and we'll exploit that to its fullest.

Using storage classes to dynamically provision persistent volumes

So far, we used static PersistentVolumes. We had to create both EBS volumes and Kubernetes PersistentVolumes manually. Only after both became available were we able to deploy Pods that are mounting those volumes through PersistentVolumeClaims. We'll call this process static volume provisioning.

In some cases, static volume provisioning is a necessity. Our infrastructure might not be capable of creating dynamic volumes. That is often the case with on-premise infrastructure with volumes based on NFS. Even then, with a few tools, a change in processes, and right choices for supported volume types, we can often reach the point where volume provisioning is dynamic. Still, that might prove to be a challenge with legacy processes and infrastructure.

Since our cluster is in AWS, we cannot blame legacy infrastructure for provisioning volumes manually. Indeed, we could have jumped straight into this section. After all, AWS is all about dynamic infrastructure management. However, I felt that it will be easier to understand the processes by exploring manual provisioning first. The knowledge we obtained thus far will help us understand better what's coming next. The second reason for starting with manual provisioning lies in my inability to predict your plans. Maybe you will run a Kubernetes cluster on infrastructure that has to be static. Even though we're using AWS for the examples, everything you learned this far can be implemented on static infrastructure. You'll only have to change EBS with NFS and go through NFSVolumeSource (`https://v1-9.docs.kubernetes.io/docs/reference/generated/kubernetes-api/v1.9/#nfsvolumesource-v1-core`) documentation. There are only three NFS-specific fields so you should be up-and-running in no time.

Before we discuss how to enable dynamic persistent volume provisioning, we should understand that it will be used only if none of the static PersistentVolumes match our claims. In other words, Kubernetes will always select statically created PersistentVolumes over dynamic ones.

Dynamic volume provisioning allows us to create storage on-demand. Instead of manually pre-provisioning storage, we can provision it automatically when a resource requests it.

We can enable dynamic provisioning through the usage of StorageClasses from the `storage.k8s.io` API group. They allow us to describe the types of storage that can be claimed. On the one hand, cluster administrator can create as many StorageClasses as there are storage flavours. On the other hand, the users of the cluster do not have to worry about the details of each available external storage. It's a win-win situation where the administrators do not have to create PersistentVolumes in advance, and the users can simply claim the storage type they need.

To enable dynamic provisioning, we need to create at least one StorageClass object. Luckily for us, kops already set up a few, so we might just as well take a look at the StorageClasses currently available in our cluster:

```
kubectl get sc
```

The output is as follows:

```
NAME                PROVISIONER            AGE
default             kubernetes.io/aws-ebs  44m
gp2 (default)       kubernetes.io/aws-ebs  44m
```

We can see that there are two StorageClasses in our cluster. Both are using the same `aws-ebs` provisioner. Besides the names, the only difference, at least in this output, is that one of them is marked as `default`. We'll explore what that means a bit later. For now, we'll trust that kops configured those classes correctly and try to claim a PersistentVolume.

Let's take a quick look at yet another `jenkins` definition:

```
cat pv/jenkins-dynamic.yml
```

The output, limited to the relevant parts, is as follows:

```
...
kind: PersistentVolumeClaim
apiVersion: v1
metadata:
  name: jenkins
  namespace: jenkins
spec:
  storageClassName: gp2
  accessModes:
    - ReadWriteOnce
  resources:
    requests:
      storage: 1Gi
...
```

This Jenkins definition is almost the same as the one we used before. The only difference is in the PersistentVolumeClaim that, this time, specified gp2 as the `StorageClassName`. There is one more difference though. This time we do not have any PersistentVolume pre-provisioned. If everything works as expected, a new PersistentVolume will be created dynamically.

```
kubectl apply \
    -f pv/jenkins-dynamic.yml \
    --record
```

We can see that some of the resources were re-configured, while others were created.

Next, we'll wait until the `jenkins` Deployment is rolled out successfully:

```
kubectl --namespace jenkins \
    rollout status \
    deployment jenkins
```

Now we should be able to see what happened through the `jenkins` namespace events.

```
kubectl --namespace jenkins \
    get events
```

The output, limited to the last few lines, is as follows:

```
...
20s 20s 1 jenkins.... Deployment            Normal ScalingReplicaSet
deployment-controller      Scaled up replica set jenkins-... to 1
20s 20s 1 jenkins.... PersistentVolumeClaim Normal ProvisioningSucceeded
persistentvolume-controller Successfully provisioned volume pvc-... using
kubernetes.io/aws-ebs
```

We can see that a new PersistentVolume was `successfully provisioned`.

Let's take a look at the status of the PersistentVolumeClaim.

```
kubectl --namespace jenkins get pvc
```

The output is as follows:

```
NAME     STATUS VOLUME  CAPACITY ACCESS MODES STORAGECLASS AGE
jenkins Bound   pvc-... 1Gi      RWO          gp2          1m
```

The part of the output that matters is the status. We can see that it `Bound` with the PersistentVolume thus confirming, again, that the volume was indeed created dynamically.

To be on the safe side, we'll list the PersistentVolumes as well:

```
kubectl get pv
```

The output is as follows:

```
NAME     CAPACITY ACCESS MODES RECLAIM POLICY STATUS CLAIM
STORAGECLASS REASON AGE
pvc-... 1Gi       RWO           Delete         Bound  jenkins/jenkins gp2
4m
```

As expected, the PersistentVolume was created, it is bound to the PersistentVolumeClaim, and its reclaim policy is `Delete`. We'll see the policy in action soon.

Finally, the last verification we'll perform is to confirm that the EBS volume was created as well:

```
aws ec2 describe-volumes \
    --filters 'Name=tag-key,Values="kubernetes.io/created-for/pvc
/name"'
```

The output, limited to the relevant parts, is as follows:

```
{
  "Volumes": [
    {
      "AvailabilityZone": "us-east-2c",
      ...
      "VolumeType": "gp2",
      "VolumeId": "vol-0a4d5cfa4699e5c6f",
      "State": "in-use",
      ...
    }
  ]
}
```

We can see that a new EBS volume was created in the availability zone `us-east-2c`, that the type is `gp2`, and that its state is `in-use`.

Dynamic provisioning works! Given that we're using AWS, it is a much better solution than using static resources.

Before we move into a next subject, we'll explore the effect of the reclaim policy `Delete`. To do so, we'll delete the Deployment and the PersistentVolumeClaim.

```
kubectl --namespace jenkins \
    delete deploy,pvc jenkins
```

The output is as follows:

```
deployment "jenkins" deleted
persistentvolumeclaim "jenkins" deleted
```

Now that the claim to the volume was removed, we can check what happened with the dynamically provisioned PersistentVolumes.

```
kubectl get pv
```

The output shows that `no resources` were found, clearly indicating that the PersistentVolume that was created through the claim is now gone.

How about the AWS EBS volume? Was it removed as well?

```
aws ec2 describe-volumes \
    --filters 'Name=tag-key,Values="kubernetes.io/created-for/pvc/name"'
```

The output is as follows:

```
{
   "Volumes": []
}
```

We got an empty array proving that the EBS volume was removed as well.

Through dynamic volume provisioning, not only that volumes are created when resources claim them, but they are also removed when the claims are released. Dynamic removal is accomplished through the reclaim policy `Delete`.

Using default storage classes

Working with dynamic provisioning simplifies a few things. Still, a user needs to know which volume type to use. While in many cases that is an important choice, there are often situations when a user might not want to worry about that. It might be easier to use the cluster administrator's choice for volume types and let all claims that do not specify `storageClassName` get a default volume. We'll try to accomplish that through one of the admission controllers.

Admission controllers are intercepting requests to the Kubernetes API server. We won't go into details of admission controllers since the list of those supported by Kubernetes is relatively big. We are interested only in the `DefaultStorageClass` which happens to be already enabled in the cluster we created with kops.

`DefaultStorageClass` admission controller observes creation of PersistentVolumeClaims. Through it, those that do not request any specific storage class are automatically added a default storage class to them. As a result, PersistentVolumeClaims that do not request any special storage class are bound to PersistentVolumes created from the default `StorageClass`. From user's perspective, there's no need to care about volume types since they will be provisioned based on the default type unless they choose a specific class.

Let's take a look at the storage classes currently available in our cluster:

```
kubectl get sc
```

The output is as follows:

```
NAME            PROVISIONER            AGE
default         kubernetes.io/aws-ebs 56m
gp2 (default) kubernetes.io/aws-ebs 56m
```

This is not the first time we're listing the storage classes in our cluster. However, we did not discuss that one of the two (gp2) is marked as the default StorageClass.

Let's describe the gp2 class.

```
kubectl describe sc gp2
```

The output, limited to the relevant parts, is as follows:

```
Name:           gp2
IsDefaultClass: Yes
Annotations:     kubectl.kubernetes.io/last-applied-
configuration={"apiVersion":"storage.k8s.io/v1","kind":"StorageClass","meta
data":{"annotations":{"storageclass.beta.kubernetes.io/is-default-
class":"true"},"labels":{"k8s-addon":"storage-
aws.addons.k8s.io"},"name":"gp2","namespace":""},"parameters":{"type":"gp2"
},"provisioner":"kubernetes.io/aws-ebs"}
,storageclass.beta.kubernetes.io/is-default-class=true
Provisioner:    kubernetes.io/aws-ebs
Parameters:     type=gp2
ReclaimPolicy:  Delete
Events:         <none>
```

The important part lies in the annotations. One of them is ".../is-default-class":"true". It sets that StorageClass as default. As a result, it will be used to create PersistentVolumes by any PersistentVolumeClaim that does not specify StorageClass name.

Let's try to adapt Jenkins stack to use the ability to dynamically provision a volume associated with the DefaultStorageClass.

The new Jenkins definition is as follows:

```
cat pv/jenkins-default.yml
```

The output, limited to the `PersistentVolumeClaim`, is as follows.

```
. . .
kind: PersistentVolumeClaim
apiVersion: v1
metadata:
  name: jenkins
  namespace: jenkins
spec:
  accessModes:
    - ReadWriteOnce
  resources:
    requests:
      storage: 1Gi
. . .
```

It's hard to spot the difference between that YAML file and the one we used before. It is very small and hard to notice change so we'll execute `diff` to compare the two:

```
diff pv/jenkins-dynamic.yml \
    pv/jenkins-default.yml
```

The output is as follows:

```
48d47
<     storageClassName: gp2
```

As you can see, the only difference is that `pv/jenkins-dynamic.yml` doesn't have `storageClassName: gp2`. That field is omitted from the new definition. Our new `PersistentVolumeClaim` does not have an associated StorageClass.

Let's `apply` the new definition:

```
kubectl apply \
    -f pv/jenkins-default.yml \
    --record
```

The output is as follows:

```
namespace "jenkins" configured
ingress "jenkins" configured
service "jenkins" configured
persistentvolumeclaim "jenkins" created
deployment "jenkins" created
```

What we're interested in are PersistentVolumes, so let's retrieve them.

```
kubectl get pv
NAME     CAPACITY ACCESS MODES RECLAIM POLICY STATUS CLAIM
STORAGECLASS REASON AGE
pvc-... 1Gi       RWO          Delete         Bound  jenkins/jenkins gp2
16s
```

As you can see, even though we did not specify any StorageClass, a volume was created based on the gp2 class, which happens to be the default one.

We'll delete the jenkins Deployment and PersistentVolumeClaim before we explore how we can create our own StorageClasses.

```
kubectl --namespace jenkins \
    delete deploy,pvc jenkins
```

The output is as follows:

```
deployment "jenkins" deleted
persistentvolumeclaim "jenkins" deleted
```

Creating storage classes

Even though kops created two StorageClasses, both are based on gp2. While that is the most commonly used EBS type, we might want to create volumes based on one of the other three options offered by AWS.

Let's say that we want the fastest EBS volume type for our Jenkins. That would be io1. Since kops did not create a StorageClass of that type, we might want to create our own.

YAML file that creates StorageClass based on EBS io1 is defined in pv/sc.yml. Let's take a quick look.

```
cat pv/sc.yml
```

The output is as follows:

```
kind: StorageClass
apiVersion: storage.k8s.io/v1
metadata:
  name: fast
  labels:
    type: ebs
provisioner: kubernetes.io/aws-ebs
```

```
parameters:
  type: io1
reclaimPolicy: Delete
```

We used `kubernetes.io/aws-ebs` as the `provisioner`. It is a mandatory field that determines the plugin that will be used for provisioning PersistentVolumes. Since we are running the cluster in AWS, `aws-ebs` is the logical choice. There are quite a few other provisioners we could choose. Some of them are specific to a hosting provider (for example, `GCEPersistentDisk` and `AzureDisk`) while others can be used anywhere (for example, `GlusterFS`).

The list of supported provisioners is growing. At the time of this writing, the following types are supported:

Volume Plugin	Internal Provisioner
AWSElasticBlockStore	yes
AzureFile	yes
AzureDisk	yes
CephFS	no
Cinder	yes
FC	no
FlexVolume	no
Flocker	yes
GCEPersistentDisk	yes
Glusterfs	yes
iSCSI	no
PhotonPersistentDisk	yes
Quobyte	yes
NFS	no
RBD	yes
VsphereVolume	yes
PortworxVolume	yes
ScaleIO	yes
StorageOS	yes
Local	no

The internal provisioners are those with names prefixed with `kubernetes.io` (for example, `kubernetes.io/aws-ebs`). They are shipped with Kubernetes. External provisioners, on the other hand, are independent programs shipped separately from Kubernetes. An example of a commonly used external provisioner is `NFS`. The parameters depend on the StorageClass. We used the `aws-ebs` provisioner which allows us to specify the `type` parameter that defines one of the supported Amazon EBS volume types. It can be EBS Provisioned IOPS SSD (`io1`), EBS **General Purpose SSD (gp2)**, Throughput Optimized HDD (`st1`), and Cold HDD (`sc1`). We set it to `io1` which is the highest performance SSD volume. Please consult *Parameters* (`https://kubernetes.io/docs/concepts/storage/storage-classes/#parameters`) section of the *Storage Classes* documentation for more info. Finally, we set the `reclaimPolicy` to `Delete`. Unlike `Retain` that forces us to delete the contents of the released volume before it becomes available to new PersistentVolumeClaims, `Delete` removes both the PersistentVolume as well as the associated volume in the external architecture. The `Delete` reclaim policy works only with some of the external volumes like AWS EBS, Azure Disk, or Cinder volume. Now that we dipped our toes into the StorageClass definition, we can proceed and create it.

```
kubectl create -f pv/sc.yml
```

The output shows that the `storageclass "fast" was created`, so we'll list, one more time, the StorageClassses in our cluster.

```
kubectl get sc
```

The output is as follows:

```
NAME             PROVISIONER            AGE
default          kubernetes.io/aws-ebs 58m
fast             kubernetes.io/aws-ebs 19s
gp2 (default) kubernetes.io/aws-ebs 58m
```

We can see that, this time, we have a new StorageClass.

Let's take a look at yet another Jenkins definition.

```
cat pv/jenkins-sc.yml
```

The output, limited to the relevant parts, is as follows:

```
...
kind: PersistentVolumeClaim
apiVersion: v1
metadata:
  name: jenkins
```

```
  namespace: jenkins
spec:
  storageClassName: fast
  accessModes:
    - ReadWriteOnce
  resources:
    requests:
      storage: 4Gi
...
```

The only difference, when compared with the previous definition, is that we are now using the newly created StorageClass named `fast`.

Finally, we'll confirm that the new StorageClass works by deploying the new `jenkins` definition.

```
kubectl apply \
    -f pv/jenkins-sc.yml \
    --record
```

The output is as follows:

```
namespace "jenkins" configured
ingress "jenkins" configured
service "jenkins" configured
persistentvolumeclaim "jenkins" created
deployment "jenkins" created
```

As the final verification, we'll list the EBS volumes and confirm that a new one was created based on the new class.

```
aws ec2 describe-volumes \
    --filters 'Name=tag-key,Values="kubernetes.io/created-for/pvc/name"'
```

The output, limited to the relevant parts, is as follows:

```
{
    "Volumes": [
    {
        ... "VolumeType": "io1",
        "VolumeId": "vol-0e0af4f2a7a54354d",
        "State": "in-use",
        ...
    }
    ]
}
```

We can see that the type of the newly created EBS volume is `io1` and that it is `in-use`.

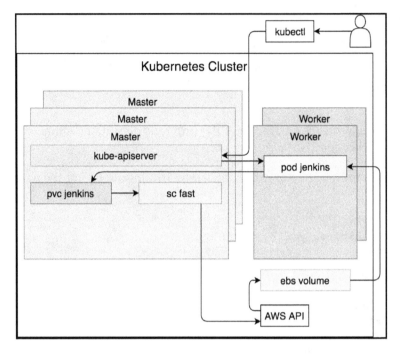

Figure 15-5: The sequence of events initiated with a request to create a Jenkins Pod with the PersistentVolumeClaim using a custom StorageClass

A simplified version of the flow of events initiated with the creation of the `jenkins` Deployment is as follows:

1. We created the `jenkins` Deployment, which created a ReplicaSet, which, in turn, created a Pod.
2. The Pod requested persistent storage through the PersistentVolumeClaim.
3. The PersistentVolumeClaim requested PersistentStorage with the StorageClass name `fast`.
4. StorageClass `fast` is defined to create a new EBS volume, so it requested one from the AWS API.
5. AWS API created a new EBS volume.
6. EBS volume was mounted to the `jenkins` Pod.

We're finished exploring persistent volumes. You should be equipped with the knowledge how to persist your stateful applications, and the only pending action is to remove the volumes and the cluster.

What now?

There's nothing left to do but to destroy what we did so far.

This time, we cannot just delete the cluster. Such an action would leave the EBS volumes running. So, we need to remove them first.

We could remove EBS volumes through AWS CLI. However, there is an easier way. If we delete all the claims to EBS volumes, they will be deleted as well since our PersistentVolumes are created with the reclaim policy set to `Delete`. EBS volumes are created when needed and destroyed when not.

Since all our claims are in the `jenkins` namespace, removing it is the easiest way to delete them all.

```
kubectl delete ns jenkins
```

The output shows that the `namespace "jenkins" was deleted` and we can proceed to delete the cluster as well.

```
kops delete cluster \
--name $NAME \
--yes
```

We can see from the output that the cluster `devops23.k8s.local` was deleted and we are left only with the S3 bucket used for kops state. We'll delete it as well.

```
aws s3api delete-bucket \
--bucket $BUCKET_NAME
```

Before you leave, please consult the following API references for more information about volume-related resources.

- PersistentVolume v1 core
  (https://v1-8.docs.kubernetes.io/docs/api-reference/v1.8/#storageclass-v1-storage)
- PersistentVolumeClaim v1 core
  (https://v1-8.docs.kubernetes.io/docs/api-reference/v1.8/#persistentvolumeclaim-v1-core)
- StorageClass v1 storage
  (https://v1-8.docs.kubernetes.io/docs/api-reference/v1.8/#storageclass-v1-storage)

That's it. There's nothing left.

16
The End

We are finished with this book, but we only started with Kubernetes. It is so vast that no single book can cover even the core components. If we extend the scope to all the members of **Cloud Native Computing Foundation (CNCF)** (https://www.cncf.io/) project as well as third-party solutions that can be added, we'd need a series of books dedicated only to Kubernetes. To make things more complicated, the Kubernetes ecosystem is growing so fast that it is almost impossible to keep the pace. Even if we could somehow learn everything there is to know today, we would be left behind a week later.

There is an almost infinite number of combinations we can use to create and use a Kubernetes cluster. We can choose to stick only with core components, or we can combine them with third-party tools. We could choose to use only "vanilla Kubernetes", or we can adopt one of the platforms like OpenShift (https://www.openshift.com/), Docker Enterprise Edition (https://www.docker.com/kubernetes#/EE), or Rancher (https://rancher.com/). There are many others we might want to explore, and the list is growing with each passing day.

Some of the Kubernetes platforms are highly opinionated while others force us to choose ourselves the components that'll constitute a cluster. We can easily spend eternity evaluating which components are the best for our use case. Take networking as an example. There are at least twenty solutions I know of, and I'm pretty sure that number can be multiplied by ten. You can easily get blocked only with that single choice. Add persistent storage, Ingress, and authentication to the mix and the amount of the things we need to evaluate is already beyond the capacity of a single person.

If we add hosting providers to the evaluation, we are faced with additional options and new constraints. Almost all realized by now that Kubernetes is going to be the norm and that it is paramount to adopt it to their offerings. They are all adding their own components to make Kubernetes work seamlessly on their infrastructure. They are trying to attract you by saying that Kubernetes works better there than anywhere else. That also means that you will face additional new components.

Kubernetes is designed to be extensible. Almost every software and hosting vendor is adding their own components to the mix. That extensibility is probably the main reason why Kubernetes got such a broad adoption, why it grew so big, but also why it is so complex and, at times, not very intuitive. It is enormous, and it will continue growing. With that growth comes complexity that can be overwhelming.

There is no reason to despair. The principles you learned are valid no matter how you set up your Kubernetes cluster or which parts of the ecosystem you choose to use. If you did not just skim through the book, you should know the essential core components. You did the hardest part. You learned some of the most commonly used resources. You know the logic behind them, and you know how to connect them. From now on, you just need to continue exploring and extending your Kubernetes knowledge. That is, if you make Kubernetes your platform of choice.

For many, what you learned so far is (almost) everything they'll need. If that's not the case, the work on *The DevOps 2.4 Toolkit* already started and I hope you'll join me for the rest of the journey.

I do not yet know the scope of the next book. What I do know is that there are too many Kubernetes-related subjects I had to leave out of this book to keep it within four hundred pages of self-imposed limit. The good news is that the next book is also going to be related to Kubernetes. Maybe it will be called "*Things you Failed to Find in the DevOps 2.3 Toolkit*" or maybe it will be "*The DevOps 2.4 Toolkit – Advanced Kubernetes*". It'll become clear soon. Maybe, by the time you're reading this text, it is already published.

Contributions

I published the book on LeanPub (`https://leanpub.com/the-devops-2-3-toolkit`) early. Around 10% was written when it went public. That allowed many of you to get early access to the material, and it gave me an opportunity to get your feedback. The result is fantastic. Many sent me their notes, reported bugs, proposed suggestions for improvements, recommended tools and processes that should be explored, and so on.

It would be tempting to take the whole credit for the book, but that would be untrue. This book is the result of teamwork between the author (me) and many of the readers (you). It proves that lean publishing works and that we can apply agile principles when writing a book. There was no fixed scope and decisions were not made in advance. I would work on a chapter and deliver it when it's finished (*sprint*). You would review it and send your notes and comments that would allow me to improve it (*sprint review*). We had a daily exchange of emails and Slack messages (*daily standups*). We did short iterations that allowed us to learn from the mistakes and improve.

Dear readers, **you made this book great!**

A few stick from the crowd.

Neeraj Kothari helped by questioning my writing, providing suggestions, and sending me comments. He thought that my sequences and diagrams were too basic, not to say incorrect. He was so persistent that I delegated them to him. Most of the diagrams you saw in the book are his as well as the explanations of the events that transpire when we execute `kubectl` commands.

I'd love to put his biography, but he seems to ignore my requests to write down who he is and what he does. He probably will. Time will tell.

Prageeth Warnak was continually sending pull requests with corrections and suggestions. He made this book much clearer than it would be if I had to rely on my, often incorrect, assumptions of what readers expect.

Prageeth is a seasoned IT professional currently working as the lead software architect for Australian *telco giant Telstra*. He enjoys working with new technologies, and he likes spending his leisure time reading books (especially those written by Viktor), watching Netflix and Fox news. He lives in Melbourne with his family. He is fascinated getting Microservices and DevOps done right.

David Jacob did his best to correct my "broken" English. Without him, you'd have a hard time understanding what I wanted to say.

David is a backend Java developer who has transformed into a system administrator over the past two years. He is focusing on becoming more proficient in Linux, networking and DevOps practices and will hopefully have more time for programming again one day. He lives in Berlin and has no cats.

Don Becker helped with Windows and troubleshooting Minikube using Hyper-V.

Don is tech industry veteran having held numerous positions in nearly every facet of IT and software development. He resides in Phoenix, Arizona with his wife, three kids and three cats. His current focus is the shift from virtual machines to containerization, microservices, OpenFAAS and of course, Kubernetes.

Vadim Gusev helped to proofread and discuss book structure from the novice point of view.

Vadim is young IT specialist that started his career as a network engineer but was so fascinated by the idea of clouds and containers, that he decided to switch his career path to DevOps. He works in a small startup and leads it to bright containerized future, guided mostly by Viktor's books. In his free time he likes to work out, play drums and procrastinate on purpose.

Other Books You May Enjoy

If you enjoyed this book, you may be interested in these other books by Packt:

The DevOps 2.2 Toolkit
Russ McKendrick, Scott Gallagher

ISBN: 978-1-78899-127-8

- Let Viktor Farcic show you all aspects in the creation of self-adapting and self-healing systems in both a practical and hands-on approach.
- Learn how to choose a successful solution for metrics storage and query, including InfluxDB, Nagios and Sensu, Prometheus and Graphite.
- Understand how to integrate Docker Flow Monitor with Docker Flow Proxy.
- The creation of cluster-wide alerts by creating alerts based on metrics.
- How to apply self-healing and self-adaptive to both services and infrastructure.

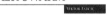

The DevOps 2.1 Toolkit: Docker Swarm
Viktor Farcic

ISBN: 978-1-78728-970-3

- Learn all aspects of Docker Swarm from building, testing, deploying, and monitoring services inside Docker Swarm clusters, available since Docker 1.12.
- Master the deeper logic of DevOps with Viktor, so that you can successfully apply that logic across any specific set of tools you're working with.
- Translate a deep understanding to different hosting providers like AWS, Azure, DigitalOcean, among others.
- You'll go beyond simple deployment: you will explore with Viktor how to create a continuous deployment process. Accomplish zero-downtime deployments, and what to do in case of a failover.
- Know how to run services at scale, how to monitor the systems, and how to make it heal itself.

The DevOps 2.0 Toolkit
Viktor Farcic

ISBN: 978-1-78528-919-4

- Get to grips with the fundamentals of Devops
- Architect efficient software in a better and more efficient way with the help of microservices
- Use Docker, Kubernetes, Ansible, Ubuntu, Docker Swarm and more
- Implement fast, reliable and continuous deployments with zero-downtime and ability to roll-back
- Learn about centralized logging and monitoring of your cluster
- Design self-healing systems capable of recovery from both hardware and software failures

Please share your thoughts on this book with others by leaving a review on the site that you bought it from. If you purchased the book from Amazon, please leave us an honest review on this book's Amazon page. This is vital so that other potential readers can see and use your unbiased opinion to make purchasing decisions, we can understand what our customers think about our products, and our authors can see your feedback on the title that they have worked with Packt to create. It will only take a few minutes of your time, but is valuable to other potential customers, our authors, and Packt. Thank you!

Index

www.ingramcontent.com/pod-product-compliance
Lightning Source LLC
Chambersburg PA
CBHW060650060326
40690CB00020B/4583